"Almost all the major elements that compose a university . . . are In an unprecedented state of change. The universities that survive will be those which learn to preserve their integrity and stability while accepting change."

To guide change, the committee submits forty-two proposals—specific recommendations concerning orientation and advising, class size, grading, educational development and innovation, new programs, undergraduate requirements, graduate education, and the problems facing the teaching assistant.

Especially timely because of widespread interest in American higher education, and in the University of California in particular, this book presents not only the recommendations of the Committee but the action taken by the Academic Senate of the University of California, Berkeley, on each of the recommendations. This is a vital and timely book, one which deserves the attention of all those concerned with higher education.

ACADEMIC SENATE, BERKELEY DIVISION
SELECT COMMITTEE ON EDUCATION

❖

CHARLES MUSCATINE, *Chairman*
English

RICHARD HERR
History

GEORGE C. PIMENTEL
Chemistry

DAVID KRECH
Psychology

SAMUEL SCHAAF
Mechanical Engineering

LEO LOWENTHAL
Sociology

PETER SCOTT
Speech

RODERIC PARK
Botany

THEODORE VERMEULEN
Chemical Engineering

UNIVERSITY OF CALIFORNIA, BERKELEY
ACADEMIC SENATE

EDUCATION AT BERKELEY

California. University. Academic Senate.
"

Report of the
Select Committee
on Education

UNIVERSITY OF CALIFORNIA PRESS

Berkeley and Los Angeles 1968

Library of Congress Catalog No. 66-63764

© 1966 by the Regents of the University of California

First Printing, 1966, by the Academic Senate,
University of California, Berkeley
Second Printing with corrections and Epilogue in
University of California Press edition, 1968
Printed in the United States of America

TO THE MEMBERS OF THE
ACADEMIC SENATE, BERKELEY:

On March 1, 1965, Acting Chancellor Martin Meyerson addressed the Senate on the subject of education at Berkeley. He challenged the Senate to consider "a pluralistic approach to education," and proposed that a new "commission on the state of education at Berkeley . . . bringing together and clarifying the many ideas being suggested on the campus could then develop for our consideration specific proposals for the revitalization of our educational aims and practice." In response to Chancellor Meyerson's proposal, the Emergency Executive Committee offered on March 8 a Resolution calling for the establishment of a Select Committee on Education at Berkeley for the following purposes:

(a) to find the ways in which the traditions of humane learning and scientific inquiry can be best advanced under the challenging conditions of size and scale that confront our university community;

(b) to examine the various changes in educational programs currently under consideration in the several schools and colleges; to seek by appropriate means to communicate information concerning these programs to the wider campus community; and to consider the implications of these programs in the light of (a) above.

The Resolution was passed, and in due course the Committee was appointed. We soon became convinced of the value of bringing out our conclusions without undue delay. We held our first meeting on April 19, and issued a brief preliminary report on May 24. Since then, with generous assistance from Chancellor Meyerson and thereafter from Chancellor Roger W. Heyns, we have been able to continue our discussions and researches uninterrupted, and we are pleased to be submitting this, our final report, in less than a year's time.

iii

The report consists of a series of discussions arranged in chapters; the discussions are punctuated by formal recommendations numbered consecutively and printed in bold face type. The Committee proposes that these recommendations not be considered in isolation, but rather in the context of the supporting arguments and in relation to each other. It has been our slow discovery that there are no simple shortcuts to good education, and none of our recommendations has full meaning or full promise taken by itself. We intend to ask this term for the Senate's formal approval of as many of the recommendations as can be accommodated on its agenda, beginning with numbers 19, 20, and 21.

The report is herewith commended to your favorable consideration.

Respectfully submitted,

Richard Herr
David Krech
Leo Lowenthal
Roderic B. Park
George C. Pimentel
Samuel A. Schaaf
Peter D. Scott
Theodore Vermeulen
Charles Muscatine, *Chairman*

March 22, 1966

Acknowledgments

So many people have taken time out from their own endeavors to help us with our task that we are unable to give them all proper credit. We are grateful to them all. We do wish, however, to mention in particular those individuals and groups without whose cooperation we could never have completed our researches.

First of all, we wish to thank the members of the Select Committee research staff: Mrs. Elizabeth Alfert, Dr. Mervin Freedman, Dr. Paul H. Heist, Dean James Jarrett, Professor Stuart Miller, Mrs. Frances Newman, Mr. David Nichols, Mr. Harold Norton, Professor Paul H. Piehler, Professor John H. Raleigh, Professor Dan I. Slobin, Mr. William Somerville, and Professor Sheldon Wolin. In conducting particular studies at our request, these men and women provided us with invaluable assistance and took many burdens from us.

We have a special debt of gratitude also to Professor Sherwood Washburn, a charter member of the Committee whose term expired on July 1, 1965, to Mr. Bruce Spiegelberg, our librarian, and to Mrs. Sandra Linebaugh, our secretary.

Throughout the Committee's career, we have had the help of numerous student assistants, who did everything from conducting particular studies to collecting figures for our many tables. For their efforts on our behalf, we thank Miss Lucretia Beltrone, Mr. Joseph Cady, Jr., Mr. Hobart Dewey, Miss Joan Glassel, Mrs. Sharon Green, Mr. John Gregory, Mr. Stefan Grotz, Mr. Christian Harrison, Miss Kristan Helmer, Miss Nuhad Kanawati, Miss Marla Ketelhut, Mr. Lawrence Loewinger, Mr. Ralph Maltés, Jr., Mrs. Susan Manso, Mr. Robert Mooney, Mr. Leigh Mueller, Miss Erna Olafson, Mr. Martin Roysher, Miss Judith Rypins, Mr. Allan Stone, Miss Diane Unis, Miss Jeanne Peterson, and Miss Elizabeth Weier.

We have benefited greatly from the personal advice and assistance generously given us by many consultants and contributors. First and foremost, we wish to express our gratitude to the deans and departmental chairmen of the Berkeley campus, who graciously and good-humoredly answered our many requests for information. In addition we wish to thank Miss Beatrix Bakker, Professor W. R. Breneman, Professor B. H. Bronson, Mr. Robert E. Brownell, Mr. William Butler, President Victor L. Butterfield, Professor James Cason, Chancellor Vernon I. Cheadle, Vice-Chancellor Earl F. Cheit, Professor Burton Clark, Mr. Clive Condren, Vice-Chancellor Robert E. Connick, Mr. Charles J. Courey, Dr. William H. Crawford, Professor William G. Dauben, Professor Louis Davis, Professor Ruth E. Eckert, Dean Sanford S. Elberg, Professor Ralph Emerson, Mrs. Deanna Falge, Mr. Edward Feder, Mrs. Alyce T. Foley, Dean William B. Fretter, Mr. David C. Fulton, Chancellor John S. Galbraith, Registrar Clinton Gilliam, Professor Nathan Glazer, Provost Edward D. Goldberg, Professor Michael A. Goodman, Mr. Morton Gordon, Mr. Richard Hafner, Dr. Ann M. Heiss, Chancellor Roger W. Heyns, Professor Joel H. Hildebrand, Professor J. L. Hodges, Jr., Professor Harold W. Iversen, Dean William A. Jensen, Miss Kim Johnson, Professor Charles W. Jones, Professor Dale W. Jorgenson, President Clark Kerr, Mrs. Barbara A. Kirk, Professor Charles Kittel, Professor Walter D. Knight, Dr. Dorothy Knoell, Dean Joseph D. Lohman, Mr. Errol W. Mauchlan, Professor Henry F. May, Dr. John Mays, Dr. Robert MacLeod, Dr. Thomas R. McConnell, Dr. Leland L. Medsker, Dean Martin Meyerson, Professor Josephine Miles, Professor Marvin Mudrick, Chancellor Franklin D. Murphy, Mrs. Beulah A. Nealson, Mr. William Nicholls, Professor Donald S. Noyce, Professor E. R. Parker, Professor Thomas F. Parkinson, Miss Elizabeth Petroff, Miss Rosemary Phaneuf, Dr. David H. Powelson, Mr. William Raley, Mrs. Dorothy W. Randolph, Professor Edward S. Rogers, Dean

Franklin P. Rolfe, Professor Franz Schneider, Professor Carl E. Schorske, Mr. Arnold M. Schultz, Vice-Chancellor Foster H. Sherwood, Mr. Dan Siminoski, Miss Alice Singer, Mrs. Edith Slater, Professor Otto J. S. Smith, Provost Page Smith, Professor Curt Stern, Professor Andrew Streitwieser, Jr., Dr. Robert F. Suczek, Mr. Sidney Suslow, Dr. Harold Taylor, Mrs. Louise Taylor, Dean Mack Thompson, Professor Martin Trow, Dean Robert D. Tschirgi, Dr. Ralph Tyler, Mr. Daniel Weiner, Mr. Burton Wolfman, and Professor Michael A. Zimmerman. We owe a great deal to the members of the Special Committee on Academic Programs of the College of Letters and Science, who worked closely with us: Professors Cyril Birch, Bernard Friedman, and Frederick Reif. The editorial staff of the *Daily Californian* also has been helpful to us: we particularly thank Miss Peggy Krause and Mr. Allan A. Metcalf.

We have learned much about national developments in educational reform through correspondence with educators throughout the country. We wish to thank particularly Professor Paul Baender, Dean Shelton Beatty, Mr. William Bentinck-Smith, Dean Wayne Booth, Dean Edward A. Carlin, Vice-President Robert L. Clodius, Dean Robert P. Cobb, Dr. Paul L. Dressel, Professor Charles J. Erasmus, Dr. Stanford C. Erickson, Mr. Thomas Fontaine, Professor Clay Gerkin, Dr. Clement J. Gresock, Dean Harold L. Hodgkinson, Dean John D. Hurrell, Dr. Harold Howe II, Professor Aaron J. Ihde, Dean Charles E. Johnson, Professor Albert R. Kitzhaber, Provost Edward H. Levi, Dean H. W. Magoun, Dean William McCormack, Dean Roger B. Page, Professor Roy Harvey Pearce, President Calvin H. Plimpton, Dean Leonard M. Rieser, Dean James H. Robertson, Mr. Stanley Salmen, Dr. Nevitt Sanford, Professor Aaron Sayvetz, Vice-President Donald K. Smith, Dean Glenn Starlin, President Richard H. Sullivan, Dean David Truman, Dean Robert J. West, Professor York Willbern, Dean Robert L. Williams, and Dean E. W. Ziebarth.

Finally, we can only thank collectively the 2,203 students who responded to our questionnaire; and the many faculty members, students, staff members, and friends of the University who gave us interviews, attended our ten open discussion meetings, and answered our public requests for assistance and advice.

CONTENTS

I.

INTRODUCTION:
A PHILOSOPHY FOR BERKELEY

I N RESPONDING to its charge the Committee has favored the pragmatic over the theoretical approach. Our discussions of educational principles have most often arisen in discussions of concrete proposals, and we have often found that we could easily agree on the same practical measure from rival philosophical positions that themselves might have been the occasion for long and inconclusive debate. This approach has meant that on most problems we have started from the given—the Berkeley campus, with its unique character and tradition, its strengths, weaknesses, and above all, its capacities. But while we have kept the present in sight, we have found few limits to the possibilities of education at Berkeley; and although we have primarily addressed ourselves to a series of concrete problems, we find that our proposed solutions are so related to each other as to suggest a satisfyingly coherent pattern of ideas—a "philosophy," if you will, of the whole. In the present chapter we attempt to provide a summary sketch of these ideas.

We are far from alone in our self-examination. Nearly every major college in the country has, or has had, or is planning similar studies by similar committees. We sense that we are part of a great national—and international—development, the response to an historical crisis in higher education. The main reasons for the crisis seem readily distinguishable: the changing role of the university (and thus of the professor) in modern society; the proliferation of knowledge; the growth of our population and the changes in our social expectations; the emergence of a new generation of students. Thus almost all the major elements that compose a university—the teachers, the students, knowledge itself, and their social setting—all are in an unprecedented state of change. The resultant dislocations have been largely inevitable; and one of our first duties has been to address ourselves to the ways of bringing the various elements of Berkeley education into better harmony and of preserving the stability of the campus in the face of the changes to come. For in this world of high-powered technology and of sweeping social and economic forces, the promise of the future is not stasis but accelerated change. The universities that survive and prosper will—like all other important institutions—be those which learn to preserve their integrity and stability while accepting change.

For the permanent health of our academic community, we would prefer to see it change gradually and continuously rather than having to suffer the shocks of drastic adjustment following periods of quiescence. Consequently, many of our concrete recommendations are for substantial experiments, not for untested wholesale changes. In this spirit, we have avoided wherever possible the temptation to frame legislation for "all" students and "every" department. We are confident that honest trial will determine where and when a given change should be permanently adopted; and we are convinced that large administrative and curricular policies should not (indeed, cannot) be imposed on our faculties from without. Changes are most likely to succeed if they remain optional, offered along with the means for their implementation or experimental trial, then left to the judgment of those for whose benefit they are intended.

We approach the education of the individual student in much the same spirit. Our student body is too large, too various, and too changing to be susceptible to many universal formulations. But if size and scale are among our foremost problems, they are also formidable assets. We do not have to limit ourselves to one kind of education. We have the means to generate a rich pluralism—a whole spectrum of kinds of education, better suited to the variety of our students than our curriculum is now. Our ideal for the student is that he be provided with rich opportunities, generous guidance, and plenty of room for experiment, and that he be enabled to make for himself as many of the important decisions about his own education as possible.

Our most important curricular proposals are designed in response to our most urgent needs. These needs have often been implied negatively in the complaints and criticisms leveled at this and other large universities: we need to give more attention to the individual student as a person, and offer him an education more sensitively adapted to his preparation and to his progress through the curriculum. For many students—both undergraduate and graduate—there has not been an adequate connection between their education and what they feel to be their primary concerns as human beings and as citizens. We need to make the connection more clear, and to replace those of our offerings that may have through obsolescence lost their contact with vital human concerns. We face the perennial danger, in an institution so devoted to professional expertise, of narrowness and provincialism. We need to offer protection, particularly to beginning students, against premature specialization. At the same time we should be able to give timely and generous scope to students who know what they want to do. We should at all levels keep our curricula flexible, open to the developments in other fields—for this is often a source of fruitful new discovery, and the surest way to help students to intellectual breadth and to perspective on their special interests.

Against the impersonality, against the feeling of "alienation" of the large campus, we make specific recommendations concerning orientation and advising, class size—including the use of seminars, tutorials, and preceptorials—and the use of student advice in academic policy-making. To clarify the relevance of the scholarly life, we recommend a number of measures; among them the "problem-oriented" rather than the "survey" approach to introductory courses; "ad hoc" courses; a program of elective "field studies;" and graduate curricula individually tailored and better adapted to prospective teaching careers. Most of these measures are also steps toward that greater pluralism which, as we have said, will contribute to the more sensitive adaptation of the student's opportunities to his needs. In our feeling that the campus urgently needs to take greater formal responsibility for the *general* education of all students, we recommend some alternative plans for professional schools, de-emphasis on grading to allow students to experiment outside their specialties, and a new concept of the "breadth requirement" for the College of Letters and Science.

Greater pluralism and increased individual attention to students means a greater call on the administrative, teaching, and advisory power of the campus. From where is this power to come? We suggest in the course of this report a large number of different sources. But nowhere do we suggest a diminution of the research activity of the faculty. Research (or creativity) is of the very character of this campus; without it Berkeley would be indistinguishable from other kinds of schools. In a state system itself devoted to a pluralism of educational institutions, the Berkeley campus has an obligation, indeed, to maintain its eminence in research. Rather than adopt some simplistic formula based on the supposed mutual exclusiveness of "teaching" and "research," we have found it more fitting to this campus to try to suggest how teaching and research can be made to nourish each other better. Our ideal here is a kind of teaching suffused with the excitement and authority of research, and a kind of research responsive to the humane requirements of teaching. Our ideal professor is like Chaucer's clerk: "gladly wolde he lerne, and gladly teche."

The close interpenetration of teaching and research should not only give a special character to the campus; it should give an ultimate unity and coherence to our pluralistic curricula and a clear definition of role to our faculty. We have been able to find very few categorical imperatives for Berkeley education. There are very few subjects that we can agree on that *every* student should know. But we have not been unmindful of the question "What about the values?" Beneath the great variety of possible educational experiences that a pluralistic system offers, what is the common denominator? What will our students have in common? Our answer is that ideally they will have in common the exposure to a noble stance, both scientific and humane, that will be exemplified in the conduct of every one of us. It is not, then, what we teach that will give final validity to education at Berkeley, but what we are. We reject for Berkeley the idea of teachers who are not also scholars. We agree with our colleagues at Yale in their report of last June that "original scholarly work is the surest proof of intellectual distinction and the surest guarantee that intellectual activity will not cease." Scholarship, then, is a promoter of good teaching, and in the long run can be justified only by the human needs of which the teaching of others is a great part.

By the same token, we find no place on the faculty for researchers who are not teachers. There are proper places in institutes and industries for the "isolated" scholar. But the ideal of the University should be one of scholarship at the service of teaching. There is no scholarly eminence that justifies contempt of students; we are pleased to observe that our very greatest scholars are men whose respect is of the kind that comes unbidden, and whose prestige is never self-proclaimed. By this central act of service—teaching—we submit our learning directly to the test of human relevance and complete ourselves as proper objects for the emulation of the young. Poor teaching or neglect of teaching cannot be defended in the University; ultimately it vitiates the meaning of our research itself, for it is inhumane and it is alien to the spirit of scholarship.

To improve teaching we recommend faculty-wide experiment with the use of student comments, greater scrutiny and recognition of the teaching ability of younger faculty members, and general improvements in the training and apprenticing of graduate students as teachers. But our recommendations, though they embody specific measures directed at specific weaknesses, are presented in the conviction that no particular measures, no devices or gimmicks, will suffice if a fidelity to teaching is not part of the atmosphere of the campus. If this fails, then we fail not only in one branch of our activity—but in the integrity of the whole.

Teaching large numbers of students well is a great challenge, and we are confident that we can meet that challenge with judicious use of the support that can reasonably be expected from the state. This will mean a gradual redeployment of some of our means, and our putting to the maximum use the great power of self-education of the students themselves. Fortunately, many of these moves make as good educational sense as they make economic sense; and where we will not be able to solve the problem of numbers completely—no large public university ever will—it is likely that we may solve the problem of quality nevertheless. For the two problems, though related, are not the same: the world-famous lecturer before a large audience has his place in good education, providing that somewhere on campus the student gets personal attention and a chance to talk back; and students keep reminding us that there are times when anonymity itself is a blessing.

But no solution will suffice if we merely settle upon corrective measures designed to "fix" things for another five or ten or twenty years. The campus should have built into it the capacity for continuous adaptation and change; it should have built into it a continuous tradition of trial and experiment. The proposals we bring forward for the perpetuation of such a tradition are perhaps the most important ones in this report. And we have reason to hope for their favorable acceptance by the faculty. For in the long run the Berkeley campus has been an adaptable and experimental one, widely hospitable to constructive change. While the campus has remained a bastion of the great traditional academic values, the programs of many of our schools and colleges are at the forefront in their respective fields. Furthermore, we exist in a University system that is the national model for educational enterprise, having just brought into existence no less than three new campuses, each bursting with energy and imagination. And as we have studied this campus in the past year, we have found on all sides a stirring toward examination and renovation, promising experiments and improvements already under way, and a general willingness to give lively consideration to the problems that still remain. We present our proposals, then, in a spirit of optimism, confident that the faculty has the means and will take the steps to perpetuate this campus in its excellence.

II.

THE BERKELEY STUDENTS

A. Ambiguous Attitudes

Dduring the turmoil of the last academic year, ostensibly caused by a dispute over whether students should be allowed to engage freely in political activity on campus, some students publicly questioned the adequacy of this University as an educational institution. Since then many observers have interpreted the events of that year as evidence of widespread dissatisfaction among students with the way they were being taught. It may come as a surprise, therefore, that surveys taken while the events were still fresh show a large majority of the students to be reasonably content with the University. In April 1965, nine tenths of a sample of students, carefully selected to be representative of the entire student body, graduate and undergraduate, agreed with this statement: "Taking everything into account, Cal is a good place to go to school." Four fifths said they were satisfied with courses, examinations, and professors.[1] In a survey conducted by the Committee in September 1965, three quarters of the undergraduate students felt that the amount of course work required of them was reasonable.[2]

---

[1] Kathleen E. Gales, "Berkeley Student Opinion, April 1965." Copy of typescript in Select Committee files. A random sample of 439 students was used and its characteristics carefully checked against the known features of the whole student body.

[2] Questionnaire Study of Returning Undergraduates conducted for the Select Committee on Education in September-October 1965 by Mervin B. Freedman and William L. Nichols II (hereafter referred to as "Select Committee Survey"). Questionnaires were distributed to one-quarter of the undergraduate students enrolled in the spring 1965 semester who returned to register in the fall 1965, in all schools and colleges at Berkeley except Forestry, Optometry, and Public Health. 2576 questionnaires were distributed and 2203 or 85.5% were returned. The high rate of return lends support to the study's conclusions, but it is somewhat offset by the fact that the procedure used did not permit contacting seniors who graduated in June 1965 and students who did not return, those most likely to be dissatisfied with the University's undergraduate program or less successful in coping with it.

In the light of events, the results of these surveys are paradoxical. A vast majority of the students said they were happy with the University; yet at the same time a good part, perhaps half, of the same students had been willing to cut classes in order to demonstrate their opposition to the administration of the University.[3] The answer is not so simple as to say that the issues were political and not academic, or that the students were swept up in a wave of youthful exuberance or hysteria. The same surveys which showed apparent student approval of the University also revealed deep discontent with specific aspects of the education provided. A third of the students who were questioned complained that some of their classes were so big that they learned very little in them. Forty-two per cent stated that the grading system reflects "only slightly" the student's actual knowledge and understanding of the subjects studied, and another 5% believed it does "not at all." Forty-six per cent said professors spend too little time with their students, and 42% held that most professors are more interested in their research than in teaching. Half of them said students should have more control over educational policies, and half also wished they had more time for non-academic activities. Finally, nearly four fifths agreed with the popular cliché that the University operates as a factory.[4]

Obviously there is ambiguity in the attitudes of many Berkeley students toward the University. They both respect it and feel dissociated from it. This ambiguity suggests that the sources of their discontent go deeper than their specific criticisms of the University, though these criticisms are at times justified. If we can understand the basis and significance of the conflicting attitudes of the students, we shall know a great deal about their nature and needs.

B. The Missing College Community

In attacking the problem, it is well to begin by describing certain features of the student body.

Few American university campuses have a larger enrollment than Berkeley, and certainly none has a more diverse one. In the fall of

[3] Eugene Bardach, Jack Citrin, et al., "The Berkeley Free Speech Controversy (Preliminary Report) Prepared by a Fact-Finding Committee of Graduate Political Scientists," Dec. 13, 1964, mimeographed, p. 15.

[4] Select Committee Survey (grading and non-academic activities); Gales, "Berkeley Student Opinion" (professors and factory). The Gales survey found that only 49% of the students agreed with the statement: "Grades at this university are an adequate measure of ability." The agreement with the Select Committee Survey percentage is close.

1965, there were 26,832 students, including 10,224 graduates, 9,952 in upper division (juniors and seniors), and 6,656 in lower division (freshmen and sophomores). About two thirds of them were men. They came in varying numbers from every state in the union, six from Mississippi to 976 from New York, besides 19,684 from California itself. Two thousand and thirty-seven were from foreign countries.

These students were in fourteen schools and colleges, each with its own curriculum and degree requirements. Each college and school has its student group with its jargon, mores, and legends. The largest, the College of Letters and Science, with 12,384 undergraduate students majoring in such varied fields as physical and biological sciences, social science, and humanities, is in itself a diverse set of groups.

This much complexity is inherent in the organization and purpose of the University. The student body is further fragmented by the mobility of today's students. Under the traditional four-year college program, most of the class that entered as freshmen in September 1961 would have graduated in June 1965. In fact only 50% of them have graduated by January 1966 or are still on campus. The other half (54% of the women and 46% of the men) have left; many of them will later complete their education here or elsewhere. On the other hand, 38% of the class that did graduate from Letters and Science in 1965 (the only college for which figures are readily available) had done half or more of their work elsewhere.[5] That is to say that only half of our freshmen graduate here within five years, while about two fifths of the graduating class (in Letters and Science at least) consist of transfer students who were at Berkeley only as upper-division students. Then, as is to be desired, there is another large influx at the graduate level. In the fall of 1964, 36% of the graduate students were new, and of these, only one fifth came from Berkeley. In other words, there were in that semester among the graduate students 3,000 faces that were new to the campus.

When a new student arrives here, he does not find a tight-knit college community. In the survey conducted by the Committee, 30% of the undergraduates stated that they live more than ten-minutes walking distance from the campus, and it is safe to assume that this is true of a higher percentage of graduate students. Most of these undergraduates spend between two and six hours per week commuting to the Univer-

---

[5] Mervin B. Freedman, "Dropouts at Berkeley," typescript in Select Committee files. Data supplied by Dr. Robert Suczek and Dr. Lise Alfert of the Department of Psychiatry, Cowell Hospital, University of California, Berkeley. Figures on graduates from the study of the graduating class of 1965 of the Letters and Science Special Committee on Academic Program.

sity. Going to class represents for many of them somewhat the same pattern of life as going to a daily job.

In such a large student body with widely scattered residences and a high rate of turnover, it is hardly surprising that many students feel alone in a community of strangers. In the April 1965 survey, almost two thirds of the students felt the University to be an "impersonal institution," and one third agreed that they "often feel lonely walking on campus even though there are crowds of people around." Loneliness is one factor behind the decision of many freshmen and entering transfer students to drop out of Berkeley. The women who transfer to other campuses of the University of California give as their main reason for leaving Berkeley their feelings of isolation because of its large size and impersonality. Loneliness is, of course, a general problem of the individual in society and is very likely to assail young persons who are leaving their homes or local schools for the first time. A residential situation that provides close relations with other students reduces the rate of drop-outs. Students living at home (and therefore presumably commuting considerable distances) or in private rooms and boarding houses are much more prone to leaving than those who enter dormitories, co-op housing, fraternities, and sororities.[6]

A dearth of close student contacts has its effect on the informal intellectual life of the campus. The opportunities for active intellectual exchange among peers are far more restricted at Berkeley than at small private colleges. Many Berkeley students find their friendships limited to a few intimates. For many of those who remain at the University, solitude or social intercourse with a few associates, which began as a necessity, ends by becoming a way of life. There is a notable tendency for students after some time here to shift to private apartments, either alone or with a roommate or two. They move into converted private homes and old apartment buildings in the flats south and west of the campus, seeking quiet and privacy and the freedom to come and go as they please.

Many of these features of student life at Berkeley have a long history. Transfer students and apartment living have long existed. In the last decade, the replacement of former boarding houses with new high-rise dormitories has counteracted the scattering of student residences. Nevertheless, the fragmentation of the student body has been magnified, if only by the sheer increase in numbers and places of origin.

As a result, a unified college community cannot be found here, even

---

[6] Freedman, "Dropouts."

among the undergraduates. When a student's year of graduation has little relation to his year of entrance, when almost half a graduating class has done most of its work elsewhere, when a third of the students live outside the vicinity of the campus, the small-college loyalty to graduating class and even to college must wither. It is not surprising that in the usual student elections for class officers only about one tenth of the eligible students vote.[7] A large proportion of this tenth lives in fraternities, sororities, and certain dormitories—havens of tradition in which the world of college spirit still finds refuge. For the other students, Berkeley is first and foremost a place to get an education. Lacking the old-fashioned sense of college community, they fall back on smaller campus groupings and limited circles of friends. Their normal activities do not imbue "Berkeley" with the connotation of shared experience that exists at smaller institutions.

A feature of many colleges which adds to the student's sense of belonging is close contact with members of the faculty. A professor can assume the role of surrogate parent for the student newly departed from home or can provide personal adult recognition of his work in preparation for life in an adult world. These needs, more than dissatisfaction with the particular method of teaching, lie behind the frequent complaints about the large lecture courses in the lower division. The same reasons account for much of the prevailing resentment expressed against undergraduate advising. Advisers spend little time with students and change all too frequently. "I can't even remember the names of my advisers for the last three semesters" is a quotation that could come from countless students in many areas of the University. In the absence of a real adviser, a student will sometimes turn to one of his professors, but these too change, and as one student put it, "You never go back to see a professor after you're out of his course." These complaints are directed especially at certain parts of the College of Letters and Science. The professional schools and colleges are smaller and frequently do provide the desired intimacy with professors.

Under these conditions the popularity of the "factory" metaphor begins to be comprehensible. Incoming students contrast their experience at Berkeley with their lives in high school or junior college. The University does not fit the common concept of what a college should be, and in their disappointment, they find "factory" an apt description.

---

[7] ASUC election, December 1965: All undergraduates eligible to vote: 16,610; Number of voters: 1,808; Per cent voting: 10.9%. In the spring of 1965, in the aftermath of the Free Speech Movement, and in the fall of 1965, for the special Constitutional Convention, all-time high records of students turned out to vote: approximately 6,000 students or about 35%. These elections were extraordinary; the 10% of December 1965 is more typical.

Few students have actually worked in a factory, but they know that it is a place where identical articles are mass-produced and workers are treated impersonally.

C. The Variety of Students

Another important reason for the fragmentation of the student body is the wide diversity among the students themselves. Variations that are common at all universities are magnified here, for Berkeley is at the same time both a community college and a world-renowned center of learning. Its students are unusually heterogeneous.

One of the most important variations is in academic potential. A comparison of the entering freshmen of 1960, for whom we have Scholastic Aptitude Test scores, with the entering classes of leading private universities and technical schools, reveals a much wider range of ability here. Although one should use aptitude tests with caution, the SAT verbal profile offers a rough indication of intellectual ability. At Harvard, Stanford, MIT, and Cal Tech, between 70 and 90 per cent of the entering freshmen had SAT verbal scores of over 600, and none of these colleges had more than two per cent of the class with scores of under 500. Berkeley had about a third with scores over 600 and the same fraction with scores under 500. Although Berkeley has a more selective admissions policy than most state universities, the mean verbal score here is still far below that at the leading private institutions. The dispersion is also much greater, and the number of students much larger. In absolute numbers, therefore, there are as many students of high academic potential here as at any of the four institutions mentioned. In 1960 Berkeley admitted 420 students with verbal scores over 650 and at the same time 500 students with scores under 450. Professor Martin Trow sums up the situation: "In other words, in this [SAT] or other measures of academic ability, we have in the same institution and within the same classrooms and lecture halls, groups that match the entering classes of some of our most distinguished colleges and universities side by side with replicas of entering classes of far more modest institutions."[8]

From 1947 to 1960 the Scholastic Aptitude scores of entering classes at Berkeley rose markedly.[9] Although complete figures have not been

---

[8] Martin Trow, "Notes on Undergraduate Teaching at Large State Universities," mimeographed, 1966, pp. 18-19.
[9] Mean SAT Scores for Freshmen Entering Berkeley:

	Verbal		Mathematical	
	1947	1960	1947	1960
Men	491	557	508	595
Women	483	543	411	518

The University of California, Office of Educational Relations, "A Review of CEEB Entrance Testing at the University of California, 1947-1963," mimeographed.

compiled since 1960, the state-wide admissions office reports that without question the quality of our entering students has continued to improve. The proportion of outstanding students is therefore higher today than in 1960. For these students to achieve their potential, they must have the opportunity to advance at a faster rate than the ordinary student. They need the opportunities provided by honors programs and responsible individual study, such as are common at selective private colleges. Only four per cent of our graduating class of 1965 had been in honors programs, and only eight per cent had received any individual instruction.

In determining varieties of students, sex is as important a distinction as academic ability, for it has a marked influence on the choice of field and the attitude toward academic work. There is a concentration of men in the sciences and professional schools (except Education), and a concentration of women in the humanities. There is only one woman to every hundred and fifty men in Engineering, one to every ten in the College of Chemistry and the College of Environmental Design, one to every seven in Business Administration. The sexes are evenly divided in the College of Letters and Science, but the men dominate the sciences (fourteen to one in Physics, three to one in Mathematics) while the women take over some of the humanities and social science majors (two to one in English, Sociology, and Anthropology). Others are evenly split (History and Psychology), and men still control the more abstract majors (Philosophy and Political Science are about two to one, Economics, seven to one). The ratio of men is also much higher in graduate school. There are three men to every two women undergraduates, but three men for every woman among graduates.

A major reason for these different ratios is the purpose for which students come to Berkeley. When asked to pick from a list of reasons for going to college those that were most important for them, a higher percentage of men than women placed first the desire to obtain "vocational training." A more detailed analysis is revealing. It was the first choice of two thirds or more of the men in Engineering and the sciences, but of only half the men in social science and of a third in humanities. The most frequent first choice of men in the humanities (and of the women too) was to obtain "a basic general education." The women showed no such clear vocational orientation as did the majority of men. Only in Engineering and the physical sciences did more than half the women give vocational training as their most important reason for coming to college. This attitude helps explain the higher drop-out rate among women noted earlier.[10]

---

[10]First Choice of 1959 Berkeley Freshmen among Goals for College Education (see p. 18):

The marked differences between the sexes in choice of major and in attitudes toward their education show that a review of the educational needs of our students must consider the different orientations of men and women. The women who come to college highly oriented toward a career are in a minority both in the majors that women dominate and in the traditionally male fields. It is not surprising that the ratio of men to women is twice as high in graduate school as undergraduate, and the ratio of men to women in the faculties vastly greater. When we consider that the Scholastic Aptitude scores of the sexes are about equal, we must question a social and educational system that does not encourage more women to develop profitably their intellectual potential.

The students in the various fields have a tendency to be differentiated not only by their vocational orientation, but also their social and political attitudes as well. A test of the entering freshmen of 1959 showed a distinct correlation between their attitudes and their intended majors, especially among the men.[11] The men students who most frequently gave answers indicating their opposition to existing social and political conditions were those entering the humanities and fine arts. The group which found existing conditions most acceptable were the potential engineers. Women showed less clear trends. Those in the humanities were on the whole more non-conformist than others, but were far less so than the men in humanities. The group most consistently in opposition to existing conditions were the men majoring in humanities. Their very choice of major (for non-vocational reasons) already distinguished them from most men, as noted above.

Differences in temperament are, in fact, related to the whole way of life of the student. They show up, for instance, in the choice of housing. According to a recent psychological survey of Berkeley students, those who live at home, particularly in their freshman year, tend to be less

I. To provide vocational training					
	Engin.	Phys. S.	Biol. S.	Soc. S.**	Human.
Men	72%	64%	72%	52%	35%
Women	62%	53%	8%*	37%	26%
II. To provide a basic general education					
Men	19%	26%	17%	35%	47%
Women	38%	28%	—*	40%	58%

*Fifty-one per cent of the women in Biological Sciences gave no answer.
**The survey placed Business Administration and the other professional schools under the Social Sciences, so that we do not have independent data for them or for the social science students in Letters and Science (Center for the Study of Higher Education).
[11] Ibid.

independent, less tolerant and more conventional than the average student. They have less "complex personalities" in psychological terms. In later years women of this kind who do not drop out are more likely to move into sororities than into other housing, the men into dormitories. At the other extreme, the more unconventional, forceful, and tolerant, that is, the more "complex" students, either start out in apartments or move into them by the time they are seniors. This type of student also moves most frequently during his years in college. High academic potential shows a similar correlation. Students with the highest *verbal* Scholastic Aptitude Test scores are most likely to be found in apartments, and those with the lowest at home or in fraternities and sororities. Dormitories occupy a middle ground.[12]

Comments by individual students interviewed by the Committee give life to these statistics. The atmosphere in fraternities is not conducive to hard study, according to students who have belonged to them.[13] Even when special places or hours are set aside for study, the group pressure is for cooperation in informal and formal activities— a basketball game that someone suddenly starts, a fourth at bridge, decorating the house for a dance or a football weekend. The serious student finds these living arrangements unsatisfactory and moves into an apartment. The women who move into apartments have much the same to say about dormitory life. Berkeley's high-rise dormitories represent to them lack of privacy and intellectual stimulus, and restrictions on their personal freedom. One young lady who had shifted to an apartment recalled the dormitory as "thirty screaming girls on one floor."

The large size of the student body, the number of schools and colleges, and the differences of intellectual ability, sex, and temperament all combine to produce vast diversity among the students at Berkeley. They need many kinds of academic programs and many kinds of teaching, especially at the undergraduate level.

D. The Academically Oriented Students

As we have seen, among these varieties of students there is a wide range of intellectual ability. Those in humanities are likely to be higher in verbal aptitude than in mathematical, those in science and engineer-

---

[12] Mervin B. Freedman, "Some Considerations of Housing at Berkeley," typescript in Select Committee files.

[13] One of the major informants of the Committee was a candidate for the ASUC Senate from a fraternity who feels that the only hope of survival of the fraternities is to become more academic.

ing higher in mathematical aptitude; among both groups, but particularly in science, there are many who are intellectually the peers of any student group in the country. Most of these students, both at the undergraduate and graduate levels, have fixed upon careers and are seizing the opportunities offered by the University to educate themselves for a lifetime of work and advancement in their fields. They are the self-disciplined, serious students who appear in every survey.

The values of these academically-oriented students are aptly described by Professors Burton R. Clark and Martin Trow:

> The essence of this system of values is its identification with the intellectual concerns of the serious faculty members. The students involved work hard, get the best grades, talk about their course work outside of class, and let the world of ideas and knowledge reach them. . . . [They are] both identified with the college and involved in learning. For these students, their attachment to the college, which may be as strong as among the collegiate crowd, is to the institution which supports intellectual values and opportunities for learning; the emotional tie is through the faculty to the college, and through campus friends of similar mind and temper. . . . The products of this culture are typically aiming at graduate and professional schools; it is not surprising that they identify so strongly with the faculty, and internalize the scholarly and scientific habits of mind and work as part of their anticipatory socialization to future professional roles.[14]

Berkeley is fortunate in having a large number of these students. The University may be imperfect, like all human institutions, but these students are more apt to make the best of the opportunities it offers than to belabor its imperfections. In a word, they are more responsive to its virtues than to its flaws. In our present efforts to devise the best possible education for all students, those who are academically oriented compel less of our attention than do the others. But if they present fewer problems, we have no less an obligation to them, and their comfortable allegiance is no guarantee that we are meeting their needs as well as we could.

E. The Drop-Out and the Rebel

Yet the needs of all students are not the same. This fact becomes clear when we observe their attitudes toward the University. Although discontent with certain aspects of the University is fairly widespread—

---

[14] Burton R. Clark and Martin Trow, "Determinants of College Student Subcultures," mimeographed, in Committee files.

even those who are most proud of it recognize that it has flaws—the majority of students express basic satisfaction with their experience here. Dissatisfaction is most prominent among the non-conformist students who are typically inclined toward the humanities and social sciences. It takes a form of alienation whose effects can be observed in certain drop-outs and in the students who demonstrated against the University during the Free Speech Movement.

The drop-out is the extreme case of the student whose education here has been unsuccessful. Some leave because of failing grades, but others do so without such a clear academic reason. That students are admitted who prove incapable of meeting our standards is a disturbing phenomenon and calls attention to the need for reviewing our admission procedures and our liaison with high school and junior college advisers. Not all the fault lies here, of course, for students may do poorly not because of inability but because they are emotionally upset. The difficulties faced by these students are often the same as those of the students who drop out with passing grades. These last offer the most direct challenge to our educational system, since they are young men and women who have demonstrated the capacity to continue at Berkeley and choose voluntarily not to do so. Their percentage in the total number of drop-outs increases with each year of college. Only one fifth of the freshmen who leave are in good academic standing, compared to two thirds at the upper-division level.[15]

There appears to be a significant relation between the probability that an academically capable student will drop out and the variety of student to which he belongs. Women are more likely to leave than men, partly, no doubt, because they lack as strong a vocational orientation. Students living in fraternities, sororities, and dormitories are more likely to remain than those in private residences. A recent study suggests also that drop-outs who have had satisfactory grades have more complex personalities and are more non-conformist than the average student. Continuing students are more conventional, show more self-discipline, and are most interested in social and religious activities.

Frequently the academically capable drop-outs have had difficulty in finding their place in the world. Many of them have experienced family conflicts and tend to be isolated from their peers, lonely, and

---

[15] Per cent of Undergraduate Drop-Outs of the Berkeley Entering Class of Fall 1961 who had passing grades:

	Men					Women			
Years	1	2	3	4		1	2	3	4
Per Cent	14	27	59	61		38	46	83	70

Freedman, "Dropouts at Berkeley."

unable to accept help from friends or counselors. Many women experience conflict in their roles as women and are more preoccupied with sex than are the continuing women. These students are more prone than the average to suffer from the loneliness of the campus, even though in their living habits they seek privacy—often at the price of loneliness.[16]

For such students the Counseling Center and the psychiatric division of the Student Health Service offer help. One bright woman in humanities told the Committee of the following experience. Although she entered a dormitory upon arrival, she disliked its life and received poor grades. She finally consulted a University psychiatrist, who analyzed her difficulty as arising from her belief that she should belong to a group. Once she could accept the desire for independence as a normal wish, she began to do the excellent work of which she was capable. Many potentially good students, unfortunately, are not motivated to seek this kind of help. When beset by serious academic or personal problems, they become drop-outs.

These students are by no means unique to Berkeley; they resemble, for instance, the alienated and uncommitted Harvard students recently described by Kenneth Keniston.[17] These young men, too, had difficulty adjusting to the world in which they lived. They sought to escape the past and ignore the future, preferring the emotional experience of the present. While they were children the fathers of many of them were absent from the home, or, if present, paid little attention to their families. To fill this void, mothers and sons drew close together. During adolescence these young men felt estranged from other boys, and they did not learn to be comfortable in the presence of girls. By the time they reached college, they had rejected social norms, yet were unable to use the freedom that they sought for any clear purpose. Their outlook included no social commitment, no desire to join with others to change the society that they disliked. Although they were unusually intelligent, their personalities prevented them from profiting fully from their education.

Such extreme alienation is the result of personal and cultural factors beyond the control of the University. Nevertheless, something can be done for students who may drop out for reasons of this kind. Advisers

---

[16] Freedman, "Dropouts at Berkeley;" and Keith Elmer Merrill, "The Relationship of Certain Non-intellective Factors to Lack of Persistence of Higher-Ability Students and Persistence of Lower-Ability Students at the University of California, Berkeley," Dissertation in Educational Administration, University of California, Berkeley, 1964.
[17] Kenneth Keniston, *The Uncommitted: Alienated Youth in American Society* (New York, 1965).

who have the time to talk seriously to them about their education, and instructors who get to know them in small classes or seminars, could offer personal help at critical moments, and, when it is called for, could encourage the use of campus facilities for professional counseling and treatment.

Most of the academically capable drop-outs continue their education elsewhere or eventually return to Berkeley. Many of those who return end up as superior students. They say that they needed a break in their education to "reevaluate things," to "think over what I am doing," to "see how I fit in the world," and the like. They were confronted with the dilemma of continuing their current academic programs or leaving the University entirely. Sometimes, a period of complete break with the University is the best possible move. Alternatively, some of these students could do educationally valuable work off-campus in various kinds of supervised field-study programs. This would save them from the trauma of interrupting their college careers and at the same time provide them with the opportunity of developing maturity and purposeful re-orientation.

Alienation from the University does not necessarily lead to dropping out. At Berkeley the uncommitted student, who has no meaningful goal for his life and who leaves college to find himself, has been less conspicuous than the student who discovers meaning in championing the downtrodden. Berkeley has a longstanding tradition of student political activity in support of radical and unpopular causes. One can recall speeches outside Sather Gate in the Thirties in support of the Popular Front, student participation in the loyalty-oath controversy of the early Fifties, the demonstrations in favor of Caryl Chessman and against the House Un-American Activities Committee in 1959-60, and civil rights activities in 1963-64. This tradition has attracted to the campus students seeking through political and social activities some kind of commitment for their lives.

These facts were brought home by the Free Speech Movement of the fall semester of 1964. Because the events of that period were traumatic for the entire University community, they gave rise to many studies of activist commitment among Berkeley students. The most obvious causes of student support of the movement were their desire to obtain freedom of political advocacy on campus and their outrage at what they viewed as foul play on the part of the University administration. But many less explicit motivations must have played a part: prior participation in civil rights causes, dislike of certain aspects of the University, an unsatisfied longing for the shared experience so lacking in the impersonality of

Berkeley life, and dissatisfaction with their own unmotivated existence.

Students tend to fall into distinct categories as regards their support or opposition to the FSM. One can consider arrest for the Sproul Hall sit-in of the night of December 2-3, 1964, as a sign of strong commitment to the FSM. Among those arrested whose majors are known, humanities and social science students were most numerous. The major with the highest percentage of its students arrested was the Social Science Field Major (14%). The next five majors, all with more than 10% of their total graduate and undergraduate students arrested, were in the humanities.[18] The departments with the largest contingent of arrested students were English, History, and Political Science. At the other extreme, the majors with the lowest percentages of arrested students were mainly professional: Law, Electrical Engineering, and Education. Finally, there were some schools with sizable enrollments and with no students identified among those arrested: Agriculture, Forestry, Optometry, and Public Health.[19] The sciences fell in the middle, with the biological sciences having a higher proportion of arrested students than the physical sciences.

Supporters of the FSM not arrested in Sproul Hall had similar characteristics. All surveys agree that there was wide support among social science majors (three quarters of whom were favorable to the movement, according to one survey), with less support by humanities and science majors.[20] In contrast, over half the students in Business Administration and Engineering disapproved. Nearly three-quarters of the students living in apartments favored the FSM, whereas a similar ratio of those in fraternities and sororities disapproved of it.

The students arrested in Sproul Hall also included an unusual percentage of scholastically able young people. Their grades were significantly higher than those of the average student. Nearly half had grade-point averages higher than 3.0, whereas only 21% of the total student body had grades this high. Among the graduate students arrested, more than two thirds had averages above 3.5; only 55% of all

---

[18] Dramatic Art, Philosophy, Humanities Field Major, Classics and Comparative Literature. The major with the highest percentage was actually Molecular Biology, with three students out of fourteen arrested, or 21%. The major is too small to be statistically significant.

[19] English: 78 students, 6.5% of undergraduate and graduate majors; History: 62 students, 5.6%; Political Science: 53 students, 5.5%; Law: 2 students, 0.2%; Electrical Engineering: 2 students, 0.2%; Education: 1 student, 0.1%. These figures are based on the self-identification of 501 of the 645 arrested students. Many of the remaining students were probably in the lower division and had not declared a major.

[20] Gales, "Berkeley Student Opinion"; and Paul Heist, "Representation of Respondents: Percentage of FSM Members and Students in Comparison Samples Distributed by Academic Year and Major Field of Specialization," mimeographed table in Select Committee files.

graduates were at this level.[21] Many of the most promising students in the College of Letters and Science and in graduate school, especially in the humanities and social sciences, were strongly enough devoted to the cause of the FSM to face arrest in its behalf.

Moreover, if we explore the reactions of the student body at large, we find that there was considerable sympathy for the FSM, though its extent would be difficult to gauge accurately. Over four fifths of the students surveyed in April, 1965, said they agreed with the goals of the FSM, although only one half approved of its tactics. Moreover, three quarters believed the leaders of the movement to be idealistic and motivated by moral values.[22] On the whole, support was greater among those students with high scholastic records than among those with low records. According to the principal study available, 80% of the surveyed undergraduates who had grade-point averages over 3.5 (more A's than B's) approved of the FSM, but only 44% of those with less than 2.5 GPA (more C's than B's) did so. Among graduate students the figures were even more startling. Only one fifth of those with less than 3.0 (B) averages approved, but nearly three quarters of those with over 3.5 averages did so.[23] These surveys show that the spirit of the FSM touched more students than simple arrest figures indicate.

For reasons already observed, many students failed to find here a community spirit, and the FSM suddenly offered them a cause with which they could identify. For them the FSM imbued the name of Berkeley with a meaning and an ethos, and gave them a feeling of belonging to an identifiable and worthwhile group.

As was seen, even during the excitement of last year, a large majority of the students expressed general satisfaction with the University. One can attribute the return of calm in the fall of 1965 in part to this spirit. Nevertheless, the experience of the FSM offers serious lessons. First of all, the ease with which a majority of students could find, however ephemerally, a commitment and a moral drive in opposing the University administration is evidence of a widespread, if latent, alienation which can be turned against the University. This alienation is different in degree, but probably not in kind, from that of the more active protestors.

[21] Ibid.
[22] Eugene Bardach et al., "The Free Speech Controversy." The information came from 598 questionnaires completed by the persons arrested, of which 537 (80%) came from currently enrolled students. Eighteen per cent were graduate students, 46% upper-division students, 36% lower-division students. In the total student population of that semester, the graduates were 35%, upper-division students 36%, and lower-division 28%. Graduate students were underrepresented in Sproul Hall, but the ratio of upper-division to lower-division students was the same as in the total population (1.3 to 1).
[23] Gales, "Berkeley Student Opinion."

Secondly, the high intellectual abilities of many strongly committed members of the FSM may mark them for positions of leadership in our society, particularly in cultural and political fields. The success of the movement demonstrated their capacity for leadership. Whatever judgment is made of their behavior, Berkeley can be proud of the presence of this kind of student. There is danger, however, that the effectiveness of their education may be lost through alienation and antagonism.

F. The Non-Conformist Students

To suggest that we should consider the needs of the discontented students is to evoke in many quarters the immediate reply that they are but a vocal minority, that we should concern ourselves with the majority of students who are satisfied with the education they receive. This reply oversimplifies the realities of the situation.

The Bay Area has become a leading cultural and scientific center of the United States, located in great natural beauty and favored with a pleasant climate. High among its attractions is the University at Berkeley. The magnetic force of such a community has attracted a diverse populace of unorthodox artists, writers, and thinkers, as well as self-appointed social reformers, seekers after excitement and notoriety, and irresponsible cranks. But it has also brought to our campus a remarkable group of intelligent and imaginative young men and women who both contribute and respond to the atmosphere of the local community.

At the same time, more restrictive admissions policies, forced upon us by the growing number of college-age youths, are reducing the number of students who keep alive the traditional college spirit. Evidence of this change is apparent in the recent marked decline in numbers of students belonging to fraternities.[24] Meanwhile, the commitment of the master plan for higher education in California, to reduce the size of the lower division at Berkeley while increasing the number of graduate students, will raise the age of our student body. Our students in the future will be more mature, more independent, and less attracted by the traditional collegiate culture.

---

[24] Berkeley Campus Fraternity Membership (Actives and Pledges):

Fall Semesters	
Year	Membership
1960	1,939
1961	1,901
1962	1,958
1963	1,859
1964	1,814
1965	1,646

Thus for various reasons, partly extrinsic, partly indigenous, the number of students who are susceptible to discontent with the University is likely to grow. It is, of course, impossible to know whether the number of alienated students will actually increase and what form alienation may take in the future. Much will probably depend on the attitude of the University. For the time being, however, we must recognize their presence, their feelings, and their influence. Even the large number of generally satisfied students cannot isolate themselves from non-conformist attitudes and ideas: they react positively or negatively. In the middle ground, there are many more students who share with the non-conformists their doubts about some aspects of the University. Educational changes that will affect the attitudes of the more intelligent and often more discontented minority will affect the attitudes of the entire student body toward the University. We need to understand the mentality of these intelligent non-conformist students.

The subject is one that calls for the illumination of time, and for a much more extensive study than the Committee has been able to make. Nevertheless, we feel that it is important enough to merit a provisional attempt now. Our description is more impressionistic than scientific and more simple than the description of a highly complex phenomenon should be. But we offer it in the belief that even in its broad outlines it may help to dispel some of the confusion and misunderstanding that has gathered about a group of our students.[25]

The most obvious feature of their outlook, which every observer notes immediately, is their outright rejection of many aspects of present-day America. They find much to fear and condemn and, overtly at least, little to praise. Essentially, they see our society as controlled by a group which has abandoned the common welfare in its own self-interest and has resorted to many techniques to disguise its activities and to manipulate the general public. As these students see it, while the dominant group claims to champion freedom, religion, patriotism, and morality, it produces and condones slums, racial segregation, migrant farm laborers, false advertising, American economic imperialism, and the bomb. In private life, moreover, the students find as much immorality and injustice as in public life. They commonly explain it as the product of an all-pervasive hypocrisy.

[25] The following analysis of the non-conformist student is based on various types of information: current articles on the subject, interviews with undergraduate and graduate students, and study of the literature and music popular among students. Several of the research assistants of the Committee contributed by observing the culture of the non-conformist students, meeting in discussion sessions with members of the Committee, and writing their own reports on the subject.

To succeed in this society, they believe, you must mask your real feelings and become an organization man, wear what you're expected to wear, say what you're expected to say, and praise the product of your company when you know it has been built to wear out. It's all a game, playing a role; and these young people find that Americans in this other-directed age have been conditioned to accept without a thought or a murmur their own falsity. They accuse Americans of sacrificing conscience to the quest for status. In this society, they say, those who claim to be moral are really immoral and those who claim to be sane are truly insane.

All this these students condemn. What terrifies them is their conviction that the failure of the individual sense of responsibility, in combination with technology and cybernation, is producing a bureaucratized, machine-run society. They find themselves in danger of losing both their freedom and their humanity to IBM machines and to those who use them. They say that a man must fight hypocrisy to live in a moral world, but he will have to halt the computers if he is to remain a man at all. The fear of 1984, common in the Forties and Fifties, of the totalitarian state based on ubiquitous terror, has reverted among the present generation of radical students to a fear of the scientifically conditioned Brave New World. In the student mind, the dominant group takes the form of the "organized system" that Paul Goodman decries, or the "power structure" opposed by civil rights organizations, or simply "the establishment." "You can't trust anyone over thirty" expresses a vague but pervasive belief that their elders have been corrupted past salvation by the system. Commonly, the students, taking an existentialist position of belief in individual responsibility, seek individuals to blame for the evil actions of society—men who through fear, weak character, or dishonesty have abdicated their moral responsibility. Student radicals find, for example, McGeorge Bundy, Robert McNamara, and ultimately President Johnson responsible for what they see as American aggression in Vietnam.

For a significant number of young people the older generation is represented most clearly by their parents, who have accepted the system and made their way in it. If the parents remain faithful to religious practices and teachings, the child may be further alienated, since he is likely to be religiously skeptical or atheistic. What most exasperates members of the new generation is their belief that their elders do not take them seriously. "How many roads must a man walk down before you call him a man?" the popular protest singer Bob Dylan asks in a song adopted by the FSM.

Ultimately the students find their society decadent and the dominant group intellectually sterile. For them, American art is created by folk singers, Negro musicians, and bohemian artists and writers. In their most pessimistic moments, America, and indeed the whole West, no longer appears to have any message for the world. Zen Buddhism offers more hope for humanity than does Christianity.

The revolt turns against the traditional ideals of America which the older generation holds up for admiration: the puritan ethic, individualism, and old-fashioned patriotism. Against the puritan ethic non-conformist students flaunt sexual and emotional freedom. They find individualism in the form of private property evil when it justifies exorbitant wealth, dishonest products, and segregated housing. The past history of America becomes for them a sordid tale of the exploitation of non-Anglo-Saxon cultures and races at home and of innocent countries abroad. They see patriotic appeals to the ideals of life, liberty, and pursuit of happiness as trappings to cover sham and hypocrisy.

Before 1960 the usual reaction of the few young people who held this view of our world was to withdraw from society, as did the uncommitted youths studied by Keniston at Harvard. They "went beat" and demonstrated their rejection of the system in their personal life and dress. Since then, this type of reaction has become much more widespread. Beards, long hair, and bare feet protest the conspicuous waste and conformity of the status-conscious society. Instead of the whiskey of their parents, many of these students prefer to use marijuana. Revolt also takes other forms which an outsider can view only as self-destructive; some students can explain laziness, procrastination, and irresponsibility as rejection of the puritan ethic of hard work. Thus many young people clothe in a quasi-moral garb the traditional student difficulty of buckling down to work. This attitude can lead brilliant students to fall behind and eventually drop out.

Another disturbing and ironic development of the new generation is its commitment to form. It has lost respect for the public-relations mentality of "the system," but it has its own admiration for style. In personal relations the highest mark of style is being "cool." Originally the praiseworthy quality of not losing one's head in a crisis, in the Fifties being cool came to mean not opening oneself up, not revealing one's weaknesses, having love affairs without becoming emotionally involved. Keeping cool involves as much role-playing as does the hypocrisy the student finds in the scorned minion of the system.

The search for style is in fact a manifestation of the internal conflict and ambiguity that plagues many of these young men and women. Freed from traditional inhibitions, they find that their new role-playing, their "cool," deprives them of the satisfying personal relationships that more traditional patterns used to foster. Paradoxically, old-fashioned romantic love remains their ideal. Some attempt pathetically to simulate love at first sight. Through the exchange of intense confidences, they seek to "communicate" completely and to "build meaningful relationships." To little avail. Instant love proves exhausting and empty.

The search for genuine experience leads also to experimenting with non-addictive hallucinatory drugs. The student hopes through them to free his mind from the shackles of reason and logic, to apprehend the ineffable truths about himself and his surroundings, and to become truly creative. This desire for instant poetry, instant psychoanalysis, and instant mysticism is a further form of escape from hard work, a translation to intellectual and emotional spheres of the American cult of the labor-saving device. The belief that experience through drugs provides more insight than hard rational thought cannot but affect the attitude of young people toward formal education.

These ways of rejecting society in one's private life are outgrowths of the patterns of the earlier "beat" or non-committed generation. At Berkeley the non-conformist has always had another avenue of protest against society: in preference to ironic withdrawal, some have chosen alienated commitment. Since 1960 the radical students of Berkeley have been at the forefront of a wave of student activism that has spread throughout the country.

The activists often reject formal ideologies as a suspect heritage from their elders and attack instead specific policies that they find evil: atomic testing, racial segregation, and, lately, American involvement in Vietnam. Admitting their admiration for anarchism and existentialism, these students assert that the individual must oppose evil directly no matter how strong the system that protects it; for to condemn without acting, as did the Germans who submitted to Hitler, is to share in the guilt. Yet they seldom act as individuals; instead they form groups to organize public acts of protest—petitions, marches, vigils, and, ultimately, sit-ins and civil disobedience. Besides giving strength to their voices, organizations with a high purpose can serve to compensate for a lack of rewarding relationships in their private lives. To join a cause is part of the anxious search for a new "sense of viable community" that makes this generation seem hardly less other-directed than its elders.

There is a similar ambiguity in their expectations. On the surface they display a quiet determination and optimism: "we shall overcome." At times, they seem to believe that a solution to society's ills is at hand if only their demands are met: "Freedom now!" Except in moments of exhilaration, however, as during the height of the Free Speech Movement, this confident appearance masks an underlying pessimism. They are not very hopeful of achieving instant freedom and instant reform. Their acts of defiance are often also acts of despair.

When one turns from description of student non-conformity to an explanation of its source, one enters more unsure territory. A thorough explanation of their alienation and their desires awaits a careful study, but some insights can be offered.

In some ways the current student protests have different origins from those of previous decades. Since the Second World War, a generation has grown up and entered college in a society of unparalleled affluence. They have been unimpressed by the possibilities opened up by wealth, but at the same time they take a certain amount of economic well-being for granted. Hence, they do not feel a pressure to achieve the traditional forms of success in business or the professions.

They have grown up under the dread, not of poverty, but of annihilation. Their childhood and youth were filled with stories of the dangers of atomic testing, of poisoned milk, rain, and air. Behind their existentialism and their pessimism lies a long awareness of the possibility of sudden death should an irresponsible adult push the wrong button. It is hard to document such a fear, but it is a recurring theme in the songs and literature that appeal to this generation of students.

This much is new. What is old is the very concept of social protest in America. Behind these students lie the examples of Thoreau and the Pilgrims. The twentieth century has seen a long and painful revolt against the established groups which have run the United States since its birth. In the end the "organized system" or "power structure" of the students is largely the traditional American Protestant society. Forces and traditions far older than today's students are behind the revolution that continues to stir America, but the students are keenly attuned to it and view it as their very own. Youths of traditional background who belong to this student culture find themselves cut off from their parents not only by the conflict of generations but also by their rejection of the traditions their parents revere. Their break is difficult, their position frequently ambiguous. They often seek to prove their liberation by forming relationships with members of other racial and religious groups.

There is much youthful impatience in the search for instantaneous remedies to public and private ills. The unconventional student is inordinately sure that his own picture of the world is the correct one. He lacks the perspective necessary for self-criticism and for an appreciation of his opponent's position. Of course, there are also some who enjoy the notoriety and power offered by leadership of protest movements.

Members of the older generation are more willing to tolerate the evils of the world, believing they can be reduced but never entirely eliminated. They may find these students immature and impatient; the students retort that to be willing to tolerate and explain is a sign of middle-aged compromise. There is a need to create a dialogue between these two points of view.

Understanding cannot be demanded only on the students' side. While their reaction is often emotional, their picture of the world has a rational structure and is not entirely a mirage. Too many highly intelligent and sincere young people are among the non-conformists for their protests to be dismissed out of hand. Perhaps one of their troubles is that they have taken seriously their school lessons on the high aims of America.

G. The Students and the University

This analysis has made students, conformist and non-conformist, appear more stereotyped and less individual than they are. Unavoidably, it may have suggested an artificial polarity between the concerns of the "conformist" and the "non-conformist." This polarity is indeed believed in by many radical students and their adversaries, but we regard it as a stereotype to be challenged. We would rather say that any student with enough motivation to "make it" at this campus is in fact committed to some aspect of our common and rather tolerant heritage, whether he would admit it or not.

Of course, no single student, however non-conformist, accepts the above picture of society in its entirety or engages in all the above forms of protest. Some of those whom the description fits most nearly have close associations with other young people who are no longer in college or graduate school but who remain near the Univeristy because of the excitement and social acceptance they find in Berkeley. Non-conformist students and alienated drop-outs of similar outlook produce much of the flavor of Telegraph Avenue. Although these students are a definite minority, their view of the world in attenuated form extends very widely through the rest of the student body. Their attitudes cannot but affect profoundly the relation of the students to the University.

The University takes pride in its devotion to finding and teaching truth and knowledge. Accepting it on these terms, the potentially alienated student expects to find within its walls idealism silencing cant and hypocrisy. Disillusioned with his elders, he comes to the faculty seeking a "prophet" or a "wise man" (the terms are quoted from students). Here he expects to fill his need for a community in which he can participate, find satisfactory communication with adults, and enlist their support in his struggle to right the wrongs of society. With such high, if unformulated, expectations, this kind of student is bound to be disappointed. Communication with the older generation often fails to materialize in large lecture courses. Few if any of his teachers even know his name. He comes to believe that his worth is measured in answers to mass examinations, not in personal assessment of his work and ideas. He learns to play a game within the University, to select his courses according to the grade he is likely to receive, to write ritual papers, and to second-guess the instructor. He decides that the University is too busy conforming to the needs of the establishment to produce men capable of opposing its evils.

In the critical student's eyes, the professors turn out to have their own system and play their own game. He sees their research as a means for their own advancement rather than as a search for truth. They turn out to be neither prophets nor wise men, only specialists in one area with all their prejudices in other areas intact.

We have seen that students who have this outlook on life are more likely to be in the humanities and social sciences than in the natural sciences or professional schools. Some of these students soon become convinced that even in the humanities and social sciences the professor's command of his specialty and fame through publication count for more than teaching the elements of a subject to beginning students. They decide that the only refuge may be outside. But while they prefer creativity in art and literature to its exegesis, the reforming of society to its analysis, most realize that they must still work to live, and in their disillusion end up playing the game.

In sum, the dissatisfied student finds the University to be just another part of the established order. His alienation from society turns into an alienation from his University. His distrust of the older generation makes it difficult for him to appreciate traditional methods of instruction or the faculty's idea of a good education, especially when some professors do in fact display insouciance in their teaching. The student's view of the University is molded to a large extent by the same unwillingness to accept human imperfection that molds his general views of our social system.

This explanation of the attitudes of alienated students collapses into simple logical sequence what is in fact a complex evolution. The potentially alienated freshman or transfer student comes with no clear idea of what to expect in the University, and with inchoate, largely traditional views of society. His images of American society and of the ideal university take shape simultaneously as a result of what he sees and hears after he arrives.

To say that the students reject the University because they regard it as an extension of the organized system is hardly a novel insight; it is a charge that has often been repeated by student leaders. There is a further, less obvious connection between the students' general outlook and their reaction to the University. Those who believe that there can be short cuts to social reform, mysticism, and love cannot conceive that there are no short cuts to learning. Difficult courses that make them pore over facts and theorems can seem a tedious waste of time concocted by unimaginative professors. There must be instant knowledge—if only the faculty would become attuned to the modern world. To overcome this attitude the University must discover how to impart once more the truth that there is no royal road to mathematics.

The anti-rational aspects of student thought contribute to this attitude. Students who hold unreflectingly the belief that feeling is a surer guide to truth than is reason, cannot readily appreciate the University's commitment to rational investigation. If they believe that Western culture is decadent, they cannot appreciate the University's devotion to its preservation and transmission.

Commitment to social action also prevents students from accepting as valuable an autonomous world of ideas. They find it hard to conceive that the purpose of the University can be to seek and preserve pure knowledge. They feel that impartiality cannot exist in the social sciences, or for that matter in any subject that deals with man and his culture. Instead of praising the impartiality of the teacher who does not relate his lessons to immediate problems, they accuse him of moral irresponsibility.

There is a contradiction in this criticism that betrays the anti-intellectual stance of the non-conformist students. They condemn the University because it is a factory that turns out the products demanded by society and trains students in the rules of the game; yet they want their education to be related to present-day life and to their personal needs, not to the abstract concerns of the humanities and sciences. They see the University as an agent of the power structure, and they want it to become instead an agent of their moral revolution. A major task of the University is to convince the students of the value of free and independent inquiry, of the need of the University for autonomy from all quarters if it is properly to serve society.

H. Conclusion

This brief look at the ferment among our students has attempted to make clearer some of the reasons for the ambiguity of their attitude toward the University that was observed at the outset. There are many varieties of students. Those who by and large approve of American society as it is, those who enjoy the culture of fraternities and dormitories, and those who come here specifically to prepare for a profession are on the whole satisfied, or at least not inclined to demonstrate their discontent by breaking with the University. Those who have more complex personalities or who are upset, those who choose to study humanities and social sciences, those whose individualism makes them prefer living alone, and those who reject important aspects of American society are more likely to react against their education, dropping out or protesting against the University. These attitudes are not mutually exclusive and the different mixture of them in different students can account for the same person's voicing expressions of both criticism and admiration. The fact that their attitudes toward the University are as much influenced by their outlook on society as by the actual nature of the education they receive makes it unlikely that any set of reforms can satisfy all of their complaints.

Responsibility for their attitudes lies in part with an older generation whose members do not try to understand them, and who go about their own lives and their teaching in the ways they learned when they were brought up. A majority of our students agree with most of these ways, and few of the dissatisfied can think of reasonable reform. It is up to the faculty, with its greater experience, to listen seriously to the students, to analyze the problems of our present system of education, and propose new directions.

We cannot think of education here in terms of a traditional four-year college at the center of the University, and a graduate school and two or three professional schools juxtaposed to it. We have at all levels a constant movement of students, with the result that many find themselves with only vaguely collegiate loyalties. To some "Berkeley" may mean a department or a professor, but for most it connotes an atmosphere of culture, and a way of life in which personal freedom counts for much.

For students to take a real interest in their education, they must feel that the educator is also interested in them as individuals, not just as an amorphous student body. In the end we must try to build bridges across that gulf between generations that separates students from their teachers and from their own past. Personal contact with professors will tend to dispel the legends that circulate about the achievement orientation of the faculty and will make the students more likely to develop respect for hard intellectual work. If students exchange views directly with teachers who accept and embody the values of our civilization, they will be more ready to respect these values than if Western culture and the American past are handed to them from above as something to memorize and regurgitate in examinations. In the process of achieving these objectives, professors may themselves re-discover the youthful spirit. We hope that a number of the proposals that follow will help accomplish these aims.*

*Prof. Peter Scott wishes to add the following comment: "I find something oblique and misdirected about the foregoing references to the problems of our society, as mirrored in the alleged 'outlook' of 'the new generation'. Not only do I question many of the judgments which ensue, I doubt the initial value of focusing on the mirror. Disillusion with this world is and always has been the beginning of heightened self-awareness; but one will learn little more from a catalogue of its outward manifestations, which may be either constructive or escapist. Nor am I happy at the tranquillizing prospect of 'teachers who accept and embody the values of our civilization'. Both students and teachers have, I think, a more vital job: not to accept values, but to make them new.

"On a more practical level, the students will only come to identify with the University when a richer, more active student culture develops, as at Harvard or Oxford. It is not so much that we do too little to educate students, as that they need to do more for themselves. 'The popular cliché that the University operates as a factory' will not be dispelled simply by a smoother program of Student-Faculty (or Administration) Relations. Facilities are not yet adequate to encourage active, self-directed student learning; they are still too efficiently linked to the preparation of a desired vocational product."

III.

THE IMPROVEMENT
OF TEACHING

A. A Homily on the Importance of Teaching

ONE OF THE MOST widely accepted ideas in modern thinking about college teaching is that the quality of teaching depends on the ethos of the campus; it matters profoundly whether a campus is or is not permeated with a care for teaching. The best campuses, large or small, have a tradition of good teaching which is felt even in manifestations of campus life far beyond the classroom. The reason that teaching becomes part of the general ethos of a place is that it goes on all the time. It cannot be turned on and off by class hours, schedules, or catalogues. Facing students—sensitive and observant young people—we cannot help but teach. The only question is what and how.

Few of us think of teaching as the mechanical transmission of knowledge X from person A to person B. In our formal courses, along with information, we consciously transmit a method, a skill, a stance toward problems; and in an age of rapidly changing knowledge, the method, the skill, and the stance may well outweigh the information in value to the student. We are sometimes less conscious that in profound ways some of the most lasting things that we also teach are qualities, abilities, and attitudes exemplified in the way we have taught, in our stance toward the student himself. A class taught by an unprepared teacher teaches the student neglect of scholarship. A department which encourages professors to hide from students, teaches the neglect of human relations. If a scholarly attitude is—as it should be—part of what we teach, the teaching process must exemplify in all its details the scholarly attitude of the teacher; otherwise the very method of teaching gives the lie to the thing taught. And if all our scholarship—our research and our publication and our teaching—is justified, as it should be, by its devotion to humane ends, no defect of humane consideration is acceptable in our transactions with students. The image of the teacher will be no trivial part of what the world is or could be in the student's mind. It will influence the student's judgment—toward hope or toward cynicism—regarding the educability of man and the power of scholarship to solve human problems; it will be a great part of his final attitude toward the University itself. Each of us has a stake, then, in the good teaching of the others, and the good teaching of each is the legitimate concern of all. A campus that lacks a tradition of good teaching by that fact casts some doubt on the ultimate meaning of its scholarship.

Large public universities are collectively under attack on the score of teaching, and we have come in for our full share of criticism by both students and the public.[1] The severity of this criticism creates a misleading picture of the Berkeley campus. We know that there is much superb teaching on this campus by professors and assistants alike; there are many students enjoying an education well suited to their personal needs, and with adequate opportunity for dialogue with members of the faculty. But it would be wrong to say that we are everywhere doing as good teaching as we would like. While there are individuals and even whole schools and departments that are distinguished for the quality of their teaching, the campus as a whole has not yet achieved that atmosphere or ethos of devotion to teaching that it must have in order to maintain its scholarly excellence.

An ethos is produced by the emulation of respected models; the responsibility for its maintenance falls most heavily, then, on the most respected members of the faculty. They, most of all, must demonstrate an ample concern with teaching, lest the whole enterprise become tainted with irresponsibility. We may take satisfaction in such fine traditions as those of the English Department, where senior professors usually

[1] See for instance, P. H. Abelson, "What Are Professors For?", *Science*, Vol. 148 (June 18, 1965), p. 1545; J. F. Boler, "Behind the Protests at Berkeley," *Commonweal*, Vol. 81 (Feb. 5, 1965), pp. 602-5; J. Cass, "What Happened at Berkeley," *Saturday Review*, Vol. 48 (Feb. 20, 1965), p. 62; John Fischer, "Is There a Teacher on the Faculty?", *Harper's Magazine*, Vol. 230 (Feb., 1965), pp. 18-28; Max Heirich and Sam Kaplan, "Yesterday's Discord," *California Monthly*, Vol. LXXVII, No. 5 (Feb., 1965), pp. 20-32; Irving Howe, "Beleaguered Professors," *The Atlantic*, Vol. 216, No. 5 (Nov., 1965), pp. 115-18; J. G. Kemeny, "Once the College Professor was a Teacher," *New York Times Magazine*, (June 2, 1963), p. 14; E. Langer, "Crisis at Berkeley," *Science*, Vol. 148 (April 9-16, 1965), pp. 198-202; Calvin H. Plimpton, *et al*, "The Student of 1965—Four Views," *Amherst Alumni News*, Vol. 17, No. 1 (Summer, 1965), pp. 2-19; *Time*, "Crassest Opportunism," Vol. 84 (Dec. 11, 1964), p. 61; *Time*, "Ubiquitous T.A.," Vol. 85 (June 4, 1965), pp. 49-50; John Walsh, "Congress: Subcommittee Surveys Effects of Federally Supported Research on Higher Education," *Science*, Vol. 19 (July 2, 1965), pp. 42-44; Max Ways, "On the Campus: A Troubled Reflection of the U.S.," *Fortune*, Vol. 72, No. 4 (Oct., 1965), pp. 140-176; Jerome C. Byrne, *et al.*, "Report on the University of California and Recommendations to the Special Committee of the Regents . . .," May 7, 1965, pp. 28-31; also Chapter II of the present Report.

teach sections of the freshman course, and of Chemistry, where the right to teach the beginning courses is an honor accorded only to distinguished members of the department. But some of our senior professors show an extreme aversion to undergraduate and especially to lower-division teaching. This feeling may be partly a matter of temperament; there are professors who are better for graduate teaching than for undergraduate. Part of the feeling may actually be symptomatic of defects in departmental offerings. A course that fails to attract the interest of an experienced and talented scholar may be failing to arouse interest in freshmen as well. Some of the Committee's recommendations for curricular reform will be found relevant to this problem. New programs, problem-oriented courses, interdisciplinary courses, and seminars should provide a style of education attractive to professors as well as to students. Perhaps extensive redesigning of some departmental programs will be needed before the best possible style of teaching can be created. But style and ethos are closely linked. An ethos hospitable to teaching will in the long run depend on the collective conscience of the faculty. Given this conscience, given an adequate commitment to teaching, the various concrete means that are recommended here for the improvement of teaching will represent genuine attacks on our problems rather than merely hopeful tinkerings with their symptoms.

The faculty has not been idle in searching for direct means to promote good teaching on the campus. Last spring's report of the Special Committee on the Recognition of Distinction in Teaching (*Minutes of the Berkeley Division,* April 5) contained many valuable suggestions. Two among them have seemed to the present Committee particularly worthy of further study: the recognition of teaching in promotion, and the use of student ratings. They are taken up in sections B and G of the present chapter.

B. Recognition of Teaching in Faculty Promotion

In emphasizing the need for better recognition of teaching in promotion of faculty, the Committee envisions fuller implementation, but not basic change, in present University policy, which states that "superior intellectual attainment, as evidenced both in teaching and in research or creative achievement, is an indispensable qualification for appointment or promotion to tenure positions, since the professorship embodies the teaching-research function of the University."

The emphasis on teaching *and* research reflects a belief widely held in the profession, but not sufficiently understood by the public or even by all of our students, that teaching and research in a University setting do not conflict but support each other. There is of course a sense in which they are activities which compete for the professor's limited time, and a proper balance should be maintained between them.[2] But otherwise, we believe, teaching and research go together. The intellectual qualities that find expression in good research will also contribute to good teaching, and vice versa. The marshalling of one's ideas in preparation for teaching often suggests fruitful research problems, and the discoveries of the library and the laboratory cry out to be shared with students. One of the official criteria for the evaluation of talent in research is that "the candidate is continuously and effectively engaged in creative activity of high quality and significance." Yet this is one of the best ways of keeping teaching fresh and up to date, and maintaining a liveliness of mind that is stimulating to students.

As we commonly interpret it, then, our policy is that high attainment in *both* teaching and research are deemed necessary for appointment or promotion, and that a candidate who falls below the acceptable scale for either does not qualify. It stands to reason that individuals will differ in their strengths, and that extraordinary achievement in one area may offset lack of great distinction in the other. For a professor whose research is sound but not outstanding, exceptionally good teaching will help to meet the requirement of "superior intellectual attainment," and vice versa.

Our major difficulty has been that since achievement in research is a very rare commodity, it tends to enjoy in a faculty that aspires to preeminence in graduate education a greater prestige than achievement in teaching. Hence our chairmen and appointments and promotion committees have given a fuller measure of attention to evidence of research. Even granting that research is itself in some measure an indicator of qualities valuable in teaching, as the system is presently implemented, there is danger that deficient performance of teaching is not adequately recognized and outstanding performance not given due credit.

Here we must deny the loosely repeated charge that teaching at Berkeley does not count for promotion at all. We believe that the Budget Committees on this campus have given significant emphasis to evidence of teaching ability in making their recommendations, and that a strong majority of the dossiers submitted for promotions have contained evidence of satisfactory teaching. But if even a small percentage of dossiers were deficient, it would be too much.

In the past year, the "Byrne Report" commissioned by the Forbes

---

[2] See below, section III. E, "Distribution of Faculty Teaching Time."

Committee of the Board of Regents,[3] and the report of our Special Committee on Distinction in Teaching have commented on our relative weakness in collecting evidence of teaching ability. The Special Committee first describes the difficulty of gathering enough evidence even to support nominations for teaching awards, then goes on to the general problem:

> ... when the departmental chairman sends forth departmental recommendations for promotion of the instructor, evidence concerning teaching tends to be perfunctory. Under these circumstances it is not surprising that promotion committees come to make their judgments upon other criteria, primarily that of research productivity.... (*Minutes,* p. 5)

The Special Committee goes on to make a number of specific recommendations, including regular class visitations, and an improvement in the handling of evidence for appointment and promotion:

> We propose that every departmental recommendation for a merit increase or promotion in rank must include well-documented evidence about the teaching of the person so recommended. This would depart from the present procedure only in the emphasis on adequate evidence. ... The evaluation of a faculty member's balance of activity among research, teaching, and university and public service will continue to be made by the appropriate committees and administrative officers, but they will have for their use much better information about teaching than has usually been offered.
>
> The evidence now supplied is often tenuous and hard to evaluate. Departmental chairmen should be asked to provide as wide a range of tangible evidence as they can get. The instructor's participation in the Departmental Groups on Teaching, student evaluations of him, and visitations of his classes are all valuable sources of such evidence. But we would strongly emphasize that "good teaching" includes a broad spectrum of activities, only one of which—albeit a major one—is classroom performance. Evidence of noteworthy achievement as a teacher might also include the following: development of a new course which makes a signal contribution to the departmental offerings; fundamental revision of curriculum, engaging in interesting educational experiments, such as special innovations in use of new kinds of instructional procedures, devices, and

---

[3] Jerome C. Byrne, "Report on the University of California," p. 29: "The net result is that almost all appraisals of teaching ability tend to be favorable, and candidates for promotion and salary increments are accepted or rejected on the basis of their published work. This fact is known to faculty, and in some cases has very likely had a negative effect on the amount of effort devoted to classroom performance. This method of selecting faculty may also prevent some talented teachers from obtaining tenure, although the number of such cases is probably low."

materials; devoting unusual effort to students by holding
special discussion sessions, preparing study guides, etc.; making
active efforts directed toward the unification of human knowledge and its effective communication to students, for example
in the writing of original textbooks which depart in stimulating ways from the traditional treatment and teaching of subject
matter. (*Minutes*, p. 7)

The present Committee realizes full well the advantages in leaving
chairmen free to use their own judgment in the submission of materials
relative to a promotion, and we are not so sanguine as to imagine that
any legislated devices will guarantee increased attention to teaching.
But the situation calls for remedies, and we are confident that more
formal documentation of teaching ability will have a good effect, particularly on those newer members of the faculty whose attitudes toward
teaching will in turn have a profound effect on the campus ethos for
many years to come. We accordingly bring forward, in implementation
of the above proposal:

Recommendation 1: **The Instructions to Appointment and Promotion**
Committees should be amended to require that every departmental
recommendation for a promotion to *tenure* rank be accompanied by a
formal dossier on the teaching performance of the candidate. Along
with the Chairman's evaluation, this dossier should include all sig-
nificant tangible evidence, such as course materials and plans, syllabi,
study guides, examinations, and textbooks written by the candidate.
It should also include written reports by colleagues, evaluating the
candidate's classroom performance on the basis of class visitations, and
a statement by the candidate describing the rationale of his teaching
efforts.

C. Some Alternatives to Lecturing

One of our most provocative consultants, Dr. Harold Taylor, former
President of Sarah Lawrence College, makes the case for the student as
his own teacher in a letter to the Committee:

There is nothing intrinsically wrong with the lecture as a
mode of communication, provided it is given to those who want
to hear it by people who have something fresh and original to
say on a subject of interest to the listener. But it has to be used
sparingly and for particular reasons. It should be a means of
starting up some self-generating thought in the student, to start
him thinking, imagining, and questioning. The reason for
shifting the entire pedagogy away from lecturing toward dis-

cussion and independent study is that discussion and independent enquiry are the natural and most effective ways to learn. They do not require the continual presence of the teacher or any kind of educational authority to be effective. The students discuss all the time anyway; it is a question of how to get them discussing matters of significance to their higher education and of teaching them how to get the most out of discussion and enquiry. The real problem is to teach them how to teach each other and how to learn from each other, from books, from experience, from their teachers, from anything. . . .

Most universities ignore the potential for undergraduate instruction which lies not only in the graduate student-body but among the undergraduates themselves. If the teaching program is turned around and considered as a learning program by the students with such help as the faculty and other students are able to give, then a new role for the student-body as a whole is immediately suggested.

It is easily possible for faculty members to choose from among students whom they have already taught, both undergraduates and graduates, those whom they wish to have join them in the teaching program. We used to do this at Wisconsin, simply by inviting students from a previous year, or even students in a present course, to work with us in leading discussions and in acting as informed advisers and tutors to the other students. . . . The variations on this pattern are multiple. From what I have seen over these past ten years in the student-body at Berkeley, there are many students capable of first-rate teaching, tutoring, supervising research papers and organizing discussions, who would be highly valuable colleagues for the faculty members interested in fresh and interesting ways of teaching.

While the Committee does not envision a sudden break with the tradition of lecturing at Berkeley, nor the early creation of a whole student population of self-propelled investigators and teachers, we agree with Dr. Taylor's principles. We find them singularly close to what the principles of a campus dedicated to original scholarship should be. Yet the campus has not been nearly enterprising enough in giving undergraduates a hand in their own education. Even the most brilliant undergraduates are relatively neglected. Nine years ago the *Report* of the Special Committee on Objectives, Program and Requirements of the College of Letters and Science commented on "The superior and self-directed student whose intellectual interests cannot be provided in any usual program. These students will always be few, and should be an object of special concern to the College. The Committee believes that in the College as it now functions there is inadequate recognition of their needs or of the possibilities for giving them the very special educational experience which they deserve" (p. 11). The College has not yet been able to implement this recommendation sufficiently. The recent proposal to liberalize the "199" courses—special studies for advanced undergraduates—still restricts their use to seniors with honors in the major. Of the 2,462 students in the College of Letters and Science graduating class of 1965, only 205 took such a course.

There are a great many more students, upper-division and lower, with perhaps lower grades but more independent souls, who are capable and willing to take more responsibility for their own education if we give them the chance. There is impressive evidence of this in some of our recent experiments with "tutorial" instruction.

The term "tutorial" can be applied to a variety of systems in which the instructor directs the studies of each of a small group of students. As used here it refers to a more formal arrangement than the preceptorial, which shades off into general curricular advising. On the other side, the tutorial is usually smaller and more informal than the seminar, and places greater emphasis on sutdent responsibility for what goes on in class meetings.

Previous to this year there was very little tutorial teaching on the campus. The Department of Psychology has had a tutorial honors course for majors during the last five years, and there has been a tutorial section of freshman English offered in a Residence Unit for the last three years. Chemistry and English have conducted summer tutorials for exceptionally able lower-division students. Last fall there was a noticeable increase of interest in this type of teaching. Psychology and English increased their offerings Comparative Literature started a freshman tutorial; ;and faculty members in French, History, Engineering, Statistics, Speech, and Biology are considering or planning tutorials for next year.

One of the leading exponents of the tutorial, Professor Paul Piehler of the Department of English, describes his method as follows:

> Ideally the class should not contain many more than 24 students, and should be taught by an instructor and a Teaching Assistant. To convert such a class to tutorial instruction, one simply arranges to meet the students in groups of four, once a week, rather than in groups of 24 three times a week. Two student papers are normally read at each meeting, and the students not reading papers will have assisted those who are reading with the preparation of their papers, and will be in part responsible for them. The student is not judged on his contributions to the class in any one week, but rather on his total

production for the whole semester, which takes the form of a preliminary manuscript of a book on some subject of general academic interest. At the moment, for example, a tutorial class in Residential Unit II is working on an anthology of essays on educational theory and practice in different civilizations, as a book of source materials for the understanding of our present problems.

There are naturally certain difficulties in switching over to the tutorial system, not unsimilar to the difficulties reported by some students in the Tussman plan. The student has to learn to take responsibility and initiative, both in and out of class. The tutor has to be primarily a good listener. He will have less time to make his own contributions than in the ordinary classroom situation, but his contributions will be made with much greater efficiency since, if he is sensitive to the development of the student's discussion, he will be making contributions only when the students are carefully prepared to absorb what he has to say.

Both tutor and students, moreover, have to adjust to a new pace of learning. Because the tutorial student is forced so much onto his own resources, he will very often make a slow start. By the end of the semester, however, the achievement of the tutorial student is likely to be far beyond that of the conventionally taught student, since the basis of his work is much more his own rather than his tutor's creation. But both tutor and students often have to exercise a good deal of faith during preliminary difficulties in regard to the final outcome. The tutor will constantly be having to consider how much or how little of his own energies to attempt to infuse into the class. Ideally he should function to the greatest degree possible on the initiative of his students.

Preliminary evaluation of the tutorial work done by freshman students shows extraordinary results both in the quality of the work produced and in the tone of student response. The graduate Teaching Fellow in one class, Miss Elizabeth Petroff, reports to the Committee in terms that make clear her own satisfaction:

Their attitude toward the class was one of intense involvement—they wanted to prove to themselves they could handle large ideas. Learning and writing were not easy and fun; this surprised them at first. They were very conscious of how little they knew. They had to learn how to use a tutorial, when it would be helpful to talk to me, when they were better off talking with each other. Occasionally a group would call me at home and ask me to have dinner with them and discuss their ideas before they began writing. They had to fight with the library, learn to use reference works and commentaries with discretion. One constant fear was—"I've learned how much I can do in this kind of course. What will I do in an ordinary course?" I had to keep telling them they had to learn to rely on themselves for an education; use the system, not beat it.

Surprisingly, I spent no more time on this 1A than on the usual 1A class, but all my time was spent more usefully. My office hours were always filled, and often exceeded three hours a week. I taught between two and three hours a week. I spent three or four hours commenting on papers. I spent four or five hours reading the material on which they were writing. Had I been teaching material I had used before, less time would have been involved.

Grades were never discussed during the term; the students were told they could inquire about a tentative grade at any time, but they never did.

D. Making Small Classes Possible

The conventional objection to a policy that insures for each student some opportunity for dialogue, self-instruction, or independent study is that it means many small classes, and intricate problems of advising, supervision, and evaluation—too expensive for a large public university. The Committee, however, is not convinced that this is so. It is possible, without reducing the due contribution of the faculty to graduate teaching and research, to increase materially the number of small undergraduate classes. At the same time we can build into the curriculum at little extra expense a generous and ready provision for that earliest moment in a student's career when with responsible advising he can be allowed (perhaps even urged) to undertake important parts of his education by himself. The trick cannot be done one way, but in a number of contributory ways:

1. A lecture can be periodically made into a discussion group, or into a whole series of "small classes" with the use of student discussion leaders. This method, currently in use, could be widely expanded in connection with graduate pedagogical seminars and undergraduate volunteers.

2. The amount of regular faculty time available for undergraduate teaching and advising can be increased by reducing the disproportionate attention now given in some departments to graduate teaching. [See Sec. E below].

3. The amount of regular faculty time available for small classes and advising can be increased by reducing the frequency with which many middle-sized courses are offered. Given the attendance patterns of most students, there is no reason why a course should be offered more often than once in two years unless it is a specifically required service course or

already has very large enrollment. If, as we often claim, the large lecture is economically unavoidable, only the seminar makes it justifiable. We should avoid wasteful middle-sized courses, too small for economy and too large for dialogue. [See Sec. E below].

4. The need to supply formal lecturing can be reduced in many fields by reducing the student's normal course load (but not the amount of work he does). Institutions like Harvard and Cornell normally require only four-fifths the number of courses that we do (i.e., four courses instead of five per semester) with no visible detriment to education. An education committee at M.I.T. envisions a shift to the quarter system just in order to enable students to have a three-course load. At Berkeley the planning for the quarter system has already enabled some departments to make precisely this change. Students working longer on fewer courses means more time for dialogue and independent study in those courses. A reduced demand for places in courses means faculty time saved for seminars, tutorials, and advising.

5. A vigorous program of genuine experiments in teaching will merit the support of outside sources of financial assistance.

6. Some very good very small classes can be expected to come as extra contributions from departments, and as personal charities from individual scholars both on campus and in the community.

7. As is clearly indicated in the table on page 51 (column 4), a sizable number of our larger departments have been operating with teaching resources well below their authorized strength. Many factors lie behind this lack of success in recruitment of faculty. Some of them—for instance, the level of faculty salaries and benefits—are beyond the control of individual departments, and depend on the backing of the administration, the Regents, and the state government. We confidently expect that this situation will improve with time, and that a due proportion of the additional teaching strength will go into small undergraduate classes. Furthermore, one may be permitted to hope that as our first experiments with new programs of small classes (e.g., freshman seminars) succeed, they will justify a larger measure of public support in the form of increased faculty.

Recommendation 2: Advisers should be authorized to permit students at any stage of their experience to undertake supervised independent study involving any proportion of their time justifiable by sound educational reasons.

Recommendation 3: It should be the policy of the administration and faculty to increase the opportunity of all students for learning based on dialogue and on cooperative student self-instruction, by decreasing the proportion of lecture courses in favor of discussion sections, small classes, seminars, tutorials, preceptorials, and similar teaching arrangements.

E. Distribution of Faculty Teaching Time

Much effort has been devoted by this Committee to a search for any significant teaching resources not now being utilized. One major question is whether faculty members do an adequate amount of teaching. The average distribution of faculty working time found in a 1960 survey, corroborated by more recent studies, is recorded below. The statistics indicate, first of all, that for virtually every faculty member the combination of activities involved in his University work leaves no spare time or energy for further duty. Faculty members now devote 41 hours a week to the activities related to teaching; so that, from the State's standpoint, their personal research and administrative, committee, and public service are all done on "overtime". Thus any alteration in the faculty's participation in teaching would necessarily come from a redistribution, rather than from an increase, in teaching time.

Average Weekly Distribution of Faculty Time
(adapted from a University-wide study for Fall 1960)

Teaching: Lectures, seminars, and laboratories,
                  preparation, course development, course-
                  connected research, and examinations . . 24 hours
              Undergraduate consultation, advising,
                  and recommendations 10
              Graduate research instruction 7
                                                        41 hours
Individual research not connected with teaching 10
Administrative and committee service 6
Public service 1
                                                        58 hours

The existing patterns of teaching at Berkeley are pertinent to any question of possible redistribution of teaching time. A survey by this Committee of Fall 1964 class enrollments in 28 large, representative departments, given in the adjoining table, shows that the typical faculty member in these departments has 8 hours per week of classroom contact with students (column 4 average divided by column 2 average), exclusive of preparation, grading, or briefing of Teaching Assistants. Among these departments the relative time devoted by regular faculty members to different levels of instruction was: lower-division, 24% (about 2 hours); upper-division, 38% (3 hours); graduate, 38% (3 hours).

Allocation of Teaching Resources within Departments

Dept. No.	St. hrs. Fac. hrs. (1)‡	W. st. hr. Fac. hrs. (2)	St. hrs. F+TA hr. (3)†	W. st. hr. Fac. FTE (4)	Faculty hrs./Student hrs. Grad. (5)	:	Upper Div.	: Lower Div. (6)
1	42	33	27	203	1.50	:	1	: .103
2	57	51	36	345	10.14	:	1	: .105
3	35	30	23	273	7.15	:	1	: .105
4	56	33	44	101	3.22	:	1	: .125
5	68	53	46	376	9.55	:	1	: .147
6	43	31	17	312*	0.95	:	1	: .162
7	58	40	16	265*	1.25	:	1	: .198
8	68	55	23	312*	10.68	:	1	: .212
9	45	42	23	256	3.56	:	1	: .215
10	43	34	18	224*	5.01	:	1	: .229
11	36	30	18	224	4.21	:	1	: .239
12	42	23	19	215*	2.93	:	1	: .281
13	55	40	24	208	3.84	:	1	: .284
14	64	62	38	420*	7.13	:	1	: .348
15	54	36	18	239*	2.35	:	1	: .393
16	47	47	31	309*	5.07	:	1	: .393
17	24	26	17	179	2.49	:	1	: .428
18	33	26	15	327*	4.60	:	1	: .434
19	17	20	14	143	1.74	:	1	: .443
20	22	18	14	171*	3.11	:	1	: .502
21	27	31	22	218	1.78	:	1	: .509
22	10	8	10	129	3.65	:	1	: .548
23	17	12	14	126	1.77	:	1	: .579
24	17	15	13	111	2.10	:	1	: .610
25	23	24	14	133	2.60	:	1	: .853
26	18	14	17	165	2.19	:	1	: 1.214
27	13	10	12	133	2.30	:	1	: 1.277
28	29	29	29	213	4.68	:	1	: 1.782
(AVG.)	(34)	(33)	(21)	(265)	(3.34	:	1	: 0.519)

* Indicates a department with currently appointed FTE's 15 to 30% under budgeted values.
† Excludes teaching assistants not having independent charge of sections.
‡ Excludes faculty and teaching assistant time in preparation, course seminars, grading, etc. The numeral in each column heading corresponds to the detailed definition of the heading as given in the explanatory text below.

The 28 departments having lower-division loads in excess of 1000 student credit hours are listed without identification. In addition, area averages have been constructed to establish norms for different types of teaching. The Committee has tabulated the following indexes of instruction time for Fall 1964.

Overall ratios of faculty to student time

Col. (1) Total student credit hours/Total faculty contact hours.
Col. (2) Weighted student credit hours/Total faculty contact hours. The usual weighting is divided by 2 to give an upper-division norm. Hence the weights used are lower-division, 0.5; upper-division, 1.0; graduate division, 1.8.
Col. (3) Total student credit hours/Total faculty plus teaching assistant contact hours.

Level of budgetary support

Col. (4) Weighted student credit hours/Resident-faculty full-time-equivalent positions. (Cases where budgeted FTE substantially exceed resident FTE are starred.)

Distribution of faculty teaching effort

Col. (5) Graduate-division ratio of faculty contact hours to student credit hours, divided by upper-division ratio of faculty contact hours to student credit hours.
Col. (6) Lower-division ratio of faculty contact hours to student credit hours, divided by upper-division ratio of faculty contact hours to student credit hours. The listing of departments is in the order of increasing values of this lower-division/upper-division index.

The average class conducted by regular faculty members comprised 35 students, and the same figure held for the average of upper-division courses. Lower-division classes averaged 70 students, and graduate classes 11 students.

In recent years the budgetary allocation of faculty "FTE" (full-time equivalent) positions has been based on a relative weighting of 1.0 for lower-division, 2.0 for upper-division, and 3.75 for graduate students. Our calculation of weighted student credit hours has been based upon nearly this proportion, but with the upper division taken as the base (to give 0.5 : 1.0 : 1.75).

From the table, the overall proportions of faculty time per student credit hour are seen to be in the ratio, for lower-division : upper-division : graduate, of 0.52 : 1.0 : 3.3. The seemingly high graduate ratio can be accounted for by considering 8 credit hours (compared to 15 for undergraduates) to be a full-time course program, with graduates' remaining work done in supervised research including (in scientific fields) sessions with a faculty member for planning and analysis of the research. The above-mentioned lower-division faculty time ratio of 0.52 : 1.0, relative to upper-division, corresponds closely to the budgetary weighting ratio.

Nevertheless, a look at the figures shows that the overall averages are not very representative of the individual departments. A few departments, largely those with the most extensive provisions for Teaching Assistants, are giving only *one-fifth* the average faculty contact to lower division students. At the other end of the list, one department is giving more than three times the average relative attention to lower-division teaching. In certain cases (notably departments 2, 3, 5, and 8 in the table), an unfavorable lower-division ratio is accompanied by an extremely high graduate ratio. In other cases (departments 1, 4, and 9), the unfavorable lower-division ratio is explained by fewer than average contact hours per faculty member. In three instances (departments 6, 7, and 8), the teaching problem in the department is aggravated by a shortage of faculty, and in three others (departments 2, 4, and 5) by a relatively low complement of Teaching Assistants.

In many departments the faculty participation in lower-division teaching is so low that a very minor shift in course assignments would greatly improve the extent of participation. Compared with an overall average of 24 percent of lower-division teaching, departments 2 and 3 have 4 percent; departments 5, 8, and 9 have about 7.5 percent; department 1 has 13 percent. While the overall staffing ratio appears to provide an equitable basis for allocation of faculty positions to campuses and perhaps even to individual colleges, it clearly becomes an inadequate guide to the needs and deserts of individual departments.

When we examine the average staffing figures in the various areas of knowledge, we find that the groups of departments in humanities, social sciences, life sciences, and physical sciences are each very close to the campus-wide average. Thus the great differences in the teaching patterns of individual departments seems to be due more to departmental preference than to the intrinsic nature of the discipline.

It should be noted that a new weighting ratio has recently been adopted for University-wide planning, allocating 1.0 to the lower division, 1.5 to the upper division, 2.5 to first-year graduate students, and 3.5 to advanced graduate students. The anticipated enrollments in these respective categories by 1970, from the estimate of the Office of Analytical Studies, January 1966, are 22%, 33%, 27%, and 18% (compared with a Fall 1964 distribution of 28% lower-division, 37% upper-division, and 35% graduate.) Because of the shift toward graduate courses, the campuswide average faculty-conducted class size should tend to drop to about 25 students, with the averages for the individual levels being: lower-division, 60; upper-division, 40; first-year graduate, 15; advanced graduate, 7.

Undergraduate instruction on this scale is by no means intimate and personal, but neither is it entirely impersonal. *The Committee would favor an eventual reduction in class size by gradual expansion of the faculty while student enrollment holds constant.* Nonetheless it will also be desirable to try collectively to get optimum teaching effectiveness within the existing budgetary constraints. If some courses are offered as large lectures, others can be divided into smaller sections. The combination of one class with 20 students and three classes each with 180 students for a student's program, corresponds to the 60 average projected for the lower division; so does one class of 15 and four classes each of 240. From these averages we deduce that if a lower-division student is enrolled in four courses during any given quarter, he could expect statistically to have one faculty-conducted small class if the other three are large ones (180 to 240, or more).

In those cases where a specialized graduate or upper-division course closely parallels other offerings and at the same time draws a very low enrollment, the department concerned should consider consolidating the course with others, or should offer it on a reduced frequency, so as to increase the overall participation of its faculty members in general departmental teaching.

The supplemental role of Teaching Assistants has not been considered here, being dealt with in another chapter. The staffing patterns discussed here show the importance of increasing, rather than decreasing, the budgetary allocations for Teaching Assistants. While this Committee views the large lecture as being both a necessary and an effective form of instruction, it believes that every student in such a course should have access to small regular meetings conducted by a Teaching Assistant. In short, virtually every course given should provide the opportunity for seminar-type discussion with either a regular faculty member or a Teaching Assistant.

Recommendation 4: **Departments with markedly low levels of faculty participation in their lower-division courses should restructure their patterns of teaching in order to give greater faculty attention to the lower division.**

F. Organized Research Units

The Committee is fully aware of the need to review the role of Organized Research Units on the Berkeley campus. It is convinced that any mechanical separation in thinking about the functions of formal teaching on the one side and organized research on the other is detrimental to both of these principal tasks of the University in general and of this campus in particular. Unfortunately time did not permit us to engage in major studies of the relationship of teaching and Organized Research Units, but we took a preliminary look at this issue within the limits of our ability.

In November we sent a letter of inquiry to the heads of Organized Research Units, asking two questions: First, how does the Unit contribute to the education of students? Second, what could and should be done to enhance the educational role of the Unit? Replies were received from twelve Laboratories, eleven Centers, nine Institutes, three Museums, two Stations, a Facility, the Bancroft Library, the Botanical Garden, and the Herbarium. From this very preliminary survey we find that without exception the responding Units are already contributing to the education of students, especially graduate students. This contribution takes a variety of forms, of which the following are a sample:

a. Academically related work for a large number of graduate students in the form of Research Assistant or other technical positions. Many student positions can properly be described as "apprenticeships;" much student work leads directly to the preparation of theses or other scholarly documents.

b. Support and supervision of independent research for many students through Grants-in-Aid.

c. Seminars and colloquia often (but not limited) to the benefit of students associated with Organized Research Units.

d. Special classes to supplement instruction available through regular departmental offerings, e.g., in languages and in statistical techniques.

e. Provision of facilities ranging from complex equipment used in some of the physical sciences through meeting rooms, special collections, and libraries.

f. Student contact with faculty members in their own and, especially, in other departments. Units also help develop contacts with other students, professionals not members of the Academic Senate, and visitors.

g. Development, testing and distribution of curriculum materials, ranging from botanical exhibits through course outlines.

These are but a sample of the educational activities of the Organized Research Units. It does seem apparent, both from this sample and from the comments of the respondents, that these activities should properly be seen as something more than a supplement to education received elsewhere on campus by other means, e.g., classroom instruction. The image conveyed is that these activities are an integral part of modern education. This is directly suggested by one respondent:

> Research work under the direct supervision of a member of the faculty or an advanced Ph.D.-level graduate student is, in my judgment, the only effective way of replicating Mark Hopkins' log in a modern university. It should be an obligation of research units, therefore, to generate this situation for every graduate-level student after the first year of graduate work. I believe that most of our better research units function this way.

Our respondents have provided information which tends to confirm this judgment; the responding Units apparently do function this way to the limits of their resources.

Many of the responding Units suggested that their main problem in the area of student education was one of limited resources. More specifically, many seem to feel that the educational role of the Organized Research Units is not officially recognized and that this contributes to undersupport of such Units through the regular University budget. This theme was recurrent:

One of the greatest services your committee could perform is to put an end to the nonsense of the diochotomy between teaching and research. The classroom is but one medium for teaching and its efficacy is certainly debatable. The research laboratory is another medium for teaching.

* * * * *

What is urgently needed at this time is explicit recognition of the educational functions of organized research units and some budgetary support for the maintenance and improvement of these functions.

* * * * *

. . . the definition of the role of these units current in some circles (a definition which maintains a rigid distinction between "education" and "research") apparently makes it difficult to justify State expenditures for support of their work.

* * * * *

The problem boils down to administrative misapprehension concerning the educational significance of research units. This and other factors raise significant questions about the morale and interest of those who participate in organized research.

The primary pleas are for recognition. This, it is held, will help resolve financial and morale problems apparently experienced by many Units. It would help the administration negotiate state support for these Units; it would enlist more fully the energies and intelligence of Unit staff members, not now members of the Academic Senate, in the educational enterprise; and it would thus encourage Unit staffs to exploit the educational possibilities of their Units more fully. It might, for example, lead to consideration of what the Units could contribute to undergraduate, as well as graduate education.

The present Committee, regrettably, has been able to conduct only this most cursory inquiry into the subject. Its recommendations must reflect this fact.

Recommendation 5: Systematic study of the educational role of Organized Research Units on the Berkeley campus should be undertaken as part of the Campus Academic Plan. Such study should attempt to document the past and current educational activities of such Units, the policy considerations that have facilitated or interfered with the development of these activities, and should consider what changes might be effected to enhance the educational functions of the Units.

Recommendation 6: Consideration should be given to giving credit to students and faculty members for the educational activities carried on within Units. To the extent that Units are engaged in educational activities—which is apparently considerable—they should be recognized as educational as well as research units. Research personnel who contribute importantly to the supervision, training, and instruction of students should be given official recognition, perhaps through increased use of appropriate titles, such as Lecturer and Senior Lecturer.

G. The Use of Student Ratings

In introducing this topic we can do no better than cite again the views of the Special Committee on the Recognition of Distinction in Teaching:

> It would seem obvious that in the instructor's conduct and appraisal of his own teaching, feedback from the student should be of prime significance. Yet under present circumstances most instructors have relatively little in the way of adequate communication of this kind with the students. This is particularly true of large lecture classes but it is true to a considerable degree even in small classes and seminars. The kind of information that the instructor now gets tends to be delayed, sporadic, unrepresentative, and relatively uninformative. To be sure, some instructors do now regularly utilize some form of student appraisal, such as in the form of rating sheets administered by them at the end of the course. But this practice is not common and even when used is not as effective as it might be.
>
> To speak of the necessity of feedback from the student is not to imply complete validity of student appraisals. Student ratings, like all ratings, are subject to bias and unreliability and may reflect other aspects of teacher performance than those most central to basic educational effectiveness of the teacher. No one would propose that the student ratings should simply be taken at face value. But at the same time it would seem absurd to deny that such expression of student reaction is a highly relevant factor to be taken into account by the teacher in governing his conduct of the course. Student apathy or discontent—no matter how ill-founded the instructor may consider them to be—is never conducive to the teacher-learning function. The purpose of student rating, therefore, is to make available to the instructor this essential kind of information about student reaction, both positive and negative. It is the instructor himself who must decide what this information signifies concerning the success or failure of his teaching and what he should seek to do about it. It is natural that many teachers tend to avoid the possibly traumatic outcome of the collection of student ratings. Yet it would not seem proper from the point of view of maintenance of high quality teaching in the Univer-

sity that the instructor should be permitted to teach in a state of blissful ignorance, or of unresolved anxiety, concerning student opinion. Accordingly, we suggest that a regular campus-wide program of providing student evaluations of all courses be established. (*Minutes of the Berkeley Division,* April 5, 1965, pp. 5-6)

The above recommendation, along with the realization that the topic is a live, controversial one in the academic community, has led the present Committee to sponsor extensive staff investigation of student ratings. Individual members of the Committee have serious reservations about the desirability of imposing such ratings on unwilling faculty members. Nevertheless, a majority of us agree that at least one large-scale campus-wide experiment with student ratings would be worthwhile; it will provide a basis on which an intelligent decision can be made on the possible long-term usefulness of the device for this campus.

The Committee's review of the institutions which at present use some form of student evaluation included Bennington College, Brooklyn College, City College of New York, Cornell University, Grinnell College, Miami University, Ohio State University, Purdue University, Queens College, Reed College, University of California at Riverside, University of Michigan, University of Washington, and Yale University. Many use evaluations for administrative purposes, but the most attractive use of student opinion emphasizes the value of providing information to the instructor himself. This is the primary aim of the program at the University of Michigan, a successful example of institutionalization of student opinion and judgment now about fifteen years old. Colleagues at Ann Arbor say that the program, sponsored by a faculty group, did meet with some initial opposition, but after a few years of experience it was accepted at large, and it now draws praise from some of its strongest former opponents.

At Michigan all courses in the liberal arts college are rated by students every third term. There is no bureaucratic apparatus encumbering the program; each instructor administers a standard questionnaire which is completed in his absence, retained in a sealed envelope in the department office, and given to him after the completion of grading. (The current Michigan form is given below, Appendix E.) All instructors are thus automatically provided with student feedback. The form has been designed with the secondary aim of stimulating the student to think of educational objectives, as can be seen in questions 2 and 3. The evaluation forms are the private property of the instructor, unless the faculty of a department vote as a whole to pass them on to their chairman.

In making its recommendation, the present Committee wishes to emphasize objectives already expressed by the Special Committee on Recognition of Excellence in Teaching: that student evaluation provide an instructor with essential information about student reaction, and that the instructor alone decide the significance of the information and govern its use. An experiment should be designed to give each member of the faculty a chance to sample and evaluate for himself the worth of student ratings. Certainly, few individual students, no matter how alert and fair-minded, have the training, experience, or perspective to tell what is right and wrong with their teachers, their courses, or the program as a whole. But the student is the only person equipped to report on his own experiences and attitudes; he is the only one who can express his own condition. Our recommendation is based on the premise that evaluation questionnaires may at the very least offer valuable information on student morale and attitudes that does not conventionally appear on term papers and course examinations. At the most, we may hope that in making even more explicit the faculty's concern for the quality of its teaching and in making the most constructive use of student comment, such evaluations will help support a teaching ethos.

The new Berkeley Division Committee on Teaching is charged to "conduct continuous study of all problems concerning the improvement of teaching in the University," and would have jurisdiction in this area. In planning the questionnaire, the Committee could depend on broad discussion within the Berkeley faculty, on outside assistance, and on the extensive information already collected by our investigators. The present Committee feels that the Michigan form is too detailed, and that fewer and more open-ended questions are desirable. We see no value in a ranking patterned and confined by the multiple-choice style. The form should encourage a free and considered response; it should reflect its purpose to engage students in responsible analysis of significant educational experience. The Committee on Teaching could distribute the questionnaire by mail to all students, with addressed return envelopes for mailing of the completed forms *to the instructor.* The Committee should then solicit faculty members for their opinion on this experimental use of student evaluation, and open discussions to consider institutionalization of a program.

Recommendation 7: **The Committee on Teaching should design and** administer an experimental student evaluation of all undergraduate courses in the winter quarter, 1967, to be sent by students directly to individual faculty members, as the basis for later faculty consideration of a permanent system of student evaluation of courses.

The present Committee does not recommend that the faculty in any way engage itself in the production of published evaluations for the use of students. It can be pointed out, though, that such publications have generated student interest and, if responsibly executed, they can gain the confidence of both students and faculty. Unfortunately, independent student efforts are often methodologically unsound. Opinions published in the student course evaluations are generally based on inadequate and highly prejudiced samples in spite of the efforts of those working on the publications. Furthermore, conclusions are apt to be expressed in personal, inflammatory terms which serve no constructive end. It is possibly desirable to have some institutional and methodologically sound evaluation system to which the abused professor or department can appeal for more objective and broadly-based student reaction on any given issue. There is room for considerable injustice where independent publications rule the field of evaluation by default.

H. Student Contribution to Educational Planning

The Committee believes that feedback of student opinion can contribute importantly not only to improvement of specific courses but also to the assessment and planning of educational programs. Though most students are inexperienced in campus affairs, and as a rule cannot master fully issues in educational policy, the orientation of student views does not preclude their validity. The students bring to discussions of educational policy and assessment both a fresh viewpoint and an acute involvement in the outcome of such discussions. By the time a student has graduated, he is often qualified to evaluate certain aspects of the curriculum better than many of the professors who teach in it. He is in a particularly good position to recognize omissions and redundancies in curriculum as well as the match or mismatch between what the department plans to teach and what is actually transmitted.

This campus is making increasing use of student opinion contributing to the evaluation and planning of educational programs. One of Chancellor Heyns' first acts upon coming to Berkeley was to propose that each department establish liaison groups between student majors (graduate and undergraduate) and the faculty, to strengthen the intellectual bonds between them and to provide valuable feedback about the efficacy of our academic programs. This process works well on the departmental scale. In response to the Chancellor's proposal, some departments already have set up liaison groups. The English Department's faculty-student advisory committee meets frequently to discuss problems ranging from changes in the Ph.D. language requirements to furnishings for the graduate meeting room. Although the committee is solely advisory in nature, so far the chairman has had to turn down none of its recommendations. In the Mathematics and Political Science Departments, the executive committees of the respective graduate student associations have met with faculty committees to discuss common concerns. The School of Education's faculty-student advisory committee holds regular monthly meetings. Graduate students in the Sociology Department also participate in an active faculty-student group.

The present Committee has also sought student opinion on many issues. In the summer of 1965 we employed fifteen student Research Assistants, graduate and undergraduate, to aid in gathering data for this report. We did so not merely because we needed technical and clerical assistance, but also because we valued the insights into the problems of the University which our students possessed. For this reason we later instituted a series of ten weekly discussion meetings open to the entire student body, and encouraged the students to communicate their ideas about campus affairs to the Committee. We also distributed a questionnaire to a random sample of some 2,500 returning students registering in the fall and received an 85% response.

So far, with the exception of active solicitation of undergraduate opinion by faculty committees and others, student contributions to educational planning and assessment have been restricted primarily to graduate students. The reasons for this are apparent: not only are the lines of communication between faculty and graduate students generally better established than between faculty and undergraduates, but the graduate students are older and more experienced both as students and as teachers.

At present, the lack of representative undergraduate opinions developed through widely based undergraduate organizations has limited departmental advisory committees to only graduate student representation; but not all departments are content with this arrangement. The Department of Comparative Literature, for example, hopes to include undergraduates on its faculty-student committee. However, the departments still need a reliable method of finding undergraduate representatives.

Although our students have most to say about the educational problems of their own departments, they nevertheless may make significant contributions toward the educational planning of the entire campus, as they have done for this Committee. Some student groups feel that they need a collective, forceful student voice to counteract the more influential voices of the faculty and administration. These groups believe that all decisions reached behind closed doors are untrustworthy. They want the presence of students on faculty and administrative committees as insurance that the committees will take no action harmful to students.

Though we are convinced that faculty committees must remain aware of and sensitive to student opinions in order to formulate successful educational policy, we are also convinced that student membership on faculty committees will not hasten improvements, but could provide the ideal mechanism for polarization and impasse. The typical faculty member does not get called for committee service until he has reached tenure rank. He has had a good deal of experience with the intellectual and pragmatic aspects of campus life. Thus student members of faculty-student committees often are at a distinct disadvantage compared to faculty members in areas outside their own experience as students; and they do not have, nor can they be expected to have, professional responsibility for educational policy. We believe that campus-wide faculty committees should consult student opinion in the same way that they consult many other sources of information before reaching decisions on educational policy. We do not believe that more direct student participation will necessarily lead to an atmosphere of greater intellectual and political trust.

Faculty-student committees work well on the departmental level because within the department professors and students share a common interest in their subject, and because the students know best the educational problems of their own departments. Campus-wide faculty-student committees would lack such advantages. For these reasons we would prefer campus-wide student committees, which should meet periodically with the counterpart faculty committees to exchange information and viewpoints. Campus-wide student groups concerned with student participation in educational policy already exist. The Student Educational and Faculty Relations Board of the Associated Students shares our concern that students become involved in the making of decisions about University affairs; reporting to this Committee, the SEFR Board has made several practical suggestions about educational reform at Berkeley, some of which run parallel to our own thought on the subject. The political parties Slate and Scope attempt to define the students' position on educational policies; the *Slate Supplement* in particular has served as a platform for students lobbying for specific reforms. Finally, the Honor Students Society has shown great interest in problems of academic reform, and has been of continuing assistance to us.

Recommendation 8: The faculty and administration should regularly consult students' views on educational policy both in campus-wide and in departmental affairs. Campus-wide, the students have the major responsibility to develop effective channels of communication; within each department, however, the chairman and faculty should take the initiative.

Recommendation 9: The Division's Student Affairs Committee should confer with student leaders to discuss the first steps in establishing a permanent means of liaison between campus-wide faculty committees and comparable committees representing the student body.

IV.

FRESHMAN ADMISSIONS

A. The Influence of Campus Atmosphere and Style

THE TABLE on present and projected University enrollments printed in Appendix A to this report indicates two critical changes in the composition of our student body. One, which has been occurring over the last five years and is virtually completed, is that the size of the student body has reached a permanent limit. The other, which will continue for another ten years, is a definite shift in proportion toward more advanced, hence older, students.

Presumably, we will never return to the situation in which each year brought some uncontrolled growth of the student body, and, inevitably a few years late, the additional faculty and facilities with which to deal with it. Formerly, both the total size of our student body and its relative distribution among the various levels and disciplines were fixed in the family living rooms of the state's high school and junior college graduates. Now we are entering a period in which the size of the student body will be static and its composition more closely under our command. We will have to make decisions as to which applicant may enter and which must be directed elsewhere, and we will have to decide whether the composition of the various disciplines is to be highly controlled or left as before to social forces outside the campus.

As to the composition of the various disciplines, the Committee has no recommendations to offer; that will have to be decided over a substantial period of trial and discussion. However, we can point to some general conclusions on admissions policy, derived from the already projected increase in the maturity of our students.

At present, roughly two thirds of our students are undergraduates, but in a few years the proportion will be reduced to less than half. In the next ten years we expect to reduce the lower division by 525 students

(8.7%) and the upper division by 2,250 (21%). Meanwhile the graduate population will increase by 3,200 additional candidates for advanced degrees, an almost unbelievable 30.8%. This change reflects our acceptance and implementation of public policy: that the University take major responsibility for graduate education in the state's educational system.

The most obvious implication is that the campus is destined to become even more graduate-oriented in its atmosphere than it is now. It means that there will be even greater pressure to select faculty members for their special interest and capability in creative research, and we must expect that the faculty will spend a smaller fraction of its total educational activity with undergraduates. While we do not expect individual undergraduates to receive less attention—indeed, we anticipate that they will receive more—the fact remains that they will be going to school in an atmosphere increasingly dominated by serious scholarship; the tone of the campus will be set increasingly by the needs and values of the graduate students. It follows that undergraduate admissions should seek students who will flourish in this atmosphere.

The Committee discussed at length the suggestion that the lower division has no place in a "graduate-oriented" campus. We feel, however, that it would be a serious defect to lose contact with younger students and with the high schools they come from, to lose their freshness and vigor and to cut off our rich opportunity to bring the flavor of university scholarship into the earliest years of undergraduate education. Nor, needless to say, do we favor an undergraduate curriculum that is merely the serviceable appanage of the graduate school. Many of our students will not be bound for graduate schools, and even those who are, deserve much more than a narrowly professional education, even if the profession be scholarship itself. Our undergraduate programs should increasingly provide for that breadth and liberality of background that give perspective and direction to specialist activities. Our aim should continue to be, for all our investment in expertness, the cultivation of creative and thinking men, no matter what careers lie before them.

But we will be forgiven if we hope that the Berkeley campus of the future succeeds in attracting an even greater share of those undergraduates who are most likely to profit from what we shall have to offer—students who, whatever their particular talents, inclinations, and humors, can catch the excitement of the intellectual endeavor.

There is reason to hope that as the style of the campus increasingly defines itself, it will have a salutary effect on student self-selection. The campus will attract more and more outstanding young people who are ready to take on the challenge of serious thinking. Admissions policy should be designed to identify these students readily and to seek out other highly desirable candidates who themselves do not seek admission.

B. Identifying Desirable Students

The student's high school grade record is at present the major (and for most students the only) source of information now used for admissions. On it we check for a list of required subjects which the student must have passed; then we require a minimum cumulative average in his grades, currently a B (3.0). This information is indispensable, but it needs supplementing. Particularly as we become more selective, the representation of the student's high school achievement by a simple, lumped grade-point average will become increasingly unsatisfactory. The high school record itself represents the culmination of approximately 12 years of schooling when a student has lived and been compared with his peers continually, has experienced and been evaluated by two or three dozen individual teachers, has piled knowledge upon knowledge and organized it in his own way. Despite its inadequacies, it is the best single document for representing the student's potential capability for engaging in higher studies. It can show steadiness, fluctuation, brilliance, stupidity, perseverance, laziness, discouragement, many things. It represents a collective judgment, by many pople over a long time, of the quality of the student's work. It is a mistake, therefore, to reduce such a historical record to a single number. The mathematical average, quite bluntly, ignores fluctuations which may be significant. The subject pattern in University entrance requirements covers a wide range of knowledge and for many persons will include areas of great competence and others of rather severe deficiency. The grade-point average obscures these details. We should not continue to allow the difficulties of evaluating thousands of records to dissuade us from examining each significant characteristic. The admissions program should be re-designed so as to make evident the areas of competence demonstrated by each student, and to indicate fluctuations in ability or performance from area to area and from time to time.

But the high school record is by itself still subject to certain defects: it does not take into account possibly significant differences in high schools. It might, of course, be possible to apply a "grade-point differential" on the basis of the performance of each high school's students on the campus, but such a device would involve great political difficulties, and is even more undesirable on other grounds. For small schools it is statistically unreliable because of the fluctuations in performance among the few students who come to us. For the large schools the subsequent grade-point record on campus is affected by certain habitual subject patterns carried over from high school to college. In any case, the method places unhealthy extra emphasis on grade points, conspires against identification of the creative eccentric, and denies the individual his own record.

The better answer lies in the aptitude and achievement tests which compare the student with a large number of similar persons in the country as a whole. A single test is by itself a poor indicator of the nature of a whole person, but, as supplementary devices, external tests serve many purposes, one of which is to detect and correct for any differences among grading practices in high schools. A selected series of tests, properly compared with the corresponding subject patterns in the high school record, provides indispensable supplementary aids in evaluating the applicant. The combination of subject patterns in high school, aptitude test, and achievement test in particular areas offers a useful picture of the state of a student's knowledge and the quality of his thinking.

But not all of our students—nor all of us—learn or communicate by conventional means. We should recognize distinguished achievement or great aptitude in a wide range of other activities—the performing arts, student leadership, public service—and be prepared to give it due weight in assessing the meaning of the scholastic record.

We presently lack a complete procedure which invites school officials to bring to our attention promising candidates whose academic records are misleading. Granted that in the public mind this campus has perhaps over-achieved in its hospitality to eccentricity, it remains true that the world is full of creative persons who lack a college education because they were too far outside the college admission pattern. Many of these people are doing perfectly well without a college degree. But the important question is not so much whether they need us as whether the campus needs them. The only way to identify these persons is to invite school officials specifically to inform us concerning them. Personal evaluations from principals, counselors, and teachers should be accepted as a valuable supplement to any student's record; they are particularly valuable when they are responses to specific questions posed by us.

Recommendation 10: **The high school student's record for admissions should include a more sensitive analysis of his course record for aca-**

demic strengths and weaknesses; the results of aptitude and achievement tests; recognition of significant extracurricular achievement; and evaluations from high school officials.

C. A Possible Selection System

Lest it be assumed that the increased complexity of the data recommended above would render the handling of large numbers of applications too difficult, there is outlined below a quite possible system of admissions designed and described for the Committee by Professor Walter D. Knight:

The following assumes that the student should be evaluated with respect to four major areas, each of which consists of several parts. The first three areas would be: English and foreign language; mathematics and natural science; social science and other academic electives. These are to be evaluated according to high school grades combined with scores on related standard aptitude and achievement tests. The fourth area includes demonstrated abilities in extracurricular activities, and other evidence of desirable skills or aptitudes. Evaluation of a record would involve the establishment of quantitative rating schemes in each area, and routine preliminary examination of the pattern for each student—probably by machine—which would call attention to extraordinary performance in any one or more areas; reject certain applications which are below predetermined levels in one or more areas; accept for admission more or less routinely those applicants whose records are satisfactory in all respects and outstanding in none; call attention to those records which are satisfactory in some respects but questionable in others. The scores should be so arranged as to distinguish as questionable most of those students who now fall in the range of 2.8 to 3.2 in overall high school grade-point average. At present, only two per cent of our entering students can be admitted outside the normal rules. This proposed change will increase the figure to twenty or thirty per cent, and have the highly desirable effect of allowing us to scrutinize all students near the margin, both above *and* below it. We should do this because some presently below are highly desirable University students, while many presently above the limit turn out to be unsuitable.

After the mechanical arithmetic has called our attention to the superior candidates and to the marginal ones, a faculty committee comes into operation, and arranges to make available to certain of the superior students special treatment after admission—advanced standing, independent study, special seminars, or the like. It also examines carefully the marginal cases, reads the principals' recommendations, consults with school officials if necessary, and admits those with the more promising records. It gives special attention to the student who, though unpromising in several respects, may be brilliant in one—providing that he meets a reasonable standard of literacy.

The suggestion that we give special scrutiny to the broad band of applicants who now score between 2.8 and 3.2 involves a substantial change in our present procedure. This and other changes require mutual agreement among the campuses before they can be implemented. Regardless of the political difficulties of realizing such a plan, it represents a valid approach to the general problem, and we should press for its acceptance. It continues the principle of having a common minimum eligibility requirement for all campuses, but assumes that each campus will have a large amount of freedom with respect to recruitment, and each will retain full discretion with regard to admission or rejection of the marginal candidates referred to above. Marginal applicants who are rejected by any one campus might be accepted by another with differing marginal criteria.

It should be recognized that any substantial changes in admission requirements and procedures are bound to be announced well in advance of their implementation so that students in the early years of secondary schools can plan their programs accordingly. This presents a real problem, since we ought to be able to effect substantial changes very soon. We should consider making at once what changes we believe are most necessary, allowing a certain flexibility in the transition period for students whose programs were underway and not easily changed at the time we decided on our modifications.

Recommendation 11: Admission standards should be made more flexible by allowing each campus full discretion in admitting or rejecting candidates whose high school grade-point averages now fall in the range 2.8 to 3.2.

D. Recruiting

An admissions program is more than receiving willing subjects for processing. It should also involve actively seeking among large numbers of possible candidates for those who we believe will be particularly congenial as students on this campus. While many will be attracted to the campus, there are other desirable candidates who might not come at all because they are unaware of what we have to offer, or because they cannot afford to come to Berkeley, or perhaps because they have somehow been discouraged from going to college at all. A passive admissions program effectively eliminates these potential students.

Certainly the representatives of the University-wide organization cannot by themselves operate a significantly enlarged program of recruiting. It may be hoped that our own alumni retain sufficient devotion to this campus to act effectively as our representatives. They are large enough in number and well distributed geographically. There is no reason why we could not establish a mutually satisfactory arrangement in which the proper faculty representative works closely with the alumni organization in order to identify and approach promising potential candidates. A limited program of faculty participation in direct contact with high school students is certainly possible and reasonable. Finally, certain registered students should be enlisted to help with the job of identifying and proselytizing among friends and acquaintances back home.

The structure of financial aid should be organized and developed in a coherent way, so that scholarships, fellowships, grants-in-aid, job opportunities, and loans bear definite relations among themselves and are properly represented to interested candidates. The Scholarship Committee of the Division should add to its present responsibilities another of enlisting the aid of alumni, students, and faculty in locating potential sources of scholarship funds. Until we are able to offer an appreciable number of prospective students sizable scholarship moneys guaranteed over two to four-year periods, we have not even understood the problem, much less solved it.

Recommendation 12: **The campus should improve its recruitment of able candidates through the use of alumni, faculty, and students, and an improved program of scholarship assistance.**

V.

ADVISING AND ORIENTATION OF STUDENTS IN LETTERS AND SCIENCE

A. The Present System: Area and Major Advising

STUDENTS NEED orientation and advising for at least
three distinguishable reasons: they need specific *information* about
academic requirements, university regulations, and their status in regard to these requirements and regulations; they need *advice or counsel*
about curricula, majors, courses, career opportunities, and discussion
of general intellectual matters; and they need some *personal relationship* with members of the faculty that will contribute to their sense of
belonging and being personally counted in the academic community.
After numerous staff interviews with faculty, students, and administrative employees all over the campus, the Committee came to the
conclusion that the professional schools and colleges provide orientation and advising that generally satisfy both the student and the faculty.
In the College of Letters and Science, however, despite heroic efforts
by administration and staff, the present advising system does not work
well, and important changes are planned for Fall 1966.

Several factors contribute to the relative success of the professional
schools in advising: smaller size; a genuine professional bond between
students and faculty; the strict sequence of courses which in many
schools leaves little need for guidance in the choice of free electives;
perhaps even the more pragmatic nature of persons who are drawn to
the applied disciplines.

Almost all the professional schools have orientation programs, in
which entering students first attend a large welcoming meeting, then go
to smaller meetings representing different subdivisions, where they can
discuss curricular offerings, graduate study, and career opportunities.
Business Administration and Engineering make use of a period of two

or three weeks around the end of each semester when tentative programs are chosen for the coming semester. Thus in the first hectic days of each semester returning students do not have to stand in long lines to see harassed professors, and the latter have time to deal with new students. In many professional schools, and notably the School of Law, there is a prevailing "open door" policy as regards advising. Students generally feel free to drop in and see their advisers or the professors teaching their courses at any time.

In considering the changes either proposed or additionally desirable in Letters and Science advising, it may help to have a brief description of the present system. The system is virtually the same as that in use at most large state universities, and its defects are the same everywhere.

Students are divided into area advisees (lower-division students who have not elected a major) and major advisees (all upper-division students and those lower-division students who have elected a major). Area advising is directed and coordinated by the College of Letters and Science. Before each semester the College asks each department to nominate a certain number of its members to serve as area advisers, the number being based upon the size of the faculty in each department. Altogether there are 255 area advisers, each adviser having about 30 assigned advisees. Assigning of advisees to area advisers is done entirely by the College, which sends to each adviser a folder on each advisee, including the past academic record if the student is a transfer student. Area advisees are encouraged to see their advisers during the advising period, and are obliged to see them at least once each term in order to obtain the necessary signatures before filing their study lists.

Departmental major advising procedures are entirely determined by the individual departments. These procedures, however, fundamentally the same in almost every department, vary only according to the amount of interest and enthusiasm put into them, with the smaller departments coming out best. Students in most departments are assigned alphabetically to major advisers, with whom they must stay the two years in the major, although in Mathematics and in some of the large social science departments the students simply choose each semester the adviser they would like to see. In almost every department in the humanities, sciences, and languages, the student meets with his adviser in the latter's study. However, in some of the social science departments students see professors in a central place, usually in the departmental office or in a small room nearby, both during the beginning advising period and during the semester for the regular weekly office hours.

In recent years some of the larger departments have been using

Teaching Assistants to do the major portion of advising. In these departments each major first talks to a Teaching Assistant, all of whom are usually seated in one small room. The Teaching Assistant completely reviews the student's major courses and tentatively plans the future program. The faculty adviser is seen for any special problems or substitution approval and for the official signature. In one department all students new to the major and all those planning to graduate that semester are interviewed by a departmental secretary, who either advises the new students of the major requirements or checks to see whether the graduating seniors have fulfilled these requirements.

Very few departments hold orientation programs for new major students. In one department, which does hold such a meeting, the chairman of the undergraduate majors talks to the students about general requirements of the major and the rationale behind them, afterwards inviting questions from the audience.

All the larger Letters and Science departments have orientation meetings for their major advisers, presided over by "chairmen of the undergraduate majors," where for the most part requirements and rules are discussed, with some treatment of departmental policy regarding the undergraduate program.

The major defect of the system of area advisers is that many of them do not know enough to be of significant help. Area advisers deal for the most part with freshmen, most of whom know nothing about campus life and regulations, let alone College and major academic requirements. The advisers themselves are often the most inexperienced members of the faculty, left over after the graduate and major advisers have been chosen. Many are brand new to the University. While advisers are armed by the College with the current bulletins and catalogues, it is obvious that new students looking to them for complete and accurate information about a welter of rules and procedures will often be disappointed, if not actually misinformed.

Students generally see their area advisers only at the obligatory study-list-signing time. With at most three or four brief meetings together during a two-year period, it is difficult for a meaningful relationship to grow up between them. Rapport is further discouraged by the annual turnover of area advisers. Theoretically, an area adviser is to have his advisee for the latter's two years in the lower division. Actually, of the 255 area advisers in the College of Letters and Science, each year 150 are new. Many students see as many as two or three advisers during their freshman and sophomore years.

Major advising is somewhat more successful than area advising. Advisers are much more familiar with major requirements than with College requirements, and often they are fully aware of the rationale behind them. In many departments, especially the smaller ones, there is a real professional bond between faculty and students and a natural concern on the part of the faculty for the intellectual development of the students. Nevertheless, major advising falls far short of satisfactory performance, especially in the larger departments. Again, a major reason is lack of knowledge on the part of advisers.

Some faculty members are not adequately familiar with the exact requirements of the departmental major and are unable to tell whether or not a student is fulfilling them. In those large departments which are divided along lines of method and conception of the discipline (as are some of the social science departments), some of the faculty are not aware of the subject matter, level of sophistication, and emphasis of courses taught within other subdivisions of their own departments. With the exception of a few very good advisers, most professors are not sufficiently aware of what courses are taught outside their own departments or how these courses might tie in with the major to give the student an integrated program of study. For a variety of reasons, professors are unable to give advice to students on the quality of teaching in their own or in other departments. The majority of students interviewed by the Committee staff report that for academic advice they rely much more heavily on other sources: the University Catalogue, friends, office secretaries, the *Slate Supplement*.

Some students complain *not* that they are not given enough time and information, but that they *do not want any advising at all* and resent having to go through the rigmarole of appointments and study-list signing. Most students, in fact, admit that they have their minds made up before approaching the adviser, and during their appointments they focus all their efforts toward the sole goal of convincing him to sign their preplanned programs as quickly as possible. Most students find it infuriating to stand for seemingly endless waits in long, chairless lines simply for the formality of a signature. Several students interviewed had gone to small liberal arts colleges before coming to Berkeley, and more than a few of these stated that they came to Berkeley to get away from what they considered a stifling atmosphere brought about by "over-advising" or too much personal concern for the students on the part of the faculty.

Almost all students admit, however, that they *would* like to discuss meaningful topics with faculty members, but that they feel that the short and obligatory appointment at the beginning of each semester does not furnish an opportunity conducive to informal discussion. Many of these say that they cannot think of anything to talk about, that they are intimidated by the professor's position as learned scholar, and that they feel they are taking up his valuable time. This report is matched by that of many advisers, who feel that students are often not interested in seeking their advice: "They come in during advising period at the last moment, only for a signature, and rarely return during the term." Yet all of the faculty members interviewed feel that advising is an important part of their academic duties, and all are willing to engage with students in the sector of advising for which they feel themselves most qualified: discussion of intellectual matters.

It is apparent that the present system thwarts rather than abets the best desires of both students and faculty. It is based on a misuse of faculty time, reducing trained scholars to routine checkers of requirements and automatic signers of study lists, often calling on them for information that they have not been given the time nor the training to acquire. Furthermore, it is based on the doubtful assumption that a spontaneous and genuine relationship will develop between a student and a faculty member within the short periods officially required for advising twice a year. There is little initial bond between the adviser and the student, especially in the lower division, beyond that of requirements and study lists. There are probably few men who are capable of forming meaningful relationships with dozens of students on short notice. Valuable relationships are built upon a true commonalty of interest, and on the nuances and rapport of character and personality—a rapport which takes time to develop, and which the fact of arbitrary assignment sometimes destroys from the first.

B. Proposed Changes

Faced with these difficulties, and with the prospect of added burdens on advisers brought on by the conversion to the quarter system, the College is considering a number of changes. The Committee finds three of them particularly promising:

1. Voluntary Advising.

Except for entering freshmen and transfer students, and students at the point of declaring a major, all advising (with the approval of the major department) will be voluntary, and departments will be urged to allow students the adviser of their choice.

This change recognizes some of the psychological defects of the present system. It relieves the advisers of much of the burden of routine study-list signing, and puts the final responsibility for choice of courses on the student. Needless to say, good educational practice will still require that students in academic difficulties be offered special attention without their asking.

2. Mechanization of Record-Keeping.

A new system of record-handling is planned, whereby each quarter a student will be given a current summary of his progress in the College and of the requirements which remain to be filled.

The Committee hopes that this modest change will be followed by others designed to mechanize the mechanical work of record-keeping on campus. There is no reason, for instance, why we cannot automate the entire process of registration. The University of Indiana is close to perfecting a computer system whereby each student can register for all his courses and sections in four or five minutes.

3. Orientation and Summer Guidance.

The College and the Counseling Center cooperatively conducted at the beginning of this term a new and highly successful orientation program for entering students and their parents. This was a pilot project looking toward a larger one in the summer, and stressed academic and career interests rather than extra-curricular interests.

Up to now, the official orientation of new students at Berkeley has been the same ineffectual kind in use at many large universities. But a few institutions have made productive advances in orientation, especially by making full use of the summer period for guidance of entering freshmen and transfer students.

During the summer before the freshman enters Pennsylvania State, he takes eight hours of aptitude and academic proficiency tests in one of many testing sites throughout the state. When the results are known, the new student, with parents if desired, goes to one of the University's campuses for an extensive interview with a professional counselor, where the discussion centers around the student's aptitudes, academic strength and weakness, career opportunities and academic programs which will prepare the student for such careers, and general information regarding the procedures and facilities of the University. Academic representatives of the various colleges are available for consultation at the same time. This program has resulted in a very noticeable reduction in the number of students dropping out of school early and a reduction also in the number of students switching from one major to the other.

In addition, the program has had a very good public response; as one counselor writes, "it is one of the best public relations programs the University has."

Registration, pre-enrollment, and advising of freshmen is now being conducted during the summer at several universities. Three separate summer weekends are set aside by the University of Rochester for this purpose, and the freshmen, divided into three large groups, come to the campus for one of the weekends to complete all pre-semester details. A similar procedure is followed at the University of Pennsylvania, where the students also receive extensive vocational counseling. The Davis campus of the University of California conducts a Summer Advising Program, where new students are advised, registered, and purchase all textbooks to be used in their first semester's classes. The Santa Barbara campus conducts a similar program. Both the University of Nebraska and Webster College (Missouri) send to the prospective new student detailed and easily understandable information on courses open to him, the basic curriculum requirements, and several examples of curricula that freshmen typically follow. He is in addition supplied with forms on which he can tentatively map out his schedule of courses for his first year at the University. Webster College goes one step beyond Nebraska in that during the summer the freshmen mail their tentatively planned schedules back to the College, where they are reviewed by faculty advisers and then sent back with corrections and suggestions attached. All students are invited to seek answers to any problems they have by means of letters, telephone calls, or visits to the campus at any time during the summer. Thus, when the student has his first meeting with the adviser, he has gone beyond the totally confused stage to the point at which meaningful questions can be asked.

The three changes listed above are a good beginning; the Committee herewith recommends additional changes, in the conviction that voluntary advising will be successful only in the context of a thorough improvement of the whole system:

4. Simplification of Requirements.

The University and College requirements themselves should be drastically simplified. At present both the student and the adviser are faced by a wilderness of special regulations and limits on what courses a student may or may not offer for graduation credit. Each of these requirements should be thoroughly reviewed with a view toward its possible elimination. The UCLA faculty of Letters and Science has eliminated the "non-Letters-and-Science course" rule. Rules concerning maximum and minimum study lists, proportions of upper and lower division work, transfer equivalents, residence, changing or dropping of courses, "honors" standing, and no doubt many others might be simplified. Where rules cannot be simplified, much greater latitude should be given to departments or advisers in administering them to students in particular circumstances.

The overriding criterion on student-program decisions must always be the educational soundness of the specific proposal for the specific student. This question of soundness is one that an adviser who knows the student and the field can perhaps judge more accurately than a dean. *Routine* checking of requirements, in any case, should not devolve upon the individual professor, but be handled mechanically or by a trained assistant.

5. Informational Literature.

The collection and dissemination of information for students and advisers must be radically improved. The literature which we send to the potential freshman during the summer before he enters the University is filled with information which will aid him in adjusting to his extra-academic surroundings, but it does not introduce him to those questions which will eventually cause him the greatest confusion once he arrives on campus and the solutions to which are at the same time of greatest importance to his academic career. Choice of an academic major is one important question which, of course, does not require an immediate answer. Nevertheless, if somewhere amongst the mass of information about recreation which the student now receives during the summer there could be included a brief listing of the departments on campus, accompanied by a general description of the nature of the various disciplines and possible careers in each field, the difficulties encountered by both student and adviser at their initial meeting could be considerably diminished. Many students arrive at Berkeley in the fall with no clear distinctions in their minds between the Social Sciences and the Physical Sciences, let alone between Sociology and Social Welfare.

Nowhere in the many publications issued by the University of California are there even general hints as to how to plan a program of courses. Why not fully acquaint the student during the summer with details of curriculum planning? A separate pamphlet should be sent to him giving full and clear details of the courses open to freshmen, the requirements of the College and the prerequisites of the majors, accompanied by several typical programs of courses which freshmen interested in different fields might adopt for their first year or two at the University.

Examples of four-year programs might also be helpful. Forms could be attached on which the student could comprehensively outline the courses he should take to fulfill requirements and prerequisites.

It would also be of the greatest assistance to students and advisers—especially with the shortened "shopping period" under the quarter system—to have available each quarter in each department a comprehensive list of courses, accompanied by full descriptions of the subject matter and emphasis of each course, the demands to be made upon the student in terms of examinations and written work, and a full list of the books to be required.

6. Campus Information Service.

There should be a single professionally staffed Campus Information Service, with generous telephone equipment and reception facilities, where students and advisers might apply for any and all kinds of other relevant information about the campus. Indeed, we suggest that a vigorously run central Information Service, perhaps combining some of the present services of the Dean of the College, the Dean of Students, the Office of Admissions, and the Registrar, would be the natural agency for publishing the printed materials so badly needed.

7. Faculty Specialists in Advising.

It is granted that every member of the faculty should engage in advising to the best of his abilities. However, the special problems of beginning freshmen and transfer students make it imperative that they have access to special advising talent. While the entire faculty should offer consultation hours throughout the year for student advising on a voluntary basis, there should be available in a central place a special group of faculty members chosen for their aptitude in dealing with new students. These faculty members should be specially trained for their duties, and be compensated in the form of released time from teaching or administrative work. Some could be available during the summer and throughout the year to answer questions coming from prospective students by letter, telephone, or in person. Both North Carolina and Wisconsin report that this system works well. Wisconsin now has a Faculty Advising Service staffed with well-trained faculty men responsible for all lower-division advising, which is now completely voluntary.

8. Advising as Teaching.

The Committee feels that in the toils of conforming to an intricate system of rules and regulations the faculty of the College has tended to lose sight of the broader functions of student advising, to lose sight of the profound and seamless connection between advising and teaching itself. To the objection that a large corps of special advisers would take men away from the teaching program, the reply is that advising *is* teaching, and to the extent that student and adviser get down to fundamental intellectual questions it is a particularly important kind of teaching.

The Committee's general recommendations on curricular change and the improvement of teaching all tend toward confirming this identification. Recommendations of the increased use of small groups—sections, seminars, tutorials, preceptorials—and independent study all mean that we should combine advising with teaching wherever possible. Members of freshman seminars—even after orientation and initial advising by a specialist—should think of their seminar leaders as their natural advisers. Students whose regular programs do not lead them to small groups should be offered the option of enrolling for credit in an "exploratory" or "advisory" course. The Committee recommends that students be allowed to offer toward the degree up to four or five quarter units in courses of this kind, taken at crucial junctures in their academic careers.

The "Exploratory" Course.

The formal combination of freshman advising with exploration of academic subjects is no new thing in American education. There is a general movement toward it in some of the best orientation programs. At the University of Pennsylvania and at Pomona College entering freshmen are sent a list of books which they can read during the summer. During the freshman orientation that fall, prominent university scholars deliver a series of four or five lectures, with discussion periods following, centering around the books on the list. The students have a free choice of which lectures to attend. It would be a relatively simple matter to continue this type of discussion in one- or two-unit "exploratory" courses taught by faculty members or experienced graduate assistants to groups of 30 or 40 freshmen according to areas of general interest. During the term, the group of 40 advisees could be divided into two or three smaller groups, each group meeting with the instructor periodically. The content of the course could consist of reading, discussion, and writing which contribute to a general understanding of the character of the area. The course could be understood as exploratory in the sense that it would both explore the nature of the academic area and at the same time explore the interests, needs, and problems of the students, each of whom could meet with the instructor for private discussions when necessary.

The advisory nature of the course could be continued throughout the quarter, with discussions in class on such subjects as the University and how it functions, theories of education, the intellectual content of the different fields of learning within the University, and the nature of various majors. The student could be invited to meet with the adviser again during the following terms, but would not be required to do so. Such a course would have some of the same character and purpose of the one-unit "Introduction to Antioch" course required of all new students at that College.

This kind of solution to the problems inherent in freshman advising would do much to avoid the pitfalls now encountered. The freshman, in his first close contact with a representative of the University, would be met with professional interest and warmth which is lacking in the present system. The adviser's relationship to the student would now be based upon substantive intellectual content and the student would no longer be a faceless figure flitting in and out of the study two or three times a year. As important is the fact that advising would no longer be a burdensome duty which would detract from one's other pursuits without the compensation of reward or recognition, since the faculty member would be given full teaching credit for the time he spent in the "exploratory" course.

These principles are already at work in two advisory arrangements for upper-division students which have come to the Committee's attention.

The Preceptorial.

The Department of English has instituted two experimental "preceptorial" groups. A group of twenty-five to thirty majors is assigned to a faculty preceptor upon their declaration of the major. The preceptor is a major adviser to this group of students for their entire two years in the major. During the junior year the preceptor meets with the preceptorial monthly in a group or in small groups determined by common courses or areas of interest. He meets with the students individually often enough to insure close supervision of their progress. Group meetings are devoted to discussion of their work in the major, the airing of questions and complaints and comments on the program, discussion of common problems, informal colloquia on the disciplines of literary study, and on the relation of the major program to elective studies. In the senior year the preceptor conducts one of the senior courses required for the major, then takes his advisees through a "199" course of special studies in a related field.

The Adviser as "Curriculum Manager".

Professor Michael Goodman of the Department of Architecture has conceived an imaginative two-unit advisory course which he terms "curriculum management". By means of this course seniors in their final term are given one last opportunity to fill out or draw together the pieces of their formal education under the guidance of a sympathetic adviser. Often the work is related to the senior architectural thesis, and it usually involves independent study or taking courses in fields which give new depth or dimension to the architectural project itself. Thus a prison design might be deepened by a study in criminology, a theatre by investigation of dramatic literature or stage history, a housing project by a course in sociology or economics. In each case the adviser assists the student in finding a project; discusses his progress with him periodically; examines and evaluates the long written report submitted at the end of the term; and organizes all his advisees into a discussion group which soon turns into a lively and autonomous body of cooperating researchers and critics.

9. Students as Advisers.

For the past two years the Orientations Board of the Associated Students has offered a Student Orientation Service for new and continuing students. Completely organized and directed by students, it has been of help to many, providing them with information which ranged from the specific details of requirements and regulations to advice on study habits, and directions for locating out-of-the-way buildings. Its usefulness has been somewhat limited thus far, however, because of its location (Fourth Floor of the Student Union) and because its availability has not been well publicized to the student body.

Officers of the Service are already organizing their program for the Fall of 1966. As has been the case with the recruitment of student counselors in the past two years, they expect an overwhelming number of upper-division students to volunteer as counselors. A rigorous spring training program is again being planned by experienced student counselors. Next year's counselors will receive instruction in academic requirements, university regulations, procedures of registration, information about scholarships, etc. In addition, the counselors will be divided into small teams, one being sent to each department on campus to seek specific and up-to-date information about major requirements, with special emphasis on the intricacies of the conversion of each major's curriculum requirements to the changed situation of the quarter system.

The College of Letters and Science plans to cooperate with Student Orientation Service by providing volunteer advisers from the faculty to help students who require additional assistance.

This is precisely the kind of student involvement in the academic purposes of the campus that the campus needs. With advising, as with teaching, the contribution of students will not diminish the duties and responsibilities of the faculty; it may even increase them; but it will contribute greatly to the quality of the work finally done.

In conclusion the Committee presents the following summary recommendation:

Recommendation 13: The advising system in the College of Letters and Science should be made largely voluntary through the adoption of such improvements as mechanizing the record-keeping, reforming the orientation procedure, simplifying the rules and liberalizing their application, providing ample printed materials, establishing a Campus Information Service, appointing advising specialists, promoting combinations of advising and teaching, and encouraging participation of student advisers.

VI.

GRADING

A. Work of the Committee

THE ESTABLISHMENT of the present Committee came at a moment when, throughout the United States, considerable debate and planning was being devoted to the problem of grading in higher education. Few would deny that, as more and more students compete for admission to our better undergraduate and graduate schools, they have become increasingly "grade-conscious." Students, faculty, and administrators alike have expressed concern about the pressure of grades; and some institutions have planned or implemented changes to free the student from the full impact of this pressure. Nearly all of these changes have moved in the direction of limited or experimental pass-fail grading in some form. Starting in 1966, students at Cornell will be allowed to elect one non-major course per semester for pass-fail; and a list of courses which can be so elected is being established at Princeton. Cal Tech has been conducting a two-year experiment in which only pass-fail grades are given in the freshman year. Two of the new University of California campuses have taken similar steps: the faculty of Cowell College at Santa Cruz plans, at least for the time being, to operate with pass-fail grades only; while Irvine allows one pass-fail course per quarter in work taken outside the student's Division.

The Committee decided at its outset that the problem of grading, and the various plans which had been considered for meeting it, merited close study. It accordingly engaged the summer services of Professor Stuart Miller, who, with a student assistant, reviewed the extensive literature in the field, conducted about one hundred interviews, and corresponded with as many colleges and universities throughout the nation. Professor Miller compiled a comprehensive review of the arguments against the present system and of proposed modifications to it, and he submitted his own recommendations for experimental pass-fail grading and comprehensive or qualifying examinations. A brief abridgement of his very extensive findings and recommendations was duplicated and made available to interested faculty members for discussion and comment. It was later published in a supplement to the *Daily Californian*. A second report, by Professor Otto Smith, outlined a plan whereby the present five-step system of recorded grades would be converted to a compatible ten-step system by the addition of "plus" grades with 0.5 grade-point extra credit. This too was duplicated and distributed to department chairmen. Some three dozen extensive comments on these documents were received from the faculty. Many of these developed additional arguments with great cogency and eloquence; and one of them, from Professor Henry May, was also published in the *Daily Californian*.

The documentation which the Committee has thus acquired attests both to the importance and to the intricacy of the problem. It does not, however, show any clear consensus as to the best path forward. In these circumstances, the Committee has been able to recommend only limited changes, together with a proposal for further experiments.

B. Student Opinions Concerning Our Grading System

Even if we cannot immediately resolve the deep differences of opinion which exist on our campus with respect to grading, it is possible and useful to suggest what these differences are. Above all, we can report that student dissatisfaction with the present system is apparently not, as sometimes alleged, confined to a small, vocal, but essentially unrepresentative minority. We gathered this and other conclusions from a questionnaire distributed last fall to a random sample of 2,576 returning students, to which 2,203, or 85.5%, replied. These students were given four possible responses to the question "How well do you thing the grading system at Berkeley reflects the student's actual knowledge and understanding of the subjects studied?". Only a bare majority seemed to believe in the efficiency of the system (3.4% answered "Very well," and 49.2% "Fairly well"). No less than 41.8% answered "Only slightly," and this result cannot be attributed solely to resentful disappointment: 35% of the honors-level students in the sample answered in this way,[1] and 26% of those with grade-point average of 3.5 or better. A more or less

---

[1] I.e., those students whose grade-point average the previous semester was 3.0 or better.

constant 5% of students at all grade-point-average levels answered "Not at all." Thirty-one out of 836 honors-level students (3.6%) believed that the system works "Very well"; another 467 (55.8%) answered "Fairly well." Obviously one should not expect enthusiastic support for any form of grading. But when two fifths of an honors-level student sample express such signficant disbelief in the system which rewarded them, it is surely time to reconsider not only the grading system itself, but the increasing emphasis which we are pressed to place upon it. The questionnaire also indicated that 43% of those replying found grades a "major" worry; this figure included 41% of the honors-level students.

Almost two thirds of the students replying took advantage of open-ended questions to suggest improvement, particularly with respect to the grading system. Almost half of those who commented on grading volunteered the suggestion that more pass-fail grading be used, especially outside the major or in the lower division. Others asked for a more sophisticated range of grades. Many students also criticized the present emphasis on final examinations; they tended to ask for more emphasis on written work, or to criticize the present reliance on "objective" questions which put a premium on memorization. The open-ended comments did not suggest any particularly significant variations among schools, colleges, or majors. They did, however, challenge the allegation that pass-fail grading is the preference of mediocre performers: in a sample of 300 open-ended replies, the highest percentages favoring some form of pass-fail grading came from the honors-level students.

C. Faculty Opinions Concerning Grading

Grading Per Se

Our correspondence from faculty members contained virtually the same range of suggestions for improvements as from the students. But most letters, inasmuch as they were written in reply to the Miller Report, were particularly interested in the principle of grading as such, and a majority of them were concerned to justify the necessity of letter-grading. Some replies pointed out the intrinsic merits of letter-grading, as an unwelcome but salutary comparison by which each student could be forced to learn something about his standing among his peers, and also to criticize himself. It was argued that personal comments on students by professors were not likely to be particularly rigorous or searching; and something rigorous was indeed required, to make both the professor offer true criticism, and the student believe it.[2]

---

[2] "It would be deplorable if the rather harsh, critical environment appropriate to an educational institution gave way to a congenial, unevaluative one, in which scholars

The limited and formal features of course grades were not only admitted, but defended: from one point of view an academic course was precisely "a formal preparation for a formal test and evaluation." Thus the course could be viewed as a device to encourage a measurable performance. It might in addition have many lasting inspirational effects, "but you cannot measure inspiration directly. You can only measure performance on a test of some sort, against more or less well-defined standards."[3] A far greater number of letters defended letter-grading as at least preferable in principle to the visible alternatives. As long as our society continues to be competitive and selective, it was argued, professors will continue to be asked for comparative evaluations among students. The present system at least gives the student a reasonably clear picture of what that comparison will be, whereas "personal evaluations" might very well be based on private grade-records, which the student could neither profit from nor question.[4] Even if the objections raised to formal grades are true—that they can be erratic and subjective, so that even the same professor will grade the same work differently at different times—these objections are no less true of any other conceivable form of evaluation.

How We Grade

Many of the same correspondents who defended the system of grading per se freely admitted that we should contemplate modifications to the system as it operates at Berkeley. Some professors who had taught large breadth courses drew attention to the anomaly that necessarily perfunctory grading of hundreds of students together counts for as much as a closely supervised grade in a major seminar.

> . . . the grading is a nightmare. I have found that I cannot mark with any pretence of fairness several hundred essays in

---

went about their business and students were simply welcome to pick up what they liked, as spectators on the intellectual scene. The most effective way of inculcating habits of self-criticism in one's students is as a critic, and only secondarily as an example. . . . But unless one is forced to do this, one will tend to avoid it: professors have much more interesting things to do than to persuade students of their mistakes. And this is my main argument for grading: it forces teachers to evaluate their student's work and to justify those evaluations in detail—activities which neither party particularly enjoys . . . since a radical reduction of the teaching ratio is not in prospect, grades are the best method we have of coercing ourselves to pay the right kind of attention." (Letter of December 14, 1965 from Prof. Thomas Nagel)

[3] Letter of Jan. 10, 1966 from Prof. James Leiby.

[4] "I would expect a conscientious teacher to make sure of the systematic accumulation of evidence for student evaluation and that he would make this become a matter of record for future reference when the much admired 'personal evaluations' might be sought. It is not likely that this would often involve a private system of 'grading' unknown to the student? And would not this hidden system generate a new set of problems?" (Letter of Dec. 27, 1965 from Prof. L. L. Sammet.)

the time alloted me, and I do not think it right to leave to inexperienced 'readers' decisions which may affect a student's whole University career. I have therefore taken to 'objective' examinations demanding factual answers, which I dislike extremely but consider less unfair than badly marked essays. I think it ridiculous that a physicist or engineer should find his career depending on whether he gets a 'B' or a 'C' in my course (as sometimes seems to happen) . . .[5]

Some professors expressed interest in the Smith proposal for more sophisticated gradations, but they represented mostly the hard sciences, where more objective discrimination can be made. However some professors asked for a more discriminating system at the graduate level. There was little support for, and much opposition to, the idea of comprehensive examinations at this campus, especially from some professors who had administered them. It was argued that we should move instead in the direction of intimate, more personal confrontations between the student and his examiner. By the same token, many professors supported the proposal made by Prof. Henry May "that we grade less often in order to grade better." Most of the concrete proposals received were for placing large lecture courses on a pass-fail basis, or even for abolishing grades in them altogether.

D. Recent Developments Toward Liberalization of Grading

In the past few months, the Santa Cruz campus, Irvine campus, and Experimental Program at Berkeley have all petitioned the University-wide faculty organization for enabling legislation to conduct experiments in pass-fail grading. By January, 1966, this had led to two independent initiatives at the University-wide level. On the one hand the Academic Council recommended that the Santa Cruz campus be granted a two-year period for pass-fail grading in all courses. At the same time the University-wide Committee on Educational Policy proposed that the University-wide Academic Assembly replace the existing Regulation 782 by the following words:

782. Under such regulations as each Division may determine, a student in good standing is authorized to undertake one

[5] Letter of Dec. 13, 1965 from Prof. J. K. Anderson. Cf. Prof. Henry May: "I have very little confidence in the grades turned in as a result of examinations read by twenty different teaching assistants, many of them grading for the first time, in a class of a thousand. Almost without regard to the seriousness of the effort by the faculty, such numbers put a premium on the easiest and most efficient methods of grading, rather than the most serious ones."

course each term on a *Passed* or *Not Passed* basis. Units thus earned shall be counted in satisfaction of degree requirements, but shall be disregarded in determining the student's grade-point average.

The Committee also recommended the encouraging of more extensive grading experiments by Divisions.

E. Recommendations

We have found from our own experience that opinions concerning grading must take into account an unusually complex and conflicting body of evidence. Our study of the very extensive literature on grading, as summarized for us by Prof. Miller and others, suggests that the results of researches to date are very far from definitive enough to justify immediate wholesale reforms of the present system. Many of us would defend the principle that letter-grading *per se* is desirable and should continue. At the same time we cannot express satisfaction with the actual conditions under which we grade on this campus; and there are grounds for challenging them on two issues, with respect to both how we grade and the use to which grades are put. By the latter we mean our ubiquitous calculation of grade-point average as a criterion for academic privileges, including honors standing and advancement to graduate study. There is no doubt that an obsession with grade points drives many of our students to choose courses for perverse reasons. (In a sample of 1789 returning students who had chosen electives in the past, 57%, including more than half of the honors students, admitted as a factor in their choice the ease or difficulty of getting a good grade.) But it is not clear that we should blame the students for being perversely grade-conscious. The same charge might be turned against the University, as long as we were to rely on grade points alone in allocating such important academic privileges as "honors" programs, stack passes, etc. One way to encourage a healthier attitude towards grades among our students is to develop a healthier attitude ourselves. This may necessitate more humanely defined and administered rules, whereby student applications for privileges can be judged on their real merits. We therefore begin with three general principles from which we derive an initial series of proposals for practical change.

In light of what has been said above, the general principles may need little defense. They are: 1) The Division should seek ways of grading less often in order to grade better; 2) The principle of counting all units equally in the calculation of grade-point averages should be seriously reconsidered; and 3) Considerations other than grade-point average should be taken into account in allocating academic privileges such as special programs, stack passes, etc.

1. A Limited Pass-Fail Option for Students

Together with the professors already cited, we agree that perfunctory grades in large breadth courses should not play their present role in advancing or retarding students in their academic careers. The increased use of pass-fail outside the major would encourage intelligent students to seek challenging courses for breadth rather than the safer surveys; in the upper division it would promote interdisciplinary studies where the present system too often discourages or even penalizes them. Above all it would de-emphasize the system itself, and thus create an academic milieu with greater freedom, diversity, leisure, and personally-motivated inquiry. It seems safe to predict that this milieu would give greater scope to the student with his own intellectual curiosity and discipline, who at present often resents the necessity to "play it safe", "shoot for minuses", and "never get carried away." We therefore consider it most important that the Division follow the lead set by the University-wide Committee on Educational Policy (as well as other universities such as Cornell and Princeton) by approving the following formal recommendation.

Recommendation 14: **A student in good standing should be authorized to take one course each term on a Pass-Not Passed basis. Units thus earned shall be counted in satisfaction of degree requirements, but shall be disregarded in determining the student's grade-point average. Except with the consent of the student's major department, courses thus undertaken shall not satisfy requirements for the major.**

The last provision, establishing local conditions for application of the proposed state-wide regulation, is designed to meet two distinct problems. We have chiefly in mind the lower-division student who has not yet declared a major. He would thus be warned not to undertake any course for pass-fail which might eventually become relevant to this major unless he had consent. We would expect that this consent would not normally be granted before the undertaking of a course for a prospective major; in some cases, however, an adviser might wish to grant it retroactively to facilitate a change of major. The wording would also grant a limited discretion to those departments wishing to allow individual cases of pass-fail grading within the major.

2. An Experimental Pass-Fail Option for Instructors

We expect the above proposal to introduce a greater flexibility into the student's curriculum under the quarter system. By itself, however, it will not satisfy the complaints of those faculty members who feel that letter-grading is inappropriate in certain courses, particularly large breadth courses which may be irrelevant to any future major. It would not of itself free professors from the obligation to determine letter grades in such courses. It would, however, make it appropriate that we move in this direction, since there is even less point in summarily determining hundreds of letter grades if great numbers of these are not subsequently to count in any way. This would in turn release the time and energy of faculty members for more discriminate grading in courses where the student's performance can be seriously evaluated.[6]

In addition we must consider the arguments of those professors, especially in graduate courses and in the humanities, who find letter-grading inimical to the more personal relationships which they attempt to establish with their students. Even if we cannot now finally establish the superior merits of pass-fail grading as a permanent institution, it is desirable that those faculty members who believe in it be given at least a limited opportunity to explore its advantages and disadvantages on the Berkeley campus. We therefore formally recommend that a limited pass-fail option be granted not only to students, but experimentally to professors, as follows:

Recommendation 15: **For the next five years, faculty members should be authorized, subject to departmental approval, to offer one course each term on a Pass-Not Passed basis. Faculty members taking part in this experiment would be expected to report their findings to the Committee on Educational Policy and the Board of Educational Development. It is understood that such courses would carry unit credit, but not grade points.**

3. Deferred Grading in Course Sequences

Another way to encourage evaluation in depth, and at the same time cut down on the frequency of final evaluation, is by the development of

---

6 Prof. J. K. Anderson, whose complaints were noted above, estimates as follows: "Upon reckoning up I find that I have spent sixteen days this year doing nothing but grade lower-division papers from six-thirty in the morning until midnight. If all was being decided as 'pass or fail,' I would feel happy to allow graduate students to pick the papers over first, selecting a few very good ones to cheer me up and reserving the very bad ones for discussion and possible damnation. By my calculations, I would then have at least 50% more time for my teaching, reading, and writing."

course sequences lasting for two or three terms, in which the final evaluation of the student can be deferred until the completion of the sequence. There will be a much stronger case for this kind of course and evaluation after conversion to the quarter system, for the ten weeks of a single quarter will often be inadequate for the student to develop such mastery of material as can be significantly evaluated. Provision must of course be made for the grading of students who are unable to complete the course sequence. However, even if instructors choose to issue grades to all students at the end of each quarter, it would be both more meaningful and in the long run more efficient to have these grades reassessed by the instructor in the compilation of a final course grade, rather than automatically transferred to the student's record. The provisional quality of the quarter grade, and the possibility of finally improving it, would allow both the student and the instructor to concentrate their energies on long-term goals. We accordingly make the following recommendation with respect to deferred grading.

Recommendation 16: **Departments and faculty members should be authorized to offer courses in sequence of two or three quarters, wherein final evaluation of the students concerned would normally be deferred until the completion of the course sequence.**

4. Postponement of Grade-Point Average in Entering Term

We also question the desirability of commencing the calculation of grade-point average immediately with the results of an entering student's first term. It is generally recognized that some excellent candidates for further academic work do poorly in their first term on this campus, whether from poor preparation at an earlier institution, or inadequate adjustment to new responsibilities. Probationary status may then impose additional requirements of performance that the student cannot yet meet. Although the time of academic reckoning should not be postponed indefinitely, we would see no harm in giving a slightly longer period of adjustment to entering students, particularly after conversion to the quarter system. The results of the first ten weeks' work will hardly merit equal consideration in determination of grade-point average with the student's later achievements, when he is not only more mature, but more skilled in meeting the various demands of the campus environment. It has been suggested that entering students be graded at first on a pass-fail basis; but in many ways it is precisely the entering student who most needs to be informed of his relative success with respect to the standards expected of him. We therefore would formally recommend that the grading of entering students continue, but that the grades of the first term be disregarded in the calculation of grade-point average.

Recommendation 17: **Courses undertaken in a student's first term of residence at any level should earn units in satisfaction of degree requirements, but should be disregarded in determining the student's grade-point average.**

5. Further Experiment in Grading

The foregoing proposals constitute our somewhat limited approach to the problem of grading. It is possible that these would by themselves result in a more profitable redirection of the energies of students and faculty alike. Only after a limited pass-fail option has been actually tried under the quarter system can the relative merits of letter and pass-fail grading be seriously evaluated. However, some members of the Committee, particularly those from the humanities, believe that there is much more positive argument for pass-fail grading per se than the rather practical considerations presented in this report. It may become apparent that, at least in certain parts of the University, the abandonment of letter-grading could make way for deeper, more constructive evaluation and rapport. At the same time disciplines such as the natural sciences may indeed offer opportunities for purely objective evaluation of performance, where a more refined letter-grading system might appropriately be tried. The Committee has copies of the very sophisticated and detailed Smith Report for those faculty members who wish to see it; and we would note that a more refined system in parts of the University would not of itself be incompatible with the present system elsewhere. The most compatible variation might be to use "plus" and "minus" grades that carry 0.3 grade point above or below the unmarked value.

At this time we are not prepared to make or support any recommendations except those which in our opinion should be adopted by the Division for the campus as a whole. We do, however, see a strong case for further innovations in grading, particularly on an experimental basis, which could be initiated by departments, colleges, schools, councils, or (in a limited way) the Board of Educational Development. (See Chapter VII.) We see nothing incongruous in the prospect that our complex and diverse campus might move simultaneously in the directions of both pass-fail and more refined letter-grading. The materials collected by our Committee will remain accessible to all those interested in the problem of grading. They will, we believe, convince most readers that we cannot be satisfied with our system as it now operates; and that we must learn, through careful and studied innovation, how best to improve it.

We accordingly make the following final recommendation.

Recommendation 18: Departments, colleges, and schools should be encouraged by appropriate legislation to conduct further experiments in grading, including refinements in the present system.

VII.

A BOARD OF
EDUCATIONAL DEVELOPMENT

A. The Need for Development and Innovation

TWENTY YEARS have elapsed since the publication, in 1945, of *General Education in a Free Society*, Harvard's so-called "Redbook," which set out the philosophy and essential features of a compulsory "core" program in general education. The "Redbook," like the earlier discussions leading to the unified curricula at the University of Chicago and St. Johns College, was an impressive and significant event in the history, not only of higher education, but of American intellectual life. Yet, it seems to mark the end of an era, rather than the beginning: since World War II innovations in American higher education, both in theory and in practice, have chiefly moved in a quite different direction. Where the "Redbook" stressed respect for the essential unity and permanence of Western civilization as a basis for common intellectual experience and communication, many college curricula have since, without intellectual fanfare, given greater scope to diversity, flexibility, and empirical or "problem-oriented" courses. Above all there has been new emphasis on experimental courses and programs. Thanks in large part to the encouragement and liberal support of foundations and the federal government, the idea is more and more widely accepted that new courses and curricula should be defined as a result of experience and of changing intellectual concerns, rather than from *a priori* intellectual principles.[1] Today even the proponents of general education admit that the search for a common body of knowledge has yielded no certain or lasting consensus.[2] And Harvard itself has

---

[1] Paul L. Dressel, "A Look at New Curriculum Models for Undergraduate Education," *Journal of Higher Education*, XXXVI, 2 (Feb., 1965), p. 89.
[2] Thomas H. Hamilton, "General Education: A Platform for the Sixties," *Journal of General Education*, XIV (Oct., 1963), pp. 149-50.

joined the growing number of major institutions (such as Yale, Michigan, Wesleyan, Indiana, Michigan State, Stanford, Wisconsin, etc.) whose catalogues now contain a variety of so-called "Special Programs."[3]

The fact of diversification does not of itself constitute a case for it. Nevertheless many if not most observers would admit the need, both in the nation and perhaps particularly at Berkeley, to offer greater varieties of educational experience, and above all to develop our capacity to adapt and innovate continuously in the light of changing conditions. Berkeley is particularly close to the cutting edge of scientific innovation where specialized courses and indeed whole curricula can be rendered obsolete by new discoveries. Indeed, the more a given discipline flourishes, the more likely that it will contribute to the obsolescence of its academic procedures. Berkeley has also been in the forefront of the search for the new roles to be played, and new services to be rendered, by the modern university in an increasingly complex society. As a public institution it feels acutely the challenge of involving students from the most diverse backgrounds in a common pursuit of excellence. More energies will be committed to this pursuit by both teachers and students if the curriculum is made flexible enough to engage the common interests of both. But perhaps the most pressing argument for change and experiment comes, paradoxically, from those whose chief concern is with the traditional values of our intellectual and human heritage.

In saying this, we mean more than the old observation that our heritage itself is in part innovative and experimental, though we deeply agree that, in one intellectual renascence after another, a conscious return to the cultural achievements of the past has helped to quicken our civilization in its search for wiser institutions and wiser men. We mean that only through recurring reforms of our public higher educational institutions have we seen, in the West, a gradual elevation from practical to theoretical, and from professional to general or liberal concerns. The sophists and rhetoricians carried the day before Plato and Aristotle; not till the last centuries of the Roman Empire did public moneys become generally committed to the instruction of philosophy. In like manner the mediaeval universities began, by and large, as professional schools; only through bitterly contested changes did some of them achieve a broader and deeper commitment to the pursuit of truth and learning. It is the classical studies of the late eighteenth and nine-

---

[3] In this connection see: Harvard University, *Courses of Instruction* (1964-65), p. 16, *The Freshman Seminar Program*, 1965-66; Michigan State University, *Catalog*, 1966, pp. 34-37, 76-78; Indiana University, College of Arts and Sciences, *Calendar*, 1966-67, pp. 54-57; *Wesleyan University Bulletin*, 1964-65, pp. 123-130; *Yale University Bulletin*, 1965-67, pp. 130-134; Stanford University, *Stanford Bulletin, Courses and Degrees*, 1965-66, pp. 302-304.

teenth century, not of the Renaissance, that seem most characteristically suffused with Arnold's sweetness and light.[4]

The same evolution has been apparent in the history of American universities (both old and new, private and public) since their dramatic adaptation to a more stimulating and exacting German discipline about a century ago. Since that time the search for a truly liberal or general education has expressed itself in the search for curricular innovations to balance the prevailing pattern of specialized departments. Indeed much of the recent debate over curricula, and of student dissatisfaction with them, can be traced to the anomaly of America's having imitated Von Humboldt's design for a specialized graduate university, without at the same time introducing his pattern for a liberal *Gymnasium* on the secondary school level. We have not yet learned how one institution can best play both a liberal and a specialized role; but it is safe to conclude that changes and innovations are bringing us slowly closer to that objective. Only gradually has Harvard College developed its characteristic formula of tutorials, residence houses, general education, and now freshman seminars. Only gradually has Berkeley developed from its land-grant origins to become a university in every sense. These evolutions are not yet complete; and indeed will never be. The acute pressures for change which we feel at the present moment derive in large part from a growing nostalgia for traditional educational values.

The concerns of educational development are, initially, those of Bacon's *Advancement of Learning:* we must study and understand our present achievements, as well as plan for their augmentation. Thus research, planning, and execution in educational development are not limited to matters of innovation. Above all we do not wish to see aimless or fragmented innovation for its own sake. As we experiment and learn, development will increasingly mean a consideration of the whole, review of whatever is in difficulty, corroboration and strengthening of whatever needs to be encouraged. But at present we should be both urged forward and held back by a spirit of humility. On the one hand the past inflexibility of our institutions has created a short-term priority for innovative

---

[4] *Cf.* J. Bronowski, "The Place of Science," *Bennington Review* (Fall 1965), p. 5: "We have therefore to change the place of science in the curriculum from a vocational to a cultural subject. Other subjects have changed their status in the same way before now. Arithmetic was first taught as if to a race of would-be bookkeepers; now we recognize it as a necessary and natural ingredient in the everyday life of everyone. English used to be taught in the old grammar schools as if to a race of grammarians; now we recognize that to write and above all to read is a normal pleasure. . . . We need to change the teaching of science in the same way, and to turn it into a subject like English and history, which students learn not to become professionals but to become civilized—to live and act with intelligent judgment as equals in the community of literate citizens."

improvement; on the other hand we know less than we should about our practices, our objectives, and ourselves. Both considerations argue for the path of diversified experiment, rather than for either a wholesale resistance, or a wholesale surrender to change.

B. The Need to Institutionalize Development

Experimental Rather than Permanent Innovation

Adaptation to changing circumstances of our advanced and complex campus community can no longer be left to our present overworked standing committees supplemented by infrequent special reviews. There must be some facility for both continuing self-study, and continuous trial change. The studies must be sustained rather than spasmodic; the changes must be experimental rather than permanent.

We anticipate a legitimate concern lest too much experiment, or too aimless a diversification, weaken our sense of intellectual community with the past, or among ourselves. To the first concern we answer that, at Berkeley if nowhere else, our institutions seem only too well adapted to withstand the virus of rapid innovation. Indeed, if the faculty is to maintain its traditional control over curriculum, it is imperative that it develop a more adequate procedure for curricular amendment and innovation. It has been argued that where there is "desuetude of the curriculum", this is largely because of "the extraordinary difficulty of getting permission from one's colleagues to try anything new and exciting."[5]

A century ago, with the irruption of the new sciences into their purview, American universities effectively committed themselves to the principle of recurring curricular revision; but they have not yet evolved an effective machinery for this. Until recently new curricula have been subjected to rigorous and time-consuming review, on the quite legitimate grounds that they are being considered for adoption in perpetuity. By the same token an established program, even when controversial, has been relatively immune from any review whatever. Since the war we have seen increasing use of the principle of experimental or trial adoption; and in 1957 a provision for experimental liberal arts cur-

[5] Christopher Jencks, "A New Breed of BA's," *New Republic* (Oct. 23, 1965), pp. 17-21 (p. 18): "On virtually every major university campus in America there are professors who want to develop an interdisciplinary science program for non-scientists, start a small residential college where undergraduates will have a common curriculum and a chance to get to know a small group of faculty, or whatever. These ideas rarely get off the ground. Often they are vetoed by the rest of the faculty, or by one or another faculty committee. Even if an idea is accepted in principle, departments are not willing to release 'their' members from conventional teaching duties to try something different."

ricula was introduced into the Regulations of the College of Letters and Science. In eight years this procedure has been invoked only once, for the Tussman Program—one two-year experiment for which, at present, no successors are apparent. The experience of the Tussman Program has revealed the dense jungle of financial and administrative problems which remain to be solved even after faculty approval has been granted. We conclude that some kind of initial encouragement and continuing institutional support is urgently needed for experimental programs; and we do not anticipate that such institutional support will lead to a tidal wave of change.

Similarly we anticipate a second legitimate concern, lest random diversification weaken still further the forces which unite an academic community. Some critics suggest that our campus offers too many courses and programs already; and in a sense we readily agree. We are moreover concerned to find a mechanism by which to foster and protect whatever programs are not well suited to the care of specialized departments. The proponents of general studies claim that the faculty should offer more leadership in defining the groundwork for a common intellectual experience; and some of them would expect this to entail a radical restructuring of the undergraduate curriculum. In our preliminary report we made clear our interest in general education; but after months of intensive thought and inquiry we have decided that it would be self-defeating to try and strengthen it simply by legislating for wholesale curriculum revision. Here we have been guided by the difficulties which other universities, notably Harvard and Chicago, have experienced in regularly staffing general education courses, and hence in maintaining both quality and appropriate class size. No matter how excellent a course in the values or great books of Western civilization, it cannot really achieve the objectives of a liberal education if the sole available professor is addressing a class of hundreds of students. At a smaller university or college, such as Wesleyan or Amherst, it is possible to change the whole tone of undergraduate education by introducing a single new course or program. An analogous single remedy at Berkeley (or even set of remedies) would be a monolith of massive proportions and bureaucratic impersonality. Like the general education programs at Chicago and Harvard, it would readily find critics to oppose it, in the name of the very values of individual excellence which general studies programs were designed to pursue. Nor, on the other hand, can we merely rely on the good will of individual faculty *entrepreneurs,* in the spirit of "letting a hundred experiments bloom." The needs are too great; our energies and resources too few.

For these reasons we have decided to address the problem of general studies by pleading the philosophy of institutional, rather than curricular change. To be sure, we have also defined what we consider to be the priorities for curriculum development at this campus. Some of these are put forward below as concrete proposals; the remainder are outlined in the next chapter as an agenda for a new body to consider. But in general we are committed to the principle that meaningful curricular development at this campus cannot, if only for reasons of scale, be abstractly legislated. A chief priority is to make undergraduate education, especially in the lower division, more attractive to both faculty and students, by making it easier to offer whatever each individual or group of individuals can do best. We believe that general studies can only prosper where there is both the special ability and the special motivation to give them intellectual content. And those of our faculty who combine these two qualities do not need from us curricular guidelines or instructions so much as the chance to develop better courses and programs by themselves. We believe new courses and curricula mature best when those who teach them have the chance to modify them liberally on the basis of their own experience. At the same time, and increasingly from year to year, there are new programs, both here and at other campuses and universities, to be considered and assessed. Many if not most of these are being supported by foundation and federal funds available for curriculum development; Berkeley, however, has not yet followed the example of other universities (and of some of our own faculty members) in putting such funds to work on our own campus. For all of these reasons, we believe it is important to establish machinery, not to implement any single curricular change, but to give continuing consideration, encouragement, and financial support to all worthy proposals for educational development. Such machinery must combine both an academic and an administrative responsibility: on the one hand it must study and plan for improvement; on the other it must help these improvements to be carried out.

C. The Need for a Board of Educational Development

1. The Need for New Machinery

In the last analysis, educational development is the concern of the whole University, including both faculty and administration. Many but not all aspects of it will continue to be the preoccupation of individual departments; the residual problems and programs cannot however be thrust upon the regular machinery of the faculty and administration.

The regular machinery is already only too busy with on-going programs, as members of the Committees on Educational Policy and on Courses can testify. We need an enduring body with its own *esprit de corps* which can devote itself to long-term review, study, and consultations, to determine the needs and possibilities for innovation on this campus. Closely associated with this should be a high-ranking administrator to facilitate and assist programs and experiments which do not readily find protection within a regular department. If only because many of these experiments will involve more than one college or school, we propose that he should be a Vice-Chancellor in the Chancellor's Office.

It might seem tidier to limit such special machinery rigorously to non-departmental and/or experimental programs. We see a disadvantage in such rigid limitations, at least for the time being: development should build from, and relate to, what is offered and needed throughout the campus. The experience of other universities suggests that we should seek a *via media* or balance between two structural models: on the one hand a separate Dean or college (too isolated and independent of the departmental structure) and on the other hand a mere faculty committee (not independent enough). Both of these relatively simple formulas for supervising the general and non-departmental concerns of the university have, when adopted elsewhere, led to the same result: a drift towards a "second-class faculty" without the same status and protection as their departmental colleagues. Thus the machinery we propose would be concerned both with general problems and with particular remedies. As a Board it would represent the whole faculty's interest in educational development, but it would also seek to promote special contacts and *esprit de corps* among those faculty volunteers who for the time being are most actively engaged in educational innovations. Moreover, to ensure that its policies are effectively pursued, and that new programs will find adequate support, we propose that the representative quality of the machinery be balanced by an administrative component: the participation *ex officio* of an administrative Vice-Chancellor.

2. Board of Educational Development: Nature and Responsibilities

We therefore recommend the establishment of a Board of Educational Development, with the following membership and responsibilities, and that the By-Laws and Regulations of the Academic Senate be changed accordingly.

Membership

1. There shall be seven members.

2. Six members shall be appointed for three-year staggered terms by the Committee on Committees, from faculty members who combine the highest scholarly attainments with a demonstrated concern for educational development. After the first year of operation, two members shall be appointed each year. Replacements, when necessary, shall be appointed for the unexpired periods of vacated terms.

3. In addition, the Vice-Chancellor for Educational Development (see below) shall sit as an *ex officio* member of the Board with voting rights.

Responsibilities

1. To stimulate continuing discussion of the principles and effectiveness of our educational programs and to receive and encourage proposals for educational experiments.

2. To determine policy in matters of educational innovation and development, to authorize proposals, on a limited and temporary basis, for experimental courses and curricula, and to recommend to the administration the allocation of funds in support of such experiments. An experimental program may be continued under the Board's authority for up to five years, after which time it will be reviewed by the Berkeley Division for possible inclusion within the regular curriculum and budget, for termination, or for further continuation on an experimental basis.

3. To prepare, for submission to the established committees of the Colleges and the Berkeley Division, reports on the desirability of transferring existing experimental programs to the regular curriculum and budget of the University.

4. Continuously to evaluate the adequacy of existing educational offerings, with a view to establishing priorities for educational development, and to authorize and carry out such studies as may be desirable.

5. To cooperate with the Graduate Council in instituting experimental graduate programs.

6. To formulate proposals for securing funds for the above purposes from private, foundation, University, and government sources.

7. To report annually to the Berkeley Division on its activities.

Recommendation 19: We formally propose the following addition to the By-Laws of the Academic Senate:

Board of Educational Development. This board consists of six appointee members who serve three-year staggered terms, and the campus-wide administrative officer most responsible for educational development, all voting. Its duties are:

1. To stimulate and promote experimentation and innovation in all sectors of the Berkeley campus; to sponsor, conduct, and direct, with use of an Office of Educational Development, continuing studies of the needs and opportunities for educational development; and to maintain liaison with the Committee on Courses of Instruction, Committee on Educational Policy, Graduate Council, and the executive committees of the colleges and schools, on matters of educational effectiveness, innovation, and for the initiation of experimental courses, programs, and curricula.

2. To receive, encourage, and authorize experimental instructional proposals for which neither departmental nor college support is appropriate or feasible; to initiate and administer such experimental instructional programs pending their adoption by a department or other recognized faculty group, for a period not to exceed five years, subject to policies prescribed by the Berkeley Division; and to provide all possible accessory services for experimental programs initiated within departments, schools, and colleges.

3. To initiate and sponsor the securing of extramural funds for the support of experimental courses and curricula, and to administer such funds for this purpose as may be allocated to the board or to the Office of Educational Development.

As part of our proposal for a Board of this nature, we also recommend the creation of an Office of Educational Development under a specially designated Vice-Chancellor for Educational Development, as follows:

Recommendation 20: Vice-Chancellor for Educational Development. It is recommended that a Vice-Chancellor for Educational Development be appointed. He shall become an *ex officio* voting member of the Board of Educational Development. Under the policy guidance of the Board of Educational Development, he shall:

1. Administer the policies and programs of the Board of Educational Development.
2. Consult with all appropriate members of the academic community concerning deficiencies in or possible development of existing offerings, and encourage new offerings where they are considered necessary.
3. Consult with Deans and Departmental Chairmen concerning desirable recruitments and promotions conducive to campus educational development.

4. Provide general administrative and incidental assistance to studies and experimental programs.
5. Secure funds for these purposes from private, foundation, University, and government sources.

3. The Authorization of Experimental Programs

The first three of the Board's responsibilities are directed to the reception, encouragement, authorization and review of experimental instructional programs. Such programs include any innovative course, curriculum (partial or total), teaching practice, or alteration of existing requirements (e.g., grades, residence, breadth). Our proposal thus envisages a new procedure for the authorization of experimental programs, on a limited and temporary basis, for a period of up to five years. Except where questions of degree-granting were involved (see below, Council for Special Curricula) this procedure would relieve the individual faculty members concerned from the responsibility of securing the consent of the established committees of the Colleges and of the Berkeley Division. The Board would maintain liaison with these; but they would be asked to give formal approval to experimental programs only after the values and deficiencies of these programs had been demonstrated through actual practice, and the Board had prepared a report on the desirability of transferring a given experimental program to the regular curriculum and budget of the University. Our intention here is that the legislative and administrative blocks to the inauguration of new curricula should as far as possible be handled by the Board and by the Vice-Chancellor, leaving the teachers involved to devote themselves to the truly educational aspects of planning and implementation. Although the Board would have to exercise its own discretion in the authorization of experimental programs, it is hoped that the conditional nature of its authorization would normally encourage it to be generous in its respect for the judgment of individual faculty proponents. In like manner we would hope that other faculty committees could normally accept the provisional endorsements of the Board.

With this atmosphere of trust and respect, the Board will normally be able to obtain acceptance of experimental courses and curricula as fulfilling some part of the requirements for an undergraduate degree (B.A. or B.S.). It is, of course, possible that differences of viewpoint may arise, especially with regard to experiments of any magnitude. We formally recommend that, where these differences cannot be resolved between the Board and the degree-granting body, they be referred to a Council for Special Curricula, with the power to insure (and if necessary grant) a limited number of undergraduate degrees on its own authority. It would be constituted as follows:

Membership

The Council shall be composed of the following members:
    The seven members of the Board of Educational Development;
    The seven members of the Committee on Educational Policy.
The Chairman and Vice-Chairman shall be selected from their membership by the Committee on Committees.

Meetings

When the Board of Educational Development is unable to obtain acceptance by a degree-granting body of an experimental program as a valid part of a curriculum leading to an undergraduate degree (B.A. or B.S.), the Chairman of the Board of Educational Development will convene the Council for Special Curricula.

Functions

1. The Council will review the experimental program in question and, if three-quarters of its membership approve, will insure the B.A. or B.S. degree to the students in the program upon successful completion of the program and such other requirements as the Council shall establish.
2. The Council will inform the Berkeley Division of all experimental programs for which it has insured the granting of degrees as soon as it has given this insurance.
3. When the students in the program have completed the requirements for the degree established by the Council, if no degree-granting body has yet accepted the program for a degree, the Council will grant the B.A. or B.S. degree to the students.
4. The number of degrees the Council may insure in any one year cannot exceed 5% of the graduating class of the previous year, except by express consent of the Berkeley Division.
5. The Berkeley Division may instruct the Council to serve as a degree-granting agency for any other experimental or temporary program.

We do not anticipate a frequent recourse to this special degree-granting machinery: ideally, it would never be convened at all. However, we consider it essential to provide for an authority to which the Board can appeal, when necessary, for the insurance of degrees to students in experimental programs. Otherwise the Division will not have significantly altered the pressures which create in our present procedures a climate inimical to flexibility and change.

Recommendation 21: We therefore formally propose the following addition to the By-Laws of the Academic Senate:

Council for Special Curricula. This council comprises the members of the Board of Educational Development and the Committee on Educational Policy, with the Registrar as its secretary. It is authorized to serve as a sponsor for the Bachelor of Arts and Bachelor of Science degrees, substituting in this capacity for a college or school, in one of the two manners specified below.

1. Where the council finds an experimental program of courses acceptable in intellectual content and quality as part or all of a four-year curriculum, but no college or school is ready to accept it, the council may take the following action to support the program.

a. The council shall insure the acceptability of credit toward a degree to students in the experimental program, subject to successful completion of the program and of other requirements established by the council in general conformity with the practice of the most relevant college or school. For administrative purposes the student shall enroll in that relevant unit. In any one calendar year the number of students whose programs the council may insure shall not exceed five per cent of the graduating class of the preceding year, except by express consent of the Berkeley Division. The decision to insure a program shall require a favorable vote of at least three quarters of the members.

b. When a student in an insured program has completed all such degree requirements within an eight-year period after starting the program, his degree shall be recommended by the council, provided that he does not qualify instead for a degree in the relevant college or school.

c. The council shall inform the Berkeley Division of all experimental programs for which it has insured the granting of degrees, as soon as it has given this insurance.

2. Where the Berkeley Division has approved a specific program and has delegated the guidance of it to this council, students completing the program shall be recommended for their degrees by the council.

4. Other Responsibilities of the Board and Vice-Chancellor

The Board would have the responsibility for recommending the allocation of funds in support of educational experiments. If its recommendations are to be well informed, then it must gradually give more and more attention to the needs of the whole campus, and the adequacy of existing programs to meet them. Moreover, the administrative and incidental assistance which the Vice-Chancellor will offer to experimental programs need not be limited *a priori* to those authorized by the Board. It would seem reasonable to extend funds and assistance, when appropriate, to experimental programs and courses already established, to non-departmental programs in need of support, and even to departmental programs where the responsible departments can establish the relevance and value of these programs to the educational development of the whole University (see below, Funds for Educational Development). It thus appears to us that the Board's immediate responsibility for the authorization of experiments will enable it and the Vice-Chancellor's Office to be helpful to any program, non-departmental or departmental, which seeks and deserves their support. And these larger responsibilities will in turn lead slowly to a more and more informed concern for the developmental needs of the entire campus, the establishment of general priorities for educational development, and the study and planning of new programs, not simply because they are offered, but because they are needed. As the Committee on Senate Policy noted in its State of the Campus Message, "it is apparent that there will be a continuing need for educational self-scrutiny by this faculty."[6] This self-scrutiny should not be confused with the responsibilities of the Committee on Educational Policy, which must provide the general educational policy for the campus. We have looked at various forms of institutional self-study at other universities; and we have concluded that what we seek should be neither too professionalized nor too amateur. Here, too, the formula of a Board with an *ex officio* Vice-Chancellor would seem to provide the *via media* between a faculty committee without adequate resources, and an Office of Educational Evaluation, remote from the actual problems which faculty members face when teaching a course.

Our recommendations, in the interest of flexibility, have said nothing about staffing, the needs for which cannot be accurately estimated at this stage. However, from our own experience on the present Committee, we would energetically endorse a flexible situation in which the Board could consult existing authorities, contract with such authorities for

6 University of California, *Minutes of the Berkeley Division, Academic Senate,* October 11, 1965, p. 10.

special studies, or conduct its own studies with research personnel drawn largely from our student body and campus community. The recent creation on this campus of a highly qualified and well endowed Center for Research and Development in Higher Education creates an especially rich opportunity for this campus to become at once a workshop and a laboratory in exploring new ways to excellence.

In this, the "research" aspect of educational development, we would also expect the Vice-Chancellor to play a role, as an enduring representative of the Board in consultations within and outside the campus community. We have, however, refrained from a close definition of the relationship between the Board and Vice-Chancellor. For example, we have left the selection of the Chairman and Vice-Chairman, by implication, to be settled by the Committee on Committees. While seeking the right balance between faculty and administrative viewpoints in the Board, we have not ruled out the possibility that the Vice-Chancellor himself might be selected as Chairman. We would not, however, expect the Committee on Committees normally to name an *ex officio* member to this important post. As we see it, neither should the Board be a mere creature of the Vice-Chancellor, nor the Vice-Chancellor a mere creature of the Board.

5. Funds for Educational Development

Operation of the Board should be greatly aided by the increased availability of outside funds, especially from foundations and governmental sources, for the support of educational research and development. We would expect the Board and Vice-Chancellor to seek large block grants in support of general developmental categories (e.g., "Interdisciplinary Courses," see below). With or without such outside support, the Board would make it easier for faculty members engaged in educational experiments to establish contact with and receive support from the various funding agencies. We do not, therefore, anticipate that educational experiments should impose any financial restrictions on the resources available for our regular programs.

At the same time, and by the same token, we would emphasize the importance of generous support for new courses and programs, because of the special problems which these invariably encounter. In some cases this support may take the form of supplemental grants for research or secretarial assistance, to be made available to departments or individual faculty members. However, when the Board has recognized a course or program as constituting a significant educational experiment, it should have the power to reimburse departments for released faculty time, both before and during the period in which such a program is taught.

VIII.

NEW PROGRAMS

A. An Agenda of Priorities

1. General Priorities for the Berkeley Campus.

I N THE HISTORY of American higher education, there have never been so many ideas and experiments in educational innovation, both outside and within this campus, as those which clamor at present for study and possible trial. Their very number is perhaps the best argument for a Board of Educational Development: such a Board, given adequate faculty support and outside funds, will help Berkeley to maintain a leading position in the educational experimentation now being carried on at both state and private institutions. Yet for the Division to establish a new formal mechanism, without any indication of the problems and programs which that mechanism should consider, would be to leave the mechanism with little direction as to where and how to proceed. We have therefore tried to give expression to what are, in our view, the priorities for educational innovation and development on this campus. This statement, and the reaction of the Division to it, may prove useful to departments, schools and colleges, many of which are already proceeding with their own plans for change. At the same time it may be allowed to stand as an indication of the priorities which the Board of Educational Development might consider when adopting its own agenda. Ultimately the Board must, when sponsoring experimental programs, be guided by the willingness of faculty to offer them; and by the possibility of their doing so without an undue increase in the total faculty teaching load. It is in this limited sense that we have put forward the following agenda of priorities.

We have already spoken of the need for an atmosphere of continuing experiment and change. The size of the Berkeley campus, and the great diversity of its student body, would seem both to require and to favor an educational environment of a rich diversity in paths and offerings, stressing options rather than requirements. With enough students to run several educational experiments concurrently with its regular programs, Berkeley would seem to be in an ideal position to learn from such experiments, while all programs would be stimulated to improve themselves under competitive conditions.

We can, however, be more specific about the priorities for educational development at a campus whose reputation has hitherto been most securely based on the excellence of departmental offerings in the major and in graduate study. Without turning from this pursuit of departmental excellence, we must seek means to develop the same institutional commitment to lower-division education and to non-major education, two separate problems which should not be confused. The demands of specialist education itself, to say nothing of citizenship and the search for a better life, will force us to raise the standards of general and of interdisciplinary studies. Here the concerns of the Harvard "Redbook" continue to be relevant, even if all its proposals have not been universally acclaimed. The Board of Educational Development ought not to interfere with the departments' development of special studies for which they are designed. By the same token, however, it will have to give special attention to the educational objectives which transcend a department's special competence. Above all it must care for the needs and excellence of a given *student* to supplement the department's attention to the excellence of a given *subject*. We must think of learning as a practice, and plan for greater attention to learning as an active process through experiences such as freshman seminars: for this dimension of learning is almost ignored in our present formula of "breadth plus depth." Therefore we shall suggest four interrelated ideas for combating a natural drift of conventional course offerings towards a specialized and fragmented greyness:

a. Special programs stressing the activity of learning.
b. New introductory, breadth, and non-departmental courses.
c. Interdisciplinary and University courses.
d. Integration of curricula.

2. Special Programs Stressing the Activity of Learning

Seminars, and Especially Freshman Seminars

We wish to reaffirm our belief in the long-term objective that, on this large and essentially impersonal campus, every undergraduate should be offered the option of close faculty contact at any and all levels of instruction. As one step towards this goal, we are submitting a formal recommendation for a program of freshman seminars (See B below); and it is our hope that this program will be expanded and supplemented rapidly.

We have also initiated studies to estimate the total number of openings in small classes which exist on this campus in each department and level of instruction. The voluminous statistical data which we have accumulated has not yet been processed sufficiently for detailed analysis in this report. However our first impression is that small classes are available in more departments and at more levels than is sometimes alleged; and that with suitable attention to this problem by the remaining departments, those students who wish small classes can be given them with a less disturbing redirection of faculty teaching energies than might have been anticipated. We are anxious that this option be made available to all entering students, not just to freshmen. In particular we should think of the "forgotten" transfer student at the junior level, who may eventually graduate without having ever identified deeply with the campus community. Thought also should be given to the establishment of senior colloquia (as at Stanford) whereby undergraduates may bring to the seminar the results of their whole undergraduate education and training.

Alternatives to the Classroom: Independent Study, Field Study, and Honors Programs

Seminars are not the only alternative to the essentially passive experience of a lecture course; and they may fail to meet the demands of the exceptionally gifted or idiosyncratically talented student.[1] We feel that the campus as a whole has not made sufficient use of field study, and the flexibility and independent study which are afforded by Honors Programs. Elsewhere we recommend that admission to special programs should no longer be restricted to those with high grade-point average; and it is our hope that 198's and 199's will in the future be used more liberally to permit supplementary credit for what is demonstrably extra course work. Such opportunities should not necessarily be restricted to the major; and we hope that the present three-line section on Honors in the Catalogue (p. 58) can be augmented and strengthened. Each department and college should, for example, consider the possibility of a free quarter in the senior year for selected honors students with tutorial

---

[1] U.S., Department of Health, Education, and Welfare, *New Dimensions in Higher Education* (1. *Independent Study*, 1960; 6. *Study Abroad*, 1960; 10. *Flexibility in the Undergraduate Curriculum*, 1962); and the literature cited therein. See VIII. C below.

supervision and an undergraduate thesis. The Scholars of the House Program at Yale, which suspends all formal course requirements in the senior year, has permitted students to conduct original research, often of an interdisciplinary nature, for the B.A. degree. Other universities (e.g., Brown) permit independent study programs outside a given major under the supervision of a non-departmental council. The Board might pursue these and other approaches toward supplying institutional support for independent study.

3. New Introductory and Breadth Courses

General Observations: Achievements and Priorities

It is widely recognized that creative research has been the stimulus to our best undergraduate teaching; and that in general it has proved difficult to communicate the intensity of this stimulus to our introductory and breadth courses. It is difficult to prescribe general remedies for improvement. On the one hand lie the ultimate advantages of a close sequential relationship to "higher" courses; but these must be balanced against the dangers of postponing for too long the creative intellectual experience for which the preparation is intended—a postponement can be demoralizing for student and professor alike. Again, we must consider the special needs of the increasing numbers of students who graduate from high schools with advanced standing; but these must be balanced against the dangers of planning separately for the gifted and the general student. The safest generalization is to recognize the particular need for continuing experiment and flexibility in the area of introductory and breadth courses. Introductory courses, especially in the natural and social sciences, must address themselves to continuously changing conditions both "above" and "below": to reflect both the consequences of recent research and, increasingly, the improved preparation in the secondary schools. The notion of superficially "surveying" a traditional subject matter must be abandoned. Instead, the best intellects of the campus must be attracted to courses which can be devoted to fundamental intellectual principles and topics, or to the chance to demonstrate the application of research to problems of special interest. But it is easier to criticize an introductory survey course than it is to enrich or replace it. The answer lies in the increased use of experimental funds for the planning and development of introductory courses, and in increased flexibility wherever these courses need not be rigorously sequential.

Berkeley has already planned or executed several significant experiments in introductory courses, particularly in the natural and social sciences. The majority of these involve sequences of courses in inter-disciplinary programs (see below) but the recent development of a new introductory physics program and textbook, with the financial support of Educational Services Incorporated, has shown the relevance of subsidy and released time to departmental courses as well. We would hope that the Board could help other departments to produce new introductory courses with a similarly intellectual fibre.

Breadth Courses

We foresee further new and stimulating "breadth" courses as well, especially in the humanities and social sciences, which should not be considered uniquely as "areas" belonging to specialists. In a certain sense the social sciences without the humanities cannot be truly scien-tifiic, and the humanities without the social sciences cannot be truly humane. Curriculum planning in these areas must furthermore consider the needs of students in science and the professions. In both humanities and social science intellectual profundity may be enhanced by address-ing the non-major student along with the ongoing specialist. With suit-able development, we can see advantages, both for the students and for the subject-matter, in an introductory course (like Social Science 1A-B) which is designed to meet the needs of all.

We must also heed the recently renewed warning that our universities are still training experts rather than educating leaders, despite so many expressions of concern about this problem.[2] One answer to the problem of breadth is precisely to give the student practice in planning and policy making. The task of relating vision to execution in life can be compared to the task of relating the various disciplines in the University. One way to do this, we shall suggest, is to develop problem-oriented, as opposed to discipline-oriented courses.

Non-Departmental and Ad Hoc Courses

We have already proposed as the Board's first responsibility that it receive proposals for experimental courses and curricula. Thus any instructor who desired to offer a new course, and was ultimately unable

[2] John W. Gardner, "The Antileadership Vaccine," in Carnegie Corporation of New York, *Annual Report*, 1965, pp. 7-9: "Very few of our most prominent people take a really large view of the leadership assignment. Most of them are simply tending the machinery of that part of society to which they belong. . . . These people may tend it very well indeed, but they are not pursuing a vision of what the total society needs. They have not developed a strategy as to how it can be achieved, and they are not moving to accomplish it . . . unfocused discouragement is of little consequence com-pared with the expert dissuasion the young person will encounter if he is sufficiently bright to attend a college or university. In those institutions today, the best students are carefully schooled to avoid leadership responsibilities."

to secure departmental or college authorization for it, would be free to submit this proposal for possible experimental sponsorship by the Board. Such proposals might be designed to pursue a novel research interest, or a personal scholarly interest with demonstrable teaching opportunities. In like manner student proposals could receive due consideration. Indeed we would recommend the immediate endowment of one or more *Ad Hoc* Courses (with or without credit) in which professors might be able to supply the relevant scholarly and intellectual background to matters which had aroused the immediate interest of significant elements of the student body. In the last year, for example, courses on "The Idea and Uses of the University", on "Vietnam", or on "Literary Censorship", might have lent intellectual resonance to subjects of active student concern. Such courses might be given either by individuals or by groups.

Recommendation 22: The administration should arrange for *Ad Hoc* Courses, the topics of which may be determined from term to term by the Board of Educational Development, to supply the relevant scholarly and intellectual background to subjects of active student concern.

4. Interdisciplinary and University Courses

Integrated and "Problem-Oriented" Courses.

Much planning is going on at this moment for new introductory or breadth courses at Berkeley; and nearly all of them are interdisciplinary. The Biology Council has sponsored studies leading to new integrated courses for both majors and non-majors. Starting in the Fall of 1966, a one-year integrated biology course for majors will replace the present Bacteriology 1, Botany 1, and Zoology 1a: instructors from something like a dozen biological departments will be involved. Under the leadership of Professors Frederick Reif and Richard Strohman, a one-year Contemporary Natural Science (CNS) course is already being initiated for non-majors, its staff being drawn from both physical and biological departments. It will cover principles of physical, chemical, and biological science, together with some of their implications for society. It is possible that other science courses for non-majors will build sequentially from this one. Meanwhile members of the College of Engineering are considering a one-quarter course in Contemporary Technology, recognizing "that many of today's most challenging social problems (e.g., poverty, population, pollution) . . . require an informed and technologically more sophisticated citizenry to initiate and to support intelligent decision making."[3] It would be designed primarily, though not exclusively, for non-engineering students; and it would call for faculty contributions from throughout the University.

As for the humanities and social sciences, a one-year interdisciplinary course on the Society and Civilization of India is planned for 1966-67 to accomplish these purposes:

> (1) to introduce students to an understanding of the modern people of India, (2) to do so in a comparative way so as to impart a broad view of human culture and society, (3) to encourage students to active participation in the building of knowledge by having each member of the course join in working on a research problem.[4]

The course will be organized about topics (in 1966, polity, identity, and family) instead of disciplines: rather than preparing students for disciplinary work as such, it will seek to impart "certain understandings about the people of India and certain ideas about how to develop knowledge." Research teams and individual reporting will guarantee active learning to the students involved; and this will culminate in the preparation of a "policy recommendation" as if to the Indian Planning Commission.

In consultation with interested members of the faculty, Professor Carl Schorske has been coordinating plans for problem-centered offerings at every level of the campus. An essential part of this program would be the institution of other problem-centered introductory courses, which would bring the methods and relevance of several disciplines to bear on challenging contemporary problems (e.g., "The City," "Sino-Soviet-American Relations"). Such courses could have greater coherence and profundity than the cursory sampling of disparate techniques and subject matters of which too many departmental introductory surveys are composed. The occasional use of panel discussions would help clarify the relationships between disciplines. Interdisciplinary courses could supply breadth not only to the students but to the participating Teaching Assistants. The undergraduate could complement his large lecture experience with that of a small "satellite seminar," to be designed and conducted by graduate Teaching Assistants in general concordance with the guide-lines of the course. Each of these could cater to some degree to the special disciplinary interests of smaller groups of students, while at the same time supplying a complement of interdisciplinary

---

[3] Letter of January 15, 1966 from Professor Charles Süsskind, Department of Electrical Engineering.
[4] Memorandum of January 17, 1966 from Professor David G. Mandelbaum, Center for South Asia Studies.

breadth to students and teachers alike. The Teaching Assistants could also exchange knowledge and experience under the guidance of one or more of the professors in charge of the course as a whole.

Analogous Possibilities in Upper Division

As the University acquires experience in the planning and teaching of interdisciplinary courses, it becomes more meaningful to conceive of them on the upper-division level as well. The Biology Council has already appointed committees to consider the consolidation of upper-division biology teaching into five core courses (covering subjects such as genetics, evolution, ecology, physiology, and behavior) which would supply the basis for a biology major. This would allow individual students a wide choice of individual programs, ranging from the presently constituted departmental majors to the general biology major with emphasis on integrated courses. This plurality of upper-division approaches illustrates the unique advantages of a large-sized campus.

We would hope that similar studies could be undertaken in other parts of the campus; and here, too, the encouragement and support of the Board might be relevant. We need not think only of core courses. For example, we can imagine interdisciplinary courses which would explore the impact of major thinkers (e.g., Marx, Freud, Sartre), or concepts (e.g., "culture," "intellectuals") which are of major but problematic relevance to more than one discipline, and concerning whose significance different disciplines are not yet in agreement. Such courses would complement the various interdisciplinary graduate courses which are now being offered or considered on the campus.

University Courses

Although many of the developments noted in the previous sections are relatively new, it is already possible to make several judgments concerning their influence on the curriculum and on departments. We have seen many different parts of the campus turning independently to interdisciplinary courses as supplements or alternatives to the departmental course system. Whether these are integrated or "problem-oriented" courses, many of them have been planned on a year-long basis to achieve greater breadth, focus, and sequential development. In at least some cases, this integration of courses will have the good effect of reducing the total number of course offerings in the Catalogue.

But as interdisciplinary courses increase in number, they become less anomalous. They must be considered as a new type of offering, with their own problems of recruitment and administrative support. It becomes increasingly difficult to subsume them under regular departmental budgets, and to establish equitable faculty work-loads by traditional formulas. Some of these courses (like analogous graduate courses) will span not only different areas but different colleges and schools. All of them, as is fitting, have been developed after an extensive period of research and planning. In some cases this planning has been supported and even subsidized by non-departmental institutions such as the Biology Council and the Center for South Asia Studies. Outside organizations such as the National Science Foundation have in some cases helped in their funding. (We see here the increased role which Institutes and foundation support are coming to play, throughout the nation, in curriculum development.) The conclusion is that these interdisciplinary programs, considered collectively, require new administrative status and support.

It would also seem appropriate to recognize a new variety of interdisciplinary or non-departmental courses in the Catalogue. Today many universities list in their catalogues a schedule of general, interdisciplinary, interdivisional, or (as at Brown) University Courses. We propose that Berkeley, too, without being in any way bound by these precedents, establish a schedule of University Courses with special financial and administrative support. This support should be granted when departmental, area, or college support is not considered appropriate or feasible. While some experimental courses might (for want of a better "home") be offered under this rubric, we do not suggest that all experimental courses be University Courses; nor, on the other hand, do we suggest that all University Courses be experimental courses. Some courses initially authorized by the Board might, after approval by the Division, be permanently established as University Courses; indeed, there might be existing interdisciplinary programs whose participants would prefer to opt immediately for this status. For all these reasons, therefore, we make the following formal recommendation.

Recommendation 23: The Division should establish a new category of interdisciplinary University Courses, each subject to the regular review of the Committee on Courses. The Division should also develop appropriate means of special administrative support for such courses, where such means do not already exist.

5. Integration of Curricula

Our undergraduate programs are largely composed of self-contained courses drawn from a variety of autonomous departments, to which a greater or less degree of intellectual focus is supplied by a specialized major. Some students and professors believe in the value of a more unified or at least more sequential program, such as the single integrated curriculum offered by St. John's College. Until recently an option of this sort has not been available at Berkeley, despite (or rather because of) the hundreds of individual course options which we offer. Our breadth requirements in particular do not usually offer the possibility of a sequential development of general studies to balance that of the major.[5]

In the Fall of 1965 Professor Tussman and four colleagues from various disciplines inaugurated the Experimental College Program for a self-selected group of 150 freshmen. As its announcement notes, the "Tussman Program" is planned as a two-year sequence:

> Its essential structural feature is that it abandons the course system and, instead, organizes the educational life of the student around the study of significant themes and problems. Each semester will focus on a single period—the first semester, Greece during the Peloponnesian wars; the second, 17th-century England; the third, the period of the adoption of the U.S. Constitution; and the fourth, contemporary America. Studies in each period will involve a wide range of material, a great deal of reading, writing and discussion, and the flexible use of lecture, seminar, and tutorial.[6]

The Program is helped in its search for a spirit of community by its location in a small non-residential building, which can be used in evenings for informal sessions discussing contemporary subjects. There is also a period of independent study towards the end of each semester. The question of whether the Program will be empowered to grade on a pass-fail system has not been resolved at the time of writing.

Other universities have experimented with integrated curricula: we may cite at random the Department of Integrated Liberal Studies at the University of Wisconsin (Madison), the Division of General Studies at the University of Chicago, the University College Program at Michigan State University, and Monteith College at Wayne State University. Such programs need not be focused on the lower division. In 1959 Wesleyan University inaugurated experimentally, with the aid of the Carnegie

---

[5] Members of the Harvard General Education Committee have shown interest in linking General Education courses sequentially, even though this would force a revision of the Redbook notion of General Education as education "not requiring prerequisites." A proposal for sequences of General Education Courses was contained in the 1964 Harvard "Doty Committee" Report, p. 44.

[6] Letter to Entering Freshmen from Dean W. B. Fretter, College of Letters and Science, University of California, Berkeley, July, 1965, p. 1.

Corporation, an interdepartmental Collegiate Major with a three-year non-residential College of Letters, a College of Social Studies, and (since 1960) a College of Quantitative Studies:

> In each the customary pattern of formal classroom work gives way to colloquiums and group tutorials and a substantial amount of independent reading and writing. No tests are given or grades assigned. Comprehensive examinations, set and evaluated by outside examiners, are given at the end of the junior and senior years.[7]

Here again, as in the Tussman Program, our attention is drawn to the greater opportunities for flexibility and diversity of educational experience, when curricular planning is based on a two-year period or longer, instead of within the limits of a single course.

We have no immediate recommendations for making more readily available the general option of an integrated program. We do not minimize the need, nor do we expect time of itself to supply it; on the contrary, in referring this question to the Board, we fully appreciate the gravity of the intellectual organizational problems involved. In this area we would prefer to "make haste slowly": the Board should, we believe, be empowered to explore the whole matter intensively for at least a two- to four-year period. We know of no partially or fully integrated curriculum which Berkeley could import immediately from elsewhere.[8] On the other hand, we welcome the efforts of men like Professor Tussman and his colleagues to help establish the kind of program that might be best adapted to our needs.

Our proposals for the Board and Vice-Chancellor of Educational Development should make it easier for other such innovations and experiments to follow in due course, and for the innovators to concentrate their energies on academic rather than financial or administrative problems. Even when such programs are designed to be self-liquidating, the Board can see to it that the fruits of their experience are not lost. Finally, the Board and Vice-Chancellor, through the latter's responsibilities in matters of recruitment and promotion, might collaborate with departments in bringing temporarily to this campus, as Visiting Professors, outstanding national figures in the area of integrated and general studies. The intention here would not be to create at Berkeley a

---

[7] *Wesleyan University Bulletin*, 1964-65, p. 123.

[8] Cf. Report of Dean's Committee on Agendum for the St. John's Proposal, College of Letters and Science, University of California, Berkeley, June, 1965. President Weigel of St. John's College agreed with the Committee that the St. John's Program should be substantially modified in any attempt to adapt it to the needs of the Berkeley campus.

"second faculty," but to enrich the capacity of this campus to become a national workshop in both the planning and the active pursuit of under-graduate curriculum development.

Meanwhile we envisage one or two steps towards more integrated curricula which individuals, departments, colleges, and the Board can embark upon concurrently. We should first of all recognize the very liberal provisions which have existed since 1957 for more integrated programs in the College of Letters and Science, especially at the upper-division level, through group, field, and individual Majors. Of these the group majors have probably, by and large, experienced the fewest problems; some of the field majors, and above all the individual major programs, have encountered difficulties which suggest that the support, facilities, and outside review of the Board of Educational Development might well be useful.

As a further step towards more interdisciplinary majors for those who desire them, the Board might also encourage departments to de-velop more feasible programs for Double Majors in related disciplines (e.g., History and Literature, Philosophy and Political Science, etc.), especially where these would be relevant to on-going specialization in graduate school. We would expect these double majors to be at least as demanding as our present departmental majors, rather than escape-holes like the former General Curriculum. Elsewhere in this report we discuss other changes which would serve to integrate the undergraduate's course experiences. As a stimulating example of this, we have already mentioned Professor Michael Goodman's "curriculum-management" course in the College of Environmental Design (Chapter V).

The Search for a Distinctive Institutional Style

Although we have now put forward four possible varieties of "New Programs," we do not conceive these to be independent and detached ventures into an ever-widening sea of diversification. On the contrary, we see them as converging together upon the search for a distinctive educational style at this campus. Harvard, after almost three centuries, has recently settled into its distinctive combination of resident houses and tutorials. Berkeley, by contrast, is a larger, less residential, and less richly endowed institution: we anticipate that the curriculum itself, rather than any residential program, can someday best develop an intel-lectual community and tradition between faculty and students. If the curriculum is to become a "home" to students, we must plan for experi-ences which can endure longer than those of a semester or a quarter course; and the integration of curricula will be recognized as a matter of high priority. But if we are to build from our present achievements and resources, we must proceed from smaller units to larger ones. Our seminars and problem-oriented new courses, wherever they best succeed, may someday be developed into new sequences with our existing course offerings and arrangements for independent study. It is through this combination of experiment and tested experience, we believe, that an organic continuity and development in the undergraduate's education can be best achieved.

B. Freshman Seminars

Consonant with the aim of providing every undergraduate the option of close faculty contact at all levels of instruction, we firmly believe that all over the campus measures should be considered and forcefully implemented to make undergraduate seminars part of each regular departmental curriculum. Where feasible and educationally desirable, seminars should also be offered to students before they major. Indeed, we believe that the experience of Harvard and Stanford, each of which now offers 35 freshman seminars a year, is sufficiently impressive to recommend the institution of freshman seminars at the earliest possible moment.

Such freshman seminars should consist of groups of no more than twelve students, taught by members of the faculty in whatever areas of intellectual discourse a faculty member is inclined to meet with entering students. The subject matter of all such seminars need not be strictly determined as long as the orientation is one of dialogue and the spirit of inquiry. Each faculty member offering a freshman seminar would act as academic adviser to the seminar students.

We suggest that the seminars be introduced as an educational experiment which might eventually become a regular option for every student during his freshman year. The Committee is confident of the value of such an enterprise both for teaching and for student morale. It is designed to bring the student to early acquaintance with the style and meaning of scholarly thought, and at the same time to alleviate the shock of entry into an organization of so large a size. Its success or failure will depend on the degree to which enthusiasm among faculty and students will be generated and sustained.

For the very reason that the Committee is convinced of the unique contribution of the freshman seminar to the formation of the scholarly attitudes of students, we do not favor tying up the mechanics of the seminar with either special rewards or requirements. Students should apply for such seminars and be accepted, not primarily on the basis of high school or college grades, but on the basis of interest and motivation. Furthermore the Committee is not recommending any kind of mechanical formula by which such seminars might fulfill general college requirements, but would rather leave this question open and have it decided on a case by case basis.

Staffing such a program might be handled as follows. Individual faculty members or departments desiring to contribute one or more seminars to the program would make their proposals to an administrative committee. The administrative committee would also actively solicit seminars from desirable sources. While freshman seminars in the campus-wide program would not carry departmental labels, in each case the use of a professor's time for a seminar would be subject to departmental approval in light of the requirements of the regular program. The department, if it approved, would assign part of the faculty member's teaching duties to the seminar program, and either make this a contribution out of its own resources or receive proportional budgetary compensation.

Proper administration and conduct of the seminars on a large-scale campus-wide basis will need funding over and beyond such allocations as the campus administration may be able to grant, but the Committee is confident that the obvious assets of this plan for the national goals of higher education are so persuasive that additional financial assistance will be provided from government and foundation sources.

For reasons of administrative expediency the organization, administration, and operation of freshman seminars should be located in the College of Letters and Science, with the proviso, however, that all other colleges and schools be invited to participate in this venture.

Recommendation 24: **An experimental campus-wide program of freshman seminars should be offered, beginning in the Fall quarter, 1966.**

C. Field Study

The College of Engineering at the Berkeley campus has for many years had a work-study program in which students have spent periods of work with public agencies and private businesses alternating with periods of regular study on campus. The program has been administered under the policy that the off-campus work must be validly educational, but of a kind not available in formal courses in the College. No counterpart of this program exists on campus for students in other disciplines, nor does there exist a ready means whereby any student may offer for credit supervised off-campus study of a validly educational nature outside his major.

Antioch College and Bennington College have for many years had as part of their regular academic programs periods in which students depart from the campus to engage in a variety of supervised activities related to their educational development. Harvard University has for seventy years offered, through the Phillips Brooks House, a widely diversified program of off-campus volunteer work by students. Projects have ranged from teaching in prisons to work on American Indian reservations. Columbia, along with Harvard, now sponsors student teaching projects abroad. The Berkeley campus similarly has many relationships with agencies local and abroad that could or do provide students with educationally valuable study in the field, but we rarely give them formal recognition, and we have not attempted to relate them on a substantial scale to our educational program.

Currently the School of Law offers off-campus summer work integrated with its regular curriculum. Students accept summer employment in institutions such as Langley Porter Clinic and San Quentin prison, and in the Fall term they convene in a regular seminar to assess their summer experiences. The School of Law is seeking other means of summer work or study which can be tied to the regular program for credit. For example, credit will now be given for participation in the International Legal Studies Summer Workshop. The Dean looks forward to the ultimate participation of as many as three quarters of the students in such summer programs.

Elsewhere on campus, plans are being considered whereby a group of student classicists may study for credit under the auspices of the American Academy at Rome; an Art major has applied for permission to present for credit a group of canvases painted in the course of a term's study in Paris; a talented sophomore is receiving course credit in Speech for organizing and training a debating team at Berkeley High School. But for the most part the educationally valuable student work off-campus goes without recognition or credit. For many years our students have participated in well planned off-campus tutoring and Teaching Assistant programs. At present over three hundred work in Berkeley public schools and in individual projects in Oakland and Richmond. For two years students from various majors have taught at the San Quentin prison elementary and secondary school under the supervision of the Marin County school district. Much of this work is of demonstrable value as intellectual training for the student, yet it must be performed on the narrow margin of time and energy left over after the demands of the regular academic program have been met.

The Committee believes that all qualified students should be permitted to present for academic credit a limited amount of supervised field study of demonstrable intellectual value. We do not wish to encourage students to present themselves to the Registrar for credit every time they learn something outside of class. On the other hand, we feel that a sustained piece of outside work which the student is qualified to undertake and which can be evaluated by the faculty for its intellectual content is a proper object of academic recognition. We feel, too, that the opportunity desired by many students to test and validate in the field the knowledge gained in the classroom should not be limited to students of law and engineering.

The field studies that students undertake might be of several kinds. Some might be full-time studies or work for a sustained period at a distance from the campus. Foreign study in one form or another has rightly been regarded as an essential element in liberal education for centuries, and our overseas campus program is one expression of this fact. But this program is restricted to a small number of linguistically qualified students; and in any case, foreign study need not be limited to established overseas campuses. It could profitably be extended to include individual and group projects of all kinds: scientific expeditions, social and linguistic research, teaching and social service projects, and the like.

Students might also undertake field study as part of the work of their regular resident terms. The Bay Area is rich in opportunities for research, teaching, and social service projects by individuals and groups.

It is evident that there are social and economic benefits as well as educational ones to be expected from a program of field studies. Many of the projects already undertaken by students, like the teaching projects described above, have great value to the community, and the campus is endowed with many more students who would contribute time and skill to community service if it did not conflict with their campus responsibilities. A very modest academic recognition of the service performed by each qualified student—no more recognition than could be justified by the component of real learning involved—would still make available to the community an impressive contribution from this campus. It is likely that in many cases such a program could also contribute to the support of needy students, and allow many to substitute intellectually valuable activity for the menial work that they do in order to stay in school. The Engineering and Law programs already provide salaries during the field study periods. Certain other projects in the program could be coordinated with the College Work-Study Program under the Higher Education Act, and other funds could be raised through various institutional and personal sources.

Supervision and accreditation of field study is already open to departments by use of courses designated for special study and individual research (e.g., courses 199 and 299). Students returning to the campus from a period of study on their own may present themselves for degree credit by examination. However, these devices are too little used, and are in any case highly restricted in their applicability. Schools, colleges, and departments should be given wider latitude in relating field study to major programs. Beyond this, we need a convenient mechanism whereby students may earn credit for field study of a complex, interdisciplinary nature (practical life, we must remind ourselves, is interdisciplinary); we need some provision for recognizing highly desirable educational experience that does not fit into established academic categories; and we need an agency whereby students and departments may be aided in the logistics of field study projects.

The responsibility for administering desirable field study projects that are outside the competence of individual departments should be given to an appropriate interdisciplinary faculty body—perhaps the proposed Board of Educational Development. This body should represent the faculty in receiving proposals for field study; referring proposals to appropriate faculty members for advice, supervision, and evaluation; and certifying successful projects for credit.

On assuming its task, the faculty body should first develop and submit to the Division for approval its general criteria for accepting projects for academic credit and its recommendations as to the limits to be set on the kind of credit that could be granted. It may be expected that credit earned in this manner would normally be limited in amount, count as elective credit only, and be graded on a "Pass or Fail" basis. In granting initial authorization for a project, the body should consider such factors as the student's maturity, his preparation for the project, the relationship of the project to his total program, and the availability of faculty supervision and of reliable means of evaluation.

In addition, there should be established on campus an administrative staff to assist in bringing worthy students and projects together. It should raise funds; disburse them to students as salary or travel grants; compensate departments for faculty time devoted to field study projects; handle records, publish reports, and publicize the program as necessary. The administrative staff could, indeed, act as a clearing house for worthy student projects of all kinds, but its direct assistance and responsibility to the faculty would be limited to projects involving academic credit.

Recommendation 25: In order to enable all qualified students to present a limited amount of supervised field study for academic credit: (a) schools, colleges, and departments should be given wider latitude in accrediting field study; (b) the faculty should appoint a body to be responsible for interdisciplinary field study; and (c) the campus should be provided with a field study administrative staff.

D. Professorships of the University

It is widely agreed in modern society that our production of new knowledge is outracing our capacity to organize and understand it. Our need for informed and responsible interpretation of what we are learning becomes more acute each year. Among the army of researchers there are too few who have either the capacity or the opportunity to take the long view, and to express themselves in terms comprehensible to a wide audience. The general public is asked to accept and support the results of research and scholarship, but is in no position to understand them; even the most well-informed citizens would remain in general ignorance of the meaning of new discoveries were it not for the occasional efforts of a few talented journalists and scholars.

An analogous situation exists on the campus itself, in our shortage of the kind of instruction that is general and at the same time intellectually respectable. We are currently not opening to our students— whether they be beginners or advanced, whether non-specialists or specialists—a sufficiently broad view of the relationship of our various special fields of research to each other and to human life generally. Demand in various quarters for instruction having a broad perspective is often dismissed as being actually undesirable. Courses "for non-majors" are widely scorned (and by the non-majors themselves) as superficial and unprofessional. Courses of a serious philosophical cast, that might be open to majors and non-majors alike and that would take a wide-ranging view of the relationships between fields, are rarely offered because, it is said, "We have no one to give such a course."

The Committee wishes to observe, however, that in each generation of scholars there are some who combine the highest distinction in scholarship with an extraordinary capacity for philosophical breath and for self-expression. There may come times in the careers of such men, when, after years devoted to successful acquirement of knowledge in a particular field, they should be called to more general studies and asked to explain the broader relevance and implications of their knowledge both to the campus and to society at large. In order to foster such studies the University should convey to scholars of requisite calibre a sense of the urgency of this task of generalization and a recognition of its difficulty and rarity. We accordingly recommend the creation of a small number of three-year, renewable professorships carrying the highest status, privileges, and emoluments, to be known as Professorships of the University. Professors of the University should be confined to no department, but be free to investigate and teach as they please. Their primary responsibility would be to study, teach, and write on the interrelations and general human significance of the results of scholarship.

Recommendation 26: **The University should create a small number of new Professorships of the University, devoted to study of the general human significance of the results of scholarship.**

E. Undergraduate Education in Professional Schools and Colleges

Professional education forms a major part of our teaching commitment. The four professional colleges and five professional schools on this campus enroll more than 25% of our undergraduate students. Professional skills are tangible, trusted products, and these professional programs are to many citizens a major justification for the existence of a state university.

There is no better evidence for the technical excellence of our professional schools than the success of our professionally prepared students as they go on to graduate school or enter industry and business. The Committee has found that the general level of advising, teaching, and morale is very high in the professional schools and colleges. Professional education here is not only so strong that there is plainly little need for "reform," but is also so strong that it is able to relax a little in the interests of another goal of university education, namely that of guaranteeing a meaningful exposure to the humanities and social sciences. Our professional schools and colleges are aware of this opportunity, and recently the College of Environmental Design has undertaken a complete curriculum revision to incorporate general education more successfully into its program. The Department of Architecture is discontinuing its present five-year program and is proposing a four-year B.A. program within the College of Environmental Design to be followed by two years of intensive professional training leading to the Master's Degree.

This increased concern with liberal education becomes all the more desirable as our society draws more and more heavily on the advice and managerial talents of professionally trained people. Whereas lawyers have traditionally assumed administrative positions in governments, now scientists, engineers, and medical doctors are being called upon as well. These leaders in professional fields are required not only to make routine professional decisions, but also to make decisions of important consequence for the rest of society. Many of the faculty in our professional colleges and schools are aware of their expanding responsibility. Professor Süsskind of Electrical Engineering has written: "Technical triumphs also may have a dark side. Dislocation of the existing labor force, pollution of water and air, and traffic congestion are some of the problems that must be tackled with the help of engineers who are aware of the broad consequences of their actions on mankind."[9] Indeed the professional school or college located within the University is fortunate that resources are at hand for producing more than competent technicians. Ideally, professional training must involve, not only acquisition of specialized knowledge, but also the capacities to grow within a field and to make sound professional judgments.

The Committee has reviewed the extent to which the age-old competition between "useful"[10] knowledge and liberal education is resolved by the undergraduate programs of professional colleges and schools on this campus. We proceeded in this study by first reviewing the course requirements of the various majors within professional schools and colleges at Berkeley. Examples of some of these programs are given in Appendix G. There some of the more rigid programs are compared with less structured curricula.

The advent of the quarter system on campus has prompted continuation of several changes already in progress in professional curricula. The most notable of these is the reduction of units required for gradua-

9 *The World of Engineering*, McGraw-Hill, 1965, p. 116.
10 "That education should be regulated by law and should be an affair of state is not to be denied, but what should be the character of this public education, and how young persons should be educated are questions which remain to be considered. As things are, there is disagreement about the subject. For mankind are by no means agreed about the things to be taught, whether we look to virtue or the best life. Neither is it clear whether education is more concerned with intellectual or with moral virtue. The existing practice is perplexing: no one knows on what principle we should proceed. Should the useful in life, or should virtue, or should the higher knowledge be the aim of our training; all three opinions have been entertained."—Aristotle, *Politics*.

tion in Engineering and Chemistry to or near to the normal 180. As might be expected this change has not led to greater flexibility of student programs.

It can be seen in Appendix G that professional major requirements vary from a minimum of 87 quarter units (this is equivalent to the number of quarter units required by the physics curriculum within the College of Letters and Science) to a maximum of 151 quarter units. The latter program constitutes 84% of the units available for undergraduate education. Humanities and social science requirements on the other hand vary between 18 and 36 quarter units. The number cannot be judged alone, but must be balanced by the number of free electives which a program makes available to the student if he wishes to continue in the humanities-social-science area. In Forestry, for example, 27 elective units are available for this area at the discretion of the student and his adviser. Professional schools (which enroll students at the junior year), Optometry and Forestry for example, have so many preprofessional prerequisites that the student's program is in fact dictated for four years, even though he spends two years in the College of Letters and Science. In the case of Optometry this rigid program results in part from state laws governing the curriculum.

The Committee has made a study of programs actually taken by students in the professional schools in the Spring and Fall semesters of 1964. The interpretation was somewhat complicated by the large number of transfer students who bring in credits at the junior level. However, in a general way the programs corresponded closely to school or college requirements; they vary greatly in structure from the relative flexibility of Business Administration and Agriculture on the one hand to the rigidity of Engineering and Forestry on the other. It would appear, particularly in the rigid programs, that a student completing four years on this campus, while undoubtedly well trained in the professional area, has certainly received a minimal education in other aspects of our knowledge. We regard such limited exposure to subjects outside the professional field as a serious deficiency where it now occurs in professional education on this campus.

We are not the only committee which has come to this conclusion when reviewing certain professional curricula. For example, the December, 1954, report "Recommendations for Revision of the Programs of General Education for Students in the College of Engineering at the University of California at Berkeley" by John E. Burchard, then Dean of the School of Humanities and Social Studies, Massachusetts Institute of Technology, gave as number one on its list of recommendations "that every engineering student shall earn not less than 24 semester units among subjects which are deemed applicable to the general education requirement." This was a proposed 30% increase in the then existing and still existing requirement of 18 semester units. Again in October, 1959, the Engineers Council for Professional Development, which accredits engineering schools in the United States, noted that "18 units of study in non-technical subjects, categorized as humanities-social-science by the faculty, are required in each undergraduate engineering curriculum. . . . It is approximately 14% of the units required for graduation. This cannot be considered entirely satisfactory." The Council then recommended that "the faculty consider increasing the requirements (humanities-social-science) to at least 24 units instead of the present 18 units." Again in May, 1964, the Committee on Undergraduate Study (a college committee within the College of Engineering) recommended that the humanities-social-science requirement be increased from 18 units to 21 units. This Committee notes that none of these recommendations has yet been implemented. The humanities-social-science requirement in Engineering under the quarter system remains at 27 quarter units, which is equivalent to 18 semester units.[11]

Liberalization of highly structured curricula is only part of the solution to what we regard as a serious problem. The College of Letters and Science must also ask itself whether it is presently offering a meaningful education in humanities and social science for undergraduate students in professional fields. The scientists have attempted with the better "10" courses and with the proposed Contemporary Natural Science course to give general relevance to their specialized areas of study; it is necessary that the humanists and social scientists do likewise.

Our recommendations to be realistic must recognize several facts. The first is that many students in the professional fields are not greatly interested in what goes on outside their fields. This observation is equally applicable to many students in humanities, and the trouble can be partly rectified through improved programs and courses available to non-majors. The second fact we must recognize is that our professional schools and colleges find themselves in competition with other such schools and colleges across the country for placing students in good positions. We wrote to the presidents of the ten largest corporations in the United States to find whether they were satisfied with undergraduate

---

[11] It should be noted that the College of Chemistry and the Department of Plant Nutrition within the College of Agriculture have as small as or smaller humanities-social-science requirements than the College of Engineering. However, these programs are less rigid in that 800% more electives are available to the student who wishes to expand his horizons in these directions.

professional education received by recent bachelor's level employees or whether the distribution between professional and breadth aspects of the education was unbalanced. The following is typical of the answers we received:

> In general we do not feel that there is a serious imbalance between technical course work and liberal arts studies pursued by recent undergraduates. IBM, both in the marketing and product oriented functions, is recruiting approximately 75% in the hard sciences (engineering, mathematics, physics, and chemistry). What we are looking for are individuals who, in addition to their technical competence, possess favorable personality characteristics and that background which induces creativity, flexibility, and a well-balanced mature individual. Sound technical education is a requirement, and liberal arts exposure does tend to develop these additional characteristics. Measurement of the value added by the liberal arts courses is much more difficult than that possible for the technical portions of a man's education.

It comes as no surprise that professional graduates appear to be hired mainly on the basis of technical competence and not on the basis of breadth of knowledge. But the University has an obligation to supply not only what society demands but also what it feels society needs. We realize that on the one hand it would be unrealistic to expect *all* students in professional colleges and schools to appreciate their professional knowledge in relation to other knowledge that exists at a university. However, it is important that students who wish to acquire other knowledge along with their professional program should not be discouraged.

Though these students may be few in number, they will have a basis for technical judgment which will be an important strength in our society. We feel that professional colleges and schools with particularly rigid requirements should invite students completing their freshman year to take an optional program, with sufficient time spent in studies outside the professional areas to receive both the B.A. and B.S. degrees. If the B.A. degree were awarded by the College of Letters and Science, such a program could usually be completed in five years or less, assuming that the College of Letters and Science would accept the professional major as equivalent to a major within Letters and Science. This appears possible to this Committee, since a very large proportion of the courses taken by students in the rigid professional majors are taken within the College of Letters and Science at this time. For example, though the bachelor's degree in Electrical Engineering requires 151 quarter units in the major, only 69 of these units are specified within the College of

Engineering. This proposed five-year program would differ from the present Letters and Science program in Chemistry, for example, in that a student would leave the University at the same level of professional competence as the student completing the four-year program in the College of Chemistry.

We also feel that the College of Letters and Science has been deficient in the past in setting up humanities and social science programs which are particularly suitable for students who will have only limited exposure to these areas. We must not, in the interest of breadth, force professional students into inappropriate programs. It will be necessary for representatives of the professional schools and the social science and humanities areas to confer about the content of such programs. Introductory courses at the freshman level are particularly important in this respect, and we are pleased that the College of Engineering is planning courses such as "Contemporary Technology," to be offered to both engineering and non-engineering undergraduates. With respect to our survey of professional education on this campus we propose two recommendations:

Recommendation 27: The professional colleges and schools should, where appropriate, formulate with the College of Letters and Science optional programs leading to a combined B.A. degree and B.S. degree in not more than five years residence.

Recommendation 28: The College of Letters and Science should explore with the professional schools and colleges means of providing more effective general courses and programs in humanities and social science; the professional schools should then take steps to raise their breadth requirements to a minimum of 20-25% of the total degree requirement.

IX.

THE UNDERGRADUATE REQUIREMENTS IN LETTERS AND SCIENCE

THE COMMITTEE has devoted much time and effort to a review of the undergraduate curriculum. The programs in professional schools have been dealt with in another section (VIII, E). Here we are concerned with the requirements of the College of Letters and Science, which enrolls about 75% of the undergraduates at Berkeley.

The College of Letters and Science has appointed a Special Committee on Academic Programs to review its curriculum in detail and recommend changes. The Select Committee has held several joint meetings with the Letters and Science Committee, and it has transmitted the results of its research and discussion to that Committee. Here we offer a new theory of the undergraduate curriculum as a basis for further planning.

The Letters and Science curriculum consists of three parts: the major, required courses for breadth, and free electives. Under the quarter system, beginning in the fall of 1966, the breadth requirements will be a sequence of courses in English reading and composition, four quarter courses in a foreign language, and four quarter courses in each of the three areas: humanities, social sciences, and natural sciences. In the last, one course must be in physical science and one in biological science. The entering student must complete the reading and composition and foreign language requirements as soon as possible. He can be exempted from some or all of the required language courses according to his performance on an examination taken upon entrance. He may do the required work in the three areas at any time in his college career. Great choice is available in the courses that can fulfill the requirements in the three areas, both introductory and advanced courses being acceptable in most disciplines. Except for some science majors, a student can normally fulfill the requirement in one of the three areas by courses taken for his major. The total breadth requirements thus constitute between ten and fourteen courses, depending on the number of quarter courses of language the student needs. This is about 25% to 35% of the total undergraduate curriculum.

Many students and advisers object that the breadth requirements, despite their apparent flexibility, are too rigid in their actual operation. Not a few students discover in their senior year that they have "terminal problems" of missing units for this or that requirement, which in some cases delay the date of graduation. Sometimes, we are told, the student is penalized not for his own errors, but for an adviser's exercise of discretion which is subsequently shown to be inconsistent with the rules or practice of the College. We have tried in part to cope with this problem in our discussion of advising, where we have called both for simpler rules and for much greater latitude to departments or advisers in administering them. But the problem is particularly acute for many transfer students, who, we recall, are almost 40% of the graduating seniors. Since the breadth requirements are not relaxed for them, those who come from colleges with different requirements frequently find themselves taking elementary courses for breadth in their junior and senior years. The experience is frustrating, for it forces them into classes filled with lower-division students and reduces the amount of advanced work they are free to take. This difficulty reveals a weakness of too rigid an adherence to a fixed pattern of breadth, however extensive the list of courses available for breadth may be.

The present curriculum at Berkeley was drawn up in *The Report to the Faculty of the College of Letters and Science by the Special Committee on Objectives, Programs, and Requirements* (1957). In establishing the breadth requirements this *Report* followed common practice throughout American colleges. A survey of the programs of over thirty leading American universities and colleges, both public and private, shows that in virtually every case the breadth requirements are broken down neatly into three areas of knowledge: natural sciences, social sciences, and humanities. Generally the amount of work required is the same in each of the areas (as it is at Berkeley), suggestive of a rule of thumb aproach rather than any deep concept of the intellectual effort involved in becoming conversant with different types of knowledge. In the other cases, the difference of emphasis among the areas is seldom great. Only two of the colleges studied require as much work in one area as in the other two: Princeton and Oberlin define the areas for breadth differently, with the result that the number of courses in humanities equals those in social and natural sciences combined.

Besides the three major areas, all the colleges studied, except Antioch, have a foreign language requirement. It varies from two to four semesters of college work, and in all cases it can be passed by examination or by courses taken in high school.

The majority of the colleges also have an English composition requirement, usually a one-year course that can be avoided by passing an examination.

One of the clearest distinctions among the various breadth programs is between those that allow a student a wide range of choice in the courses that fulfill the requirements and those that determine the breadth courses fairly rigidly. The majority of today's curricula are of the former type, but some outstanding colleges, like Amherst, Columbia, Brooklyn, and Antioch, fall in the second category. Colleges such as Harvard, where breadth must be taken in specified general education courses, and Stanford, where all students are required to take a year course in Western Civilization, are in an intermediary position. Berkeley's vast list of courses acceptable for the breadth requirements puts it among the more permissive of all colleges.

The Committee believes that the principle behind the pattern of insisting on courses in the three major areas of knowledge should be questioned. The 1957 *Report* defined the three areas as those which a "liberally educated person" is expected to know about. The phrase indicates in a nutshell the purpose of present day breadth requirements: to insure a general or liberal education for the student. A liberal education is usually defined as the education befitting a free and responsible human being, a member of the ruling group, who must have the broad wisdom to see beyond frontiers, both geographic and disciplinary, in order to make sound plans and judgments. The advent of democracy has extended membership in the ruling group to all people, and liberal education is now seen as preparing young persons for their future role as citizens.

Renaissance writers regarded the mind as an organic whole to be cultivated or exercised, not as an empty bottle to be filled. Since that time, with the growth of the scientific and historical outlook, there has been a change of emphasis. Increasingly in the last three centuries, a liberal education has come to be conceived less as a practice of the mind than as familiarity with broad areas of knowledge which are judged essential to a full intellectual and cultural life. The classics were the first component, what we would call today the humanities. After the scientific revolution of the seventeenth and eighteenth centuries, natural science became part of this knowledge. In the last hundred years, as the concept of social sciences has developed, they have also become a part of a well-rounded or encyclopedic education. As stated in *General Education in a Free Society: Report of the Harvard Committee* (1945), natural sciences seek to understand our physical environment and adjust man to it; social sciences study human society and institutions and relate man to them; and humanities "enable man to understand man in relation to himself, that is to say, in his inner aspirations and ideals" (p. 59).

General education, or breadth, can be contrasted to specialization, or the major. The latter has usually been conceived as preparing a man for a vocation, an art, or a profession. In Continental Europe in modern times, liberal education traditionally has been imparted in the secondary school, and specialized education has begun when the student enters the university. The American undergraduate curriculum, on the other hand, combines general education with specialization in a major. To a great extent this combination was at the outset a response to inadequate liberal education at the high school level.

State universities were founded in the nineteenth century primarily to provide technical education in such subjects as agriculture, mining, and engineering. Presidents and faculties soon appeared who insisted that liberal education could not be the monopoly of private colleges and the wealthy class. They waged a struggle with tight-fisted state legislatures for money to implement programs to educate young men of modest means in the liberal arts as well as the professions and vocations.[1]

Elements of the European pattern hang on in many American colleges, which require that breadth be fulfilled in the first two years, and that work for the major begin in the junior year. Whereas in Europe a sharp educational break comes between secondary school and university, in the United States the major academic transition of the student is usually between lower division and upper division. The present Berkeley curriculum, which permits both breadth and major to be spread over the entire undergraduate curriculum, makes the transition smoother and more natural.

The whole question of educational philosophy behind the breadth requirement requires thought. If the purpose of breadth is the well-rounded man, a carefully structured program would seem to fill the need best. Even if the content of such a curriculum were not open to question, this kind of curriculum is open to the criticism that it inhibits the development of the student's individuality. A tradition-oriented

[1] Alan Nevins, *The State Universities and Democracy* (Urbana, 1962).

program may furthermore influence the student to believe that liberal education and present life are unrelated. Many Berkeley students would find such an approach unpalatable. The current tendency in American colleges to increase the number of courses available to fulfill breadth requirements, which Berkeley exemplifies, offers an answer to such criticism.

On the other hand, the requirement for work in the three major areas reflects still the illusion of the well-rounded man, conversant with all the important fields of knowledge. One can question both the logic and the results of such a compromise. How conversant with any of the areas of knowledge is a person whose experience is made up of four courses that more often than not are unrelated to each other? Clearly it is nonsensical to aim at introducing undergraduates to all major areas of knowledge. The effect of the attempt could be only the kind of superficiality and dilettantism that we condemn in the old-fashioned introductory survey course. The rationale behind the present Berkeley curriculum is to introduce students to different types of knowledge and different methods of acquiring knowledge. The Committee believes that this conception of breadth is more realistic and fruitful than the chimerical and unduly passive one of the well-rounded man. Such a goal fits unfortunately only too well with a prevailing emphasis on breadth-knowledge as objective matter to be passively assimiliated. Man, in our view, was made to be angular, but the proper knowledge of one's incompleteness should serve as a stimulus, not as a deterrent, to mental inquiry. College education should not be conceived as a complete product, a package the student wraps up and stores away with his diploma. For many, formal education will continue in graduate and professional schools and in their vocations. The graduating students should want to continue disciplining and exercising their minds in fields other than their vocation. The undergraduate experience should equip them with the confidence, ability, and curiosity that will encourage them to do so. We should recognize, however, that few people are good in all types of intellectual and aesthetic activities, and that the individual student is best able to know what kinds of activities he is good at, enjoys most, and is likely to pursue after graduation. At the same time, the college has the obligation to broaden his mind with types of knowledge he has not experienced.

A new approach to the problem of breadth is called for. Breadth is properly contrasted to depth, or work in a major. The aim of breadth is to prevent narrow specialization. If this is so, then breadth should logically be determined in relation to the work in the major. It should provide the kind of intellectual perspective which the area of specialization fails to do. This need will vary from student to student depending on his major discipline.

Conceived in these terms, breadth is of two kinds: disciplines that are outside the major of the student but related to it in subject matter, methods, and type of aptitude needed, and disciplines that are unrelated or little related to the major in these ways. One can call these two kinds "inner breadth" and "outer breadth." Inner breadth would include those subjects that, while outside the major, offer related or background material and methods for it, and provide a broadening and deepening effect on the major itself. Once the amount of course work within a major is limited, a student can be expected to take subjects in this area without the need of strict requirements. Outer breadth, on the other hand, is the kind of subject with which the student might feel ill at ease in competition with students whose aptitude is different from his. If the student is to gain the experience of college work in those subjects so that he will feel at home in types of learning otherwise mysterious to him, college requirements are called for.

The Committee does not pretend to be the first to question the use of the three traditional areas as a way to define breadth. The Harvard Committee in 1945 already substituted for the three areas two "methods of knowledge," which it finds epitomized in the natural sciences and the humanities. The former deals with the realm of physical reality and judges propositions as true or false; the latter deals with the realm of values and judges statements as good or bad. The social sciences lie between and combine the two methods.[2]

The Committee feels that while such a solution may be an improvement, it is basically a different version of the same approach. It therefore recommends that the College of Letters and Science study the feasibility of redefining breadth in terms of "inner" and "outer" breadth, with the categories of inner and outer to be specified for each major or group of majors. Sufficient work in "outer breadth" should be required, while the acquisition of "inner breadth" can be left much more up to the student, preferably in consultation with an adviser. If responsibility for the administration of "inner breadth" can be delegated from the College to the department or adviser, then it might be much easier to ensure that administrative decisions concerning students are made humanely with a full and intimate knowledge of all the facts.

In order to make breadth, and particularly "outer breadth," yield perspective to the student, the Committee advocates the establishment

---

[2] *General Education in a Free Society*, pp. 59-62.

of further courses designed to provide outer breadth. Rather than coverage, such courses should stress concepts, methods, human and social relevance, and the pleasures that may derive from intellectual activity. In this way we may more truly embody the Renaissance objective of cultivating the mind. At present, a student seeking breadth finds himself too frequently in an introductory course leading into a specific discipline which is not his own. The need is readily apparent in the sciences and has already been met with Social Science 1, Physics 10, and the new Contemporary Natural Science course. The College should study the possibility of adding similar courses in other areas of study.

Since the Special Committee on Academic Programs of the College of Letters and Science will examine the College requirements in detail, the present Committee limits itself to recommending the following general guidelines.

Recommendation 29: The College of Letters and Science should reconsider the breadth requirements in terms of "inner" and "outer" breadth related to the programs of the various majors or groups of majors rather than in terms of the three traditional areas of knowledge.

Recommendation 30: The College of Letters and Science should encourage the establishment of courses that will provide the "outer breadth" needed by students in various areas.

Recommendation 31: The breadth requirements should be applied to transfer students in such a way as to widen the student's intellectual horizons without burdening him with restrictions merely in the interest of uniformity.

X.

GRADUATE EDUCATION

A. Introduction

GRADUATE EDUCATION is a special concern of this faculty. It is our special responsibility in the statewide system of education, and it has a special importance to the future of the University and of college education generally. The present generation of graduate students will succeed us; their achievements and shortcomings as teachers and scholars will be deeply affected by our conception of their education. Even now, as large numbers of graduate students teach and help form the attitudes of undergraduates, the quality of graduate education makes itself felt in every corner of the campus. And beyond the campus, our reputation in graduate work will attract or fail to attract to California young scholars—as graduate students and as teachers—of the quality necessary to maintain the excellence of higher education in the state.

This campus may take justifiable pride in the achievements of its graduate program. Many departments enjoy national and international prestige for the quality of their training. Nevertheless, the available evidence suggests that there is need to reconsider certain aspects of graduate education. It would be wrong to suppose that the student upheavals of last year represented the dissatisfaction of undergraduates alone. Many of the complaints made familiar by the undergraduates are echoed by the graduates: excessively large courses, infrequent contact with faculty members, disappointment with the quality of instruction, and unchallenging educational programs. We quote from a study made by Ann M. Heiss, "Berkeley Doctoral Students Appraise Their Education," reported by the Center for the Study of Higher Education in April 1964:

> Some estimate of the degree of student satisfaction—or dissatisfaction—with the University may be read in the data, which

159

show that 22 per cent of the social science respondents, 19 per cent in the biological sciences, 16 per cent in the humanities, 15 per cent in the physical sciences, and 14 per cent in the professional schools reported that they would not select the University of California if they were to start their doctoral programs over.

The degree of student satisfaction with major professors may be seen in the responses of 22 per cent of the physical science respondents, 20 per cent in the biological sciences, 18 per cent in the social sciences, 16 per cent in the professional schools, and 9 per cent in the humanities, who said that they would not select the same major professor if they were to start their programs over. About three-fifths in all fields would select the same person and the remainder either had no adviser or did not answer the question.

The fairly large number of students who said they had no adviser may be a critical factor in the student's lack of identification with the University and his image of it as an impersonal, bureaucratic institution. (pp. 39-40)

Many graduate students, too, are profoundly critical of the shortage of study space and of the system of Teaching Assistantships. Many faculty members have expressed similar views. There are reasons for believing that the structure and content of graduate training are in need of reexamination.

B. The Meaning of Specialization

Discussions of graduate education begin with an agreed understanding that its purpose is to train students for the tasks of scholarship. This starting-point determines in large measure the nature of the enterprise: first and foremost it is training, and only as a by-product is it education. The graduate is viewed primarily as an initiate undergoing preparation for a defined vocation: historian, economist, or physicist. The task of the faculty, it is felt, is to ensure that the student acquires the qualifications and special skills appropriate to the particular vocation. The justification for viewing graduate education as a form of specialized apprenticeship is that specialization is the precondition for the discovery of new knowledge or for making a contribution to a given field. If there is to be cumulative knowledge, specialization seems inevitable and graduate education will have to be defined accordingly. In this view specialization is the academic version of the economic division of labor which has been the basis for the technological, scientific, and industrial achievements of our society. But it may also be the case that the human costs of academic specialization are as severe as those described by industrial sociologists and psychologists. If this is so, the time has come to reconsider our conception of specialization, and to devise ways in which it may be made to serve better the growth of the individual graduate student both as a scholar and as a teacher.

There are various discrepancies between the operative meaning of specialization and the actual form that it takes in graduate education. One major discrepancy is that created by too rigid observance of departmental boundaries in setting both the requirements and limitations of graduate programs.

C. Departmental Programs

At the present time too many departments, especially in the social sciences and humanities, still adhere to an obsolete concept of the Ph.D. as a master of all the fields within the department and of nothing else.

Departmental boundaries can, in the first place, be too inclusive. Some fields become lodged within departments as much by accident as by design; others have acquired their present status relatively recently, and their future is by no means assured; still others are there because they have always been there. Add to this the rapid growth and obsolescence of knowledge and it becomes clear that the program aimed at omniscience within the departmental area often confronts the graduate student with an unpleasant dilemma: he is required to accumulate rapidly a good deal of superficial knowledge, often unrealistically grouped and liable to instant obsolescence; or he faces an endless course of study in more fields than he can master.

The solution is not to discard entirely the ideal of competence represented by the departmental organization of knowledge, but to recognize that it cannot achieve its professed goal. In some fields the ideal of comprehensive coverage may be a positive barrier to genuine inquiry. As an alternative way of looking at this problem, the Committee proposes the ideal of specialization in breadth. The present tendency is to think of the Ph.D. as someone who contains a vast amount of information which he need merely draw on when he confronts a problem of inquiry. In truth, the knowledge, skills, and above all, insight, which he will need will not be a possession acquired at a given period of his life, but will entail a dynamic process of continuous learning.

The objective should be to prepare the student with the ability to solve problems of the kind which will occupy him throughout his entire career beyond graduate school. The emphasis should be on diverse ways of looking at problems; an awareness of what he must learn in order to deal with a problem; and an understanding of the bodies of evidence, the concepts and theories which are relevant to a particular problem.

The main impediment to flexibility and individuality of programs appears to be the comprehensive examinations, which inevitably dictate that the student regard his studies as a means of passing examinations rather than equipping his mind. In keeping with this Committee's viewpoint, it is urged that comprehensive examinations be required only at a very early stage of the student's training; that later departmental examinations concentrate upon testing the student's grasp of a more restricted field more deeply studied, or his success in pursuing the ramifications of his specialty in a program of interdisciplinary studies; and that each department devise appropriate procedures for encouraging students to prepare individual programs which may comprise or combine individual fields within the department in ways that deviate from the standard program. It is essential, of course, that these individual programs be formulated with the assistance and approval of a group of faculty advisers. To achieve this emphasis, we make the following recommendation:

Recommendation 32: **Departments should provide graduate programs in which comprehensive coverage of the department's territory gives way early in the graduate student's career to individually designed, integrated programs of study suited to the student's special interests.**

In departments which characteristically have exacted many years of study for general examinations, this approach would provide a more sensible approach to the dissertation, which would now come as the natural culmination of a period of progressively deep study. The Department of Philosophy has just instituted a new Ph.D. program of this design. The student is required to demonstrate competence in logic and "to pass a comprehensive examination based on a short reading list" by the end of his second year; thereafter he pursues and is examined in "studies in the area of his choice."

This idea has implications for the foreign language requirement for the Ph.D. There is no need to review this problem in great detail; the difficulty is widely recognized. In the majority of cases, the language requirement does not achieve its objective of providing the graduate student with an integral part of his equipment. Because the student is compelled to "learn" a language in a way that is unrelated to his intellectual preoccupations, it remains formal and external baggage. But, again, the solution is not to discard the requirement but to seek ways of integrating it with the actual inquiries being conducted by the student. If languages can be shown to be a necessary adjunct to on-going inquiry, students will quickly realize their value.

Recommendation 33: Departments should have wide latitude in determining requirements for foreign languages and other skills and should consider relating the requirements flexibly to the actual studies being conducted by individual graduate students.

D. The Period of Study

There is good reason to believe that the notion of the "comprehensive" departmental curriculum has contributed to the excessive number of years which most students spend in graduate school. Although it is difficult to establish reliable averages in this matter, it is apparent that departments differ markedly in their capacity finally to produce Ph.D.'s (see Appendix H); the period of study in departments may range anywhere from three to eight years. The shorter period is characteristic of the natural sciences, where the comprehensive approach is not generally used. The Committee has doubts about the wisdom of legislating time limits. There are ineradicable differences between the historical and the scientific disciplines in their requirements of time; and individual students may differ in the paces they wish to adopt. But we have little doubt of two things: first, that most doctoral programs in social science and humanities require too long a period; and, second, that there is a negative correlation between the length of time spent in a graduate program and the intellectual growth of the student. The sooner the student can be freed of the formal demand to fill unrelated gaps in his learning, the sooner he is asked to meet the challenge of concrete inquiry, the better.

The Committee is pleased to note that the proverbially long Ph.D. program in Romance Languages is being simplified in each of the three departments that offers it, and that the French and Italian departments now offer separate shorter programs in their respective fields as well.

If the faculty does not legislate a time limit, it may still practice some surveillance and guidance on the relative demands of degree programs.

Recommendation 34: Departments should make certain that capable full-time students having a sound preparation can earn the Master's degree in three to five quarters, and the Ph.D. in three to four years. The Graduate Council should periodically review all current graduate programs and report whether these norms are in effect.

E. Interdisciplinary Courses

The comprehensive departmental program can be not only too inclusive, but also too limiting. Today the practice of research and scholarship is almost universally understood to require constant contact with related fields. There is probably no single aspect of graduate training that lags further behind the actual needs of contemporary scholarship. At a time when practicing researchers are borrowing from other fields to the point of promiscuity, graduate education has treated the problem as one of "the outside field;" when dealing with students, faculties assume that the problems of the world have been predefined to accord with departmental boundaries. The fact which must be confronted is that for students too there are no sharp distinctions between "inside" fields and "outside" ones; instead there are only questions, problems, and puzzles whose solutions require a wide variety of approaches. The task is to translate this fact into the structure of graduate training.

At the present time, most departments require only the most perfunctory fulfillment of the "outside field" requirement, and in many instances, as almost every faculty member can testify, the oral examination in the outside field is set at a low level of competence. In preparation for these examinations, the student enrolls in various courses in other departments. If the student's main interest, for example, is in newly emerging non-Western societies, he is sent to the Anthropology, Sociology, Economics or Political Science Departments. Without questioning the quality of such courses, the fact remains that their effect upon the student is to cause him to lapse into the mentality of "taking courses" rather than to engage his attention upon problems that call for the simultaneous application of the diverse approaches represented by the departments previously mentioned. A better alternative, which actually implies a more useful view of knowledge itself, is to offer the student interdisciplinary courses organized around specific problems. An interesting example that conveys something of our thinking on this matter is the interdisciplinary Forestry seminar designed by Dr. Arnold M. Schultz, which attempts to bring a wide variety of perspectives to bear upon ecological problems. Philosophy, sociology, organizational theory, economics, and engineering are utilized in an effort to acquaint the student with the ramifications of forest management.

The educational value of interdisciplinary courses organized around problems is that it gives the student an intellectual reason for pursuing work in related fields. Once his interest is aroused by seeing how related fields can contribute to his understanding of substantive problems, he should be more receptive to investing the time and energy necessary for acquiring genuine competence in these fields.

To achieve these objectives, there will have to be greater experimentation at the level of graduate courses and seminars. Departments must be willing to release faculty members for joint courses of the type suggested; students from the related departments will have to be encouraged to take such courses; and the educational results of these undertakings should be checked at the level of the preliminary examinations. If this direction is followed out, the benefits will extend beyond the graduate student. The outlook encouraged by courses of this kind will inevitably be carried by Teaching Assistants to their undergraduate sections.

The logic of interdisciplinary work can also be extended in other ways which will attract the interest of the student and make him feel that he is an active participant in his own educational experience. A frequent complaint of faculty advisers and students alike is that the student is prevented from developing whole programs of study which would combine fields within the department with one or possibly two fields outside the department. Here again, the problem is the delayed preliminary examination which, because of its lateness, places undue emphasis upon work done within the department.

In order to encourage breadth of graduate education, departments should allow graduate students, in close consultation with faculty advisers both inside and outside the department, to develop individual programs for advanced interdisciplinary study as a substitute for the major field usually offered for the Ph.D. qualifying examination. In addition, departments should also encourage individual faculty members to develop programs which, in respect to their interdisciplinary character, may depart from the prevailing departmental program. These new programs would be considered as leading to the traditional degree, but they would be freer to experiment with interdisciplinary seminars and colloquia.

Recommendation 35: **The faculty should encourage interdisciplinary graduate study by promoting courses organized around specific problems, and by permitting students to pursue interdisciplinary programs of study under departmental or interdepartmental supervision.**

F. Teaching as Graduate Study

Another discrepancy between the shape of the student's ultimate activities and his graduate training is the divorce between research and teaching. This is an even greater problem in the graduate student's life than it is in the professor's. In another part of this report we take up the problems of the Teaching Assistant; it is very difficult for him to bring his teaching and his training for research together. In the case of the graduate student who is not a Teaching Assistant, the matter is far worse. He receives little or no training for teaching at all. While professors are swift to point out that teaching and research mutually support and enrich each other (see above, pp. 6, 42), we rarely offer our graduate students a chance to interrelate them. Yet many enter the Graduate Division with at least as great a motivation for teaching as for research, and one dispiriting element of their experience here is that their formidable training in research is so weakly brought to bear on the problems they will face as teachers. Some experience in relating research to teaching should be made available as part of each department's program.

The connection between teaching and research can be strengthened if we enlarge the idea of research to include forms of inquiry which are not intended to produce new knowledge in a given field, but are intended to increase the knowledge of the inquirer for the purpose of enabling him to communicate it to students. The kind of knowledge which many college teachers, and many Teaching Assistants as well, are attempting to convey is usually a subtle combination of the well-established and the newly-discovered. This is a demanding activity, a form of inquiry which, while it adds little to the existing stock of knowledge, is at the center of the teaching enterprise and is crucial to the development of the graduate student. This idea of research is involved whenever a teacher assumes the responsibility for organizing a course and preparing lectures and discussions; for the basic purpose of most courses is to introduce a student to the definable techniques of a given field, to apprise him of the current state of knowledge in it, and to suggest new or unresolved problems. What is all important to the development of the graduate student is that this form of research become a continuing part of his education.

It might be organized in the form of colloquia or seminars attached to undergraduate courses. All Teaching Assistants in a specific course along with graduate apprentices would be members of such a seminar, and the faculty member in charge of the course would have the responsibility for conducting the seminar along with it. The basic purpose would be to conduct inquiry of a kind suitable to the level of the course and to discuss the best ways of communicating such knowledge to the undergraduate students. The purpose would not be to re-hash stale knowledge, but to revitalize it in the light of developing knowledge and to relate it in ways that will engage the attention of the student. A progression could be embodied in the apprenticeship. Departments could develop a system of teaching seminars related to selected undergraduate courses and make it possible for graduate students to advance from the level of introductory courses to more advanced ones. A promising move in this direction is being considered by the Department of History with the teaching pro-seminar proposed for future Teaching Assistants in the History 17 seminar program. This course will introduce graduate students to problems of American history, and of teaching it, one term *before* they begin their own teaching assignments.

Recommendation 36: **Departments should allow all graduate students to participate in undergraduate teaching appropriate to their skills, and should grant course credit to graduate students for work designed to relate the graduate curriculum to the problems of teaching.**

G. Selection of Students: Admissions vs. Hurdles

To bring graduate students on to the earliest possible assumption of genuinely scholarly research and teaching, we should try as much as possible to mute the "provisional" character of the early graduate years. The actual operation of our system is sometimes quite contrary to the intention, and seems more preoccupied with the administration rather than the education of the student. For example, in several departments the first year's work is tailored to the Master's degree and is viewed as a device for thinning out the graduate student body and leaving only those deemed suitable for doctoral work. The first year's work is thus meant to compensate for inadequate admissions procedures. The Ph.D. preliminary examinations provide another hurdle at a still higher level for determining who shall proceed to the thesis. The net effect is to harass the student with endless examinations whose primary purpose is to settle the question of competence which ought to have been decided earlier, and to compel him to arrange his course of study for the primary objective of passing examinations. The overall thrust of the system, particularly outside the sciences, can be to discourage intellectual curiosity, self-motivation, and playful creativity.

Because of the diverse needs of the many fields and departments, it is impossible to propose any explicit remedy. Nevertheless, there is reason to believe that in the all-important function of evaluating the achievements and progress of graduate students, greater emphasis should first be placed on admissions, and then upon the record of the student's performance in designated graduate courses and seminars. The more certain we are of the initial quality and preparation of our students, the more we will be free to regard their progress as our own responsibility and to substitute assistance for hurdles. The Department of Economics is moving in this direction with a new policy of higher standards for admission and a corresponding simplification in the qualifying examinations.

Recommendation 37: **We should decrease the number of hurdles in the graduate curriculum by elevating admissions standards, then simplifying examination requirements correspondingly.**

H. Institutes for Community and Support

One of the most neglected phases of graduate education concerns the last year or two when the student is engaged primarily in writing his thesis. At this stage his life is dominated by the thesis, and contact with the department is usually limited to conferences with his thesis supervisor. The student has passed all of his initiation tests, save one, and he should be ready for full membership in the community of scholars. At this point we encounter two typical but quite different problems: either the student remains on campus and discovers that the only existing community consists of himself and his thesis; or worse yet, he is forced by economic circumstances to find a teaching job which gives him neither the time nor the facilities to finish his thesis, nor the professional recognition due him as a scholar who has progressed far beyond the level of the Master's degree. Fortunately, this is not true of all students; many of them receive financial support throughout their graduate years and find intellectual community in the numerous research institutes on the campus. But the problem of graduate student support continues severe, especially in the social sciences and humanities (see Appendix I). The Graduate Division has made a small but promising beginning in sponsoring a program of sustained support combining periods of Teaching Assistantship and periods of unencumbered study. What needs to be explored further is the possibility of utilizing a system of research institutes to provide places where advanced graduate students may possibly find supporting stipends, and carry on research in an atmosphere of intensely professional education and conversation. In many respects research institutes form a natural home for graduate students at the last phase of their careers. Moreover, there now exists a strong sentiment for integrating institutes more closely into the educational process. Professional concentration has its place in graduate education; the major question is, what is the proper place? It is our suggestion that this matter be approached from the point of view of using the institutes as the final stage in the graduate student's preparation. The institutes are probably better equipped to acquaint the student with the very latest developments in his field and to suggest where exciting new areas of inquiry are opening.

At the present time there are many departments for which there is no obvious institute to receive graduate students. Nevertheless, it is possible to conceive of the creation of new institutes of advanced study for those departments currently without them, which can relate them to their teaching responsibilities. Two or three departments might cooperate to establish an institute to serve their common needs. If such institutes were more closely connected with departments than is presently the case, other possibilities would be opened up. In another part of this report we make general recommendations for further study of the use of organized research facilities in teaching (See sec. III.F).

I. A New Degree: Doctor of Arts

The extent to which the research paradigm has dominated graduate education has been a constant source of uneasiness for most faculty members. The actual number of true research scholars produced is probably only a fraction of the total number of successful doctoral candidates. More disturbing still, there is the large number of unsuccessful candidates who complete all requirements save for the thesis. There are also many able students who decide to leave graduate study or who never enter it because they are unable to sustain the necessary motivation for completing a research degree. The extreme demand for teachers cannot be met by the present form of doctoral training, except at the cost of diluting its quality. At the same time, there is the irony that while many institutions refuse to hire teachers who do not possess the doctorate, the heavy emphasis upon teaching and lack of research prevailing at those institutions inevitably prevents the Ph.D. from conducting research for which he has been trained. Such institutions require the doctorate as proof of intellect and learning, not as proof of research potential. The time has come to question the whole system which makes the Ph.D. the only acceptable form of certification for college teaching. Unless this question is raised, there is grave danger that the doctorate will continue to be devalued and, above all, that serious students wishing to make a career in college teaching will be discouraged because of the research-oriented character of doctoral training.

No sooner had the Committee come to this conclusion than there appeared in *College English* for November, 1965, an article by the eminent bibliographer Professor Fredson Bowers which puts the whole matter plainly and persuasively, and offers a solution with which we agree:

> ... let us combat the shortage of college teachers not by further debasing the Ph.D., as we inevitably shall, but by also awarding a learned but non-research degree, the Doctor of Arts. This new degree will retain the doctoral standards of critical preparation and the accomplishment of the demanding examinations that represent everything that is best in the Ph.D. for the needs of good undergraduate teaching. I think a program would be satisfactory and it would certainly be practical, that would include all that is now required by the Ph.D. except for the dissertation and its accompanying specialized final examination.
>
> This proposal would leave the M.A. where it now is, and where it is likely to remain. It cannot be restored to its old prestige. On the other hand, the Ph.D. as a research degree that is necessary for university instruction as well as for the advancement of national progress in other fields, would be saved from the constant pressures of attrition that now assail it because of its unsuitability when spread too thin for too many disparate purposes.
>
> In a practical manner, therefore, the Doctorate of Arts would permit graduate students to be trained together up to the point where the narrow specialization required by the research exercise of the dissertation takes over. After three years of advanced study, it would send students out into the college and junior-college teaching world at the point where so many now leave graduate school (all other requirements satisfied) to write their dissertation in absentia while engaged with a full-time teaching job. But for such teachers the degree would offer a superior criterion to justify a higher salary than the present M.A., and it would remove the serious penalty placed on those who never succeed in finishing the dissertation under these difficult conditions—a relatively common occurrence. In fact, the most serious academic waste comes here, in the dismissal or in the low academic status and lack of promotion for those who can never quite manage to carry a heavy teaching load, raise a family, and finish a dissertation far from encouragement, supervision, and the resources of a university library.
>
> Finally, if a teacher decided that he wanted to be trained for specialized research work and that his abilities lay in this direction, he could always add the Ph.D., in the British manner, by

writing a dissertation and passing the special examination that accompanies it.

Individual departments might be permitted to administer the Doctor of Arts in different ways. The doctoral emphasis on written work, however, is in the Committee's opinion an appropriate one in principle, and we would accordingly expect that departments would require a "learned paper" (possibly the candidate's best seminar paper, suitably edited as if for publication) in lieu of a dissertation. The Department of Comparative Literature is considering some such alternative within its doctoral program. It is understood that a recipient of the Doctor of Arts might undertake a research project at a later date in order to complete the final requirement for the Ph.D.

Recommendation 38: **The Graduate Council should frame necessary legislation creating a new degree of Doctor of Arts, to require preparation equivalent to that normally required for advancement to candidacy for the Ph.D., but without requiring a dissertation.**

XI.

THE TEACHING ASSISTANT

A. Introduction

A DETAILED STUDY of the individual programs of the graduating class of 1965 shows the heavy responsibility for their education that was borne by the Teaching Assistant. When we total the number of classes every student took and divide them among the different types of instructors, we find that 31% of the total number of classes were sections regularly taught by Teaching Assistants or were laboratories in which supervision is usually in their hands. Of the lower-division classes 41% were of this kind. The role of the Teaching Assistant becomes even more significant when we consider the smaller classes by themselves. Sixty-five per cent of the classes and laboratories of 15 students or less were taught by Teaching Assistants, as were 63% of the classes and laboratories of 16 to 30 students. By any standards, then, the quality of the instruction by Teaching Assistants is important to the quality of education at Berkeley.

There is perhaps no more widely agreed-upon opinion, however, than that the Teaching Assistant system is one of our major problems. A year ago President Kerr set in motion University-wide study of the problem by both administrative and faculty agencies. The Committee on Educational Policy brought recommendations to the Berkeley Division on November 8, 1965, and an administrative report, particularly intended for various officers of the state government, was issued in December. Various schools and departments have already made substantial improvements in their handling of Teaching Assistants, and the current wide concern with the matter will no doubt have good results for teaching in the University.

The present Committee has cooperated closely in this University-wide effort, and has sponsored extensive research on the Berkeley campus. Our staff has interviewed some 35 administrators (department chairmen, deans, and division chairmen), 80 faculty members, and 55 teaching graduate students. In addition, they have spoken to about 35 administrative assistants and secretaries, to other persons with special knowledge or interest in college teaching, and to many undergraduate students. Interim staff reports have been made available to the other agencies mentioned above, and some of the findings have already been used. Some of our recommendations here will accordingly be found to agree closely with recent Senate and administration re-statements of policy.

We believe that the system of using graduate students in the instruction of undergraduates—if conceived broadly—is educationally sound and organizationally indispensable. What has been faulty has been in local applications of the system: too many Teaching Assistants have not taught well enough, and too many have not profited sufficiently from the experience.

The need for graduate students to assist in teaching is brought about by the size and quality of the campus. The ratio of regular faculty to students at Berkeley is extremely unfavorable as compared with liberal arts colleges or with the leading private universities with which we compete for faculty. In order to give undergraduates the requisite minimum of personal attention, we can either attempt to impose a heavier burden of undergraduate teaching on the regular faculty, or depend for some of the teaching on qualified assistants. As to the first alternative, we make elsewhere in this report recommendations for some redistribution of faculty teaching time and for greater variety in the teaching functions of the regular faculty. However, even under optimum conditions of time distribution, a faculty of our size cannot simultaneously discharge its obligations to graduate teaching and research, maintain its quality in the face of increasing competition from other institutions, and still provide students a good undergraduate education, unless it makes substantial use of the great teaching power of the student body itself. As the most capable and learned of student teachers, the graduate Teaching Assistant is the key to high-quality education in the public university.

To call on students to help in teaching is justifiable on other counts: for example, it provides indispensable financial support for the students; it is the best method we have of training college teachers; above all, it is a fine instrument for educating the student-teacher himself.

To teach your specialty to younger students provides excellent occasion for clarifying your own ideas, plugging gaps in your knowledge, and re-examining the basic assumptions and the relevance of your discipline. Particularly under the "problem-oriented" kind of teaching which we hope will become more prevalent—in which the Teaching Assistant can become a scholar-leader in a "seminar" rather than a drill-master in a "section"—the Teaching Assistant can develop as a scholar while he learns as a teacher; at the same time he is contributing to the intellectual growth of younger students.

The trouble with the system in past years has been that in the rapid growth of the campus, amidst chronic shortages of help, we have tended to regard the Teaching Assistantship too much as merely a paid temporary job, and not enough as a regular part of the education and training of scholar-teachers. As a result the various parts of the Teaching Assistant's experience have often not had the coherence that should characterize the life of scholarship. In the case of the faculty member we have argued that under appropriate conditions his teaching and research will reinforce each other to the benefit of both. For the graduate student, intent on first acquiring the necessary techniques of research, the argument is more difficult. He must not only acquaint himself with a wide variety of complex skills and absorb them, but he must simultaneously assume the difficult task of teaching undergraduates who expect him to measure up to a high standard of teaching. While the faculty member may find himself divided between the demands of research and teaching, the Teaching Assistant is torn by them. We have not been sufficiently sensitive to this dilemma; we have not offered the Teaching Assistant programs that make exciting and fruitful connections between learning and teaching. Lacking this, what may appear to be cynicism towards undergraduate teaching on the part of Teaching Assistants may in reality be a laudable preference for graduate study over the drudgery of a routine part-time job.

To make matters worse, we have been unable to appoint the best possible Teaching Assistants and to evaluate their performance by standards fitting to scholar-teachers. Some of our very best graduate students, who would have learned much and been excellent assistants, have by holding fellowships and research assistantships been excluded from teaching. In some departments Teaching Assistantships have been awarded by default; there have been too few graduate students to choose from, and some have been appointed before they were professionally competent to take on teaching responsibility. We have sometimes scanted the training and supervision of Teaching Assistants, and have regarded them too much as employees rather than as junior colleagues. Insecure, neglected, sometimes exploited, Teaching Assistants have responded in ways detrimental to the education of undergraduates. The creation of a Teaching Assistants' union, in opposition to the University as "employer", is a symptom of their dissatisfaction.

We need to move toward a state in which the ideal of the scholar-teacher is as applicable to the Teaching Assistant as it is to the professor.

B. Appointment, Training, and Supervision

The Berkeley Division on November 8, 1965, adopted the policy that "Each department should give serious attention to appropriate measures for assisting graduate students to become effective teachers of undergraduate courses. Departments should be enabled, if they think proper, to require all graduate students to participate in undergraduate teaching, or to grant course credit to graduate students for work designed to improve teaching ability." This policy has great merit as a contribution to graduate education generally, and is substantially repeated in our Recommendation 36, above (page 167). It is also a necessary background to proper appointment of Teaching Assistants, for it provides both for training and for some prior evaluation of the teaching potential of candidates. It is true that some of the most enlightened instruction on the campus is done by Teaching Assistants. At their best they offer energy, a zest for their subject, and a sympathy with undergraduate problems quite comparable to that of the best regular professors. However, it is the rare department that takes teaching potential seriously into account in the first appointment of Teaching Assistants. With no evidence to go by, selection committees choose Assistants not for teaching promise but for academic prowess. In the future, an apprentice period offered to all graduate students should make it more possible for us to recognize promise of teaching ability and to eliminate from responsible service those who have defects in professional competence, in capacity to communicate, or in personality or motivation for teaching.

During last November's discussion of Teaching Assistants in the Academic Senate, some scepticism, if not hostility, was expressed by faculty members toward the idea of teaching Teaching. In the same vein, although the Berkeley General Catalogue lists several courses devoted to university teaching in departments outside the School of Education, none has actually been given for years. The Committee's canvassing of academic departments yielded only one, the Department of German, which plans to offer a purely pedagogical course of this nature. Faculty members offer several reasons for the unpopularity of courses in teaching: graduate students' indifference, resistance to "educationese," overloaded graduate requirements, the lack of a concrete subject. This Committee, however, while it admits to a modest distrust of abstractions, and would not recommend to all departments the teaching of Teaching in general, is certain that teaching in some senses can and must be taught.

We have already sketched (in section X.F above) the possibilities in a graduate seminar or colloquium formed to study the problems of teaching a specific undergraduate lecture course and taught simultaneously by the same professor. The subject matter of the seminar would be the considerations that go into the researching, structuring and presentation of a subject; the choice, order, and pacing of its materials; the decisions on proper emphasis, omission, summary, or elaboration; the examining and evaluating of student work; and the evaluation of the progress of the course itself. These are not abstractions; relating the content of graduate study to the problems of teaching, they are no more beneath the interest of a graduate student than of a full professor. Students in the seminar could act as informal discussion leaders with small groups of students in the lecture course, to the benefit of both, and they could be depended upon to bring back to the professor valuable observations on the progress of the course.

The History Department is considering just such an experimental innovation for the first half of the general sophomore course in United States history, History 17. In weekly two-hour sections, Teaching Assistants would select aspects of the successive course topics for treatment, being responsible for reading and paper assignments and examinations. Two lectures a week would provide integration and continuity. Simultaneously the lecturer would conduct for the Teaching Assistants a special graduate reading seminar, devoted to the topics being covered in History 17 and the teaching of these topics. The lecturer would be assisted, in lectures and in the seminar, by other members of the Department who are specialists in the topics dealt with. A similar experiment is being initiated by a professor in the Department of French. He plans to give a graduate course that combines the study of linguistics with a practical approach to techniques of teaching the language.

The device of gathering Teaching Assistants into a regular colloquium to follow the progress of the course is already being successfully used in Physics, Political Science, Anthropology, and in various other parts of the campus. It is coming into use at other institutions as well. For instance, in the Department of History at Washington University (St. Louis), where teaching is required of all departmental graduate students, the first year includes auditing the introductory course, visiting discussion sections led by the senior instructors, and doing limited practice teaching in the sections. Only in the second year do the graduates begin to do regular supervised teaching, when they lead sections and are apprenticed to lecturing by being permitted to deliver some of the review lectures before exams. Some University of Michigan departments, including Chemistry and English, maintain active training programs of this kind, and the Psychology Department conducts a term-long pre-teaching seminar, part of an especially lively, successful system under a keenly interested chairman.

More modest, more pragmatic, or shorter-term periods of training are also feasible and desirable. Our German Department provides a full week of training for all its Teaching Assistants in the elementary courses, including films on methods, demonstrations of classroom techniques, and discussions of a detailed syllabus for every class meeting. "The scheduling plans were impeccable," commented one Teaching Assistant. Next summer new Teaching Assistants will take a course covering the use of language laboratories, instructional materials, and also including class visits.

The connection between the proper supervision of Teaching Assistants and their training for teaching is obvious, and we have found some exemplary instances of successful supervision on campus. A Physics professor, in addition to meeting his Teaching Assistants regularly, visits a section of each one as discussion leader. Many faculty members sit in periodically on classes taught by each Teaching Assistant. An economist who prefers informal contact talks over the course with his Teaching Assistants during visits in the hall, or at coffee or lunch or Sunday supper, on the average of twice a week. A young Spanish professor held three meetings with his eleven assistants before classes began, taught one group of students in classes paralleling the Teaching Assistants', and met with them each week to talk over mutual problems. A French professor in charge of 63 Teaching Assistants has recently started them visiting each others' classes and learning the classroom techniques of senior faculty members. The Departments of Italian and French have devised "pilot classes" which Teaching Assistants must attend to observe the methods of master teachers.

One of the best-trained and supervised groups of graduate student teachers are the eighteen assigned the thankless task of teaching Subject A, the remedial course in English Composition. Before classes start the Subject A teachers, new and old, receive ten days of intensive training in grading, classroom procedures, and teaching methods, and conferences continue through the term. "We discussed how to conduct classes, demonstrated our own techniques, talked over the dittoed handouts we had used. The meetings were a first-rate education in pedagogy, with a Subject A slant. By our second time around even those of us who had not known grammar at the beginning knew it cold." Strongly encouraged are visiting others' classes, exchanging successful assignment topics, and consulting with the faculty supervisor, who also periodically evaluates his assistants' theme comments and the justice of their grading.

Where Berkeley's Teaching Assistants have lacked supervision and training, the usual explanation has been lack of faculty time. Good supervision does take time, a fact that is beginning to be recognized in assigning faculty teaching loads. Our Psychology Department, for example, now gives "teaching credit" for supervising. In Humanities courses on the San Diego campus every professor (who is expected to meet individually with each of his Teaching Assistants every week in addition to a weekly meeting with all six) is given double credit.

But some Berkeley faculty members and a minority of Teaching Assistants feel that "too much supervision" makes Assistants "nervous." or that "they are mature enough to act independently." Actually, our research shows that most Teaching Assistants welcome interested guidance, and some are dismayed not to have it.

Supervision is not to be confused with smothering, however, and here we return to the idea that we should accept the Teaching Assistant as a partner. More than one professor has commented to us on the great store he puts in scholarly discussion with Teaching Assistants, and the mutual benefits of discussing ideas with them. The Berkeley Speech Department conducts joint Teaching Assistant-faculty meetings. Other faculty members look upon their Teaching Assistants as active colleagues in planning and conducting courses, and as special advisers in their own fields of interest, but few professors actually give Teaching Assistants responsibility and independence proportional to their talents. One Mathematics professor considers responsibility for planning an important ingredient of training and encouraging his Assistants, though he cautions against assigning more independence than they can properly handle, and suggests that only the most highly capable should be allowed to plan largely on their own. His department is experimenting with allowing five of its best Teaching Assistants to have sole charge of lecture-discussion classes in five different courses. Normally professors lecture to the total enrollment of these courses, over 200 each, and Assistants have small discussion sections. In the experiment each Assistant has his own class of 20 students and provides the lecture himself. A History professor, also experimenting with Teaching Assistants as course planners, has given his twelve section leaders a free rein in running their classes. At his regular Teaching Assistant meetings he calls for resumés of their plans, and follows up with postmortems on how well they succeeded.

A requisitely creative role for the Teaching Assistant is made possible by a creative attitude from the professor. Among the most satisfying experiences for Teaching Assistants recently has been their participation in teaching innovations. In the tutorial sections started this year by professors in English, Comparative Literature, and Psychology, classes have been held in student dormitories and houses, and professors and assistants have been free to experiment with size of classes, original modes of presentation, forms of examinations, length and number of sessions, and the like. All the participants in this program are unblushing in their enthusiasm (See section III.D above).

Recommendation 39: **Teaching promise should be a major criterion for student appointments that involve teaching or tutoring, and teaching responsibilities should always be commensurate with the student's state of preparation. It follows that sustained classroom teaching should generally be reserved to the second year of graduate study and later.**

Recommendation 40: **Frequent regular meetings between professors and Teaching Assistants, including graduate teaching colloquia or teaching seminars where appropriate to the discipline, should be part of the regular program in each department, and should be counted as teaching credit of faculty and course or service credit of students.**

C. Morale

Teaching Assistants should perform their duties at a level of good teaching practice comparable to that of the regular faculty. Attendance at scheduled classes, scrupulous observance of office hours, and giving extra attention and special assistance to students as needed should be regarded as among the normal duties for which Teaching Assistants are compensated. Expecting a high level of professional performance from Teaching Assistants, we must ensure that they are treated in such a way as to give them a sense of professional pride. While Teaching Assistant morale is by no means universally dismal, our staff found too many Teaching Assistants who testified that in one way or another their treatment had been lacking in professional respect. We believe that the measures recommended above, to the extent that they will improve the atmosphere of the entire system, must also improve morale.

But there still are other measures that can be taken, the simplest and most obvious being to improve the physical surroundings in which Teaching Assistants work.

Faculty members in some departments have recognized their assistants' needs as akin to their own, and have provided well-lighted offices, desks, conference rooms, and other morale-lifting amenities. The instance of the professor who makes available his office, phone, and private library to his one Teaching Assistant or Reader could hardly be duplicated for all 1.800 graduate assistants. But some groups in some departments are well taken care of. The Economics Department gives Teaching Assistants for certain courses a fair-sized office with a phone extension, individual desks, newspapers, journals, and free coffee; the Psychology Department provides hourly phone-message service, and a spacious lounge shared with the faculty, plus access to private conference rooms when the occasion demands. In neither department is the office *more* than adequate—one cannot help turning a sympathetic ear to mumblings about claustrophobia (neither has windows) and distractions (one has been dubbed "the zoo"). And in the Economics Department Teaching Assistants in *other* courses must share desks and office hours.

Most Teaching Assistants do not have any of these advantages; many work under exceedingly trying conditions. Cramped quarters and shared desks are typical.

Some departments, especially those in which demand exceeds supply, have found it expedient to handle their Assistants with great consideration, keeping their teaching hours and busy work to an acceptable minimum; and most departments no longer regularly ask their Teaching Assistants for more than the stipulated 20-hour-a-week maximum. But with a few exceptions truly conscientious Assistants spend more than 20 hours, especially during their first year of teaching. And even among the less conscientious, too many are still excessively burdened, particularly when they work in more than one course at a time. Even a 20-hour job, when it is not geared to his education, may be a questionably large diversion from the graduate's own academic goals. The Committee has received complaints from Assistants in many departments about the kind of work they are asked to do. Professional respect is reflected in a department's care in keeping menial tasks to a minimum. We heartily endorse last November's recommendation by the Committee on Educational Policy:

> The current emphasis on routine assignments in the correcting of student problem work should be eliminated. Simpler ways should be sought to verify the students' performance of

assigned work (for instance, posted solutions should become the primary means for illustrating problem-solving methods) in order to increase the personal responsibility of undergraduates for such matters. Such changes will greatly reduce the "busy work" done by graduate Assistants, and will reorient them toward a responsible and creative role in teaching, better matched to their abilities and energies.

Tradition does not justify perpetuating ineffective and dispiriting Teaching Assistant assignments in any course. Large courses that customarily divide the enrollment into sections, as well as those using Teaching Assistants in other patterns, should be frequently reviewed to make sure that Teaching Assistants are in a position to contribute substantially to the students' understanding. If they do not, the sections should be dropped, or new patterns constructed. Variations in section assignments, such as rotating or exchanging Teaching Assistants' sections, Teaching Assistants working in pairs, encouraging students to visit different sections, offering Teaching Assistants and students a choice as to type of section, or dividing the term between the large lectures and the small section meetings (all of which have been successfully tried by a few professors) can mitigate the trapped feelings of assistants in uncongenial assignments, capitalize on their specialties, and help maintain their pride and interest in teaching.

Professional respect is also reflected in a department's willingness to discuss matters of appointment. Several, like Economics, have taken the lead in setting up student-faculty committees and issuing detailed outlines of appointment policies and ways of handling students' requests. Such measures have been sparked by student discontent, but the increase in friendly communication has pleased students and professors alike. We see no reason why departments should not enlarge the assistants' sense of participation in the common enterprise by also bringing into discussion matters of curriculum, and even of the selection and evaluation of junior assistants.

Recommendation 41: **All departments using Teaching Assistants should foster a climate of professional respect through (a) providing assistants with adequate physical facilities for both their teaching duties and their own studies; (b) assigning work with careful attention to avoiding duties that are too heavy or unnecessarily menial, and with periodic review of appropriateness of assignments; and (c) establishing student-faculty discussions of standards of appointment, workable ways of handling students' requests, and other matters of common professional concern.**

D. Gradations and Compensation

The policy approved by the Division last November envisions a gradation of levels of instruction by graduate students:

a. At the initial level ... the graduate student should assist a regular faculty member in such duties as searching the literature, developing new problem material, meeting informally with students in the course, or helping to supervise undergraduate laboratory work. Simultaneously he should be mastering (by observation, discussion, independent study, and participation in seminars on teaching) the subject matter and teaching techniques he will need for the next level of teaching.

b. At the second level ... he should carry on classroom teaching in the discussion sections of a course, accompanied by scheduled seminars or planning sessions with the course instructor, and under extensive constructive supervision.

c. At the third level . . . he should have the responsibility for an entire section of a lower-division course, or other assignment of considerable difficulty and responsibility. In such work, he should still serve under the general direction of a tenure faculty member, to ensure continuity in the way the course is given. Only the very best of the graduate-student teachers would be eligible for this rank.

Under this system students at the initial level—first-year Teaching Trainees—might be of three kinds: (1) Students receiving no support or compensation, but taking training either voluntarily or as part of a degree program; (2) Fellowship holders who are taking training with no extra compensation, either voluntarily, or as required by a degree program or the terms of the fellowship; (3) Students who in the course of training do more than the pedagogically prescribed amount of work and are formally appointed and compensated (perhaps at one-quarter time) as "Teaching Assistants."

Teachers at the second and third levels would all be compensated directly or receive compensation as part of an integrated program of teaching and study covering a number of years.

We have expressly made no mention of the Reader in this conception, because we feel that the Readership as it is now used on the campus should be discontinued. The Readers' hourly pay scale, presumably designed for routine chores, seems acceptable to those whose duties actually are routine. But in many departments Readers have drifted into key roles in judging the work of undergraduates. In some departments they have been used to do the sensitive grading, tutoring, and occasional classroom teaching that closely resembles Teaching Assistant work. Under these circumstances the gap in pay and the relative lack of training and supervision make the maintenance of Readerships unfair to both Readers and their students. The funds presently devoted to Readerships should be diverted to the graded system described above. The present duties of Readers should be partly taken over by regular Teaching Assistants and partly by unpaid supervised Trainees, whose activities should strictly exclude menial assistance.

But no discussion of the subject would be complete without taking into consideration the prior question of recruitment, and the capacity of the assistantship to attract and hold the best graduate students. Most of our proposals for improving instruction would be congenial to prospective assistants too; a campus whose departments all sought to inspire and reward the student assistants, to treat them as professional colleagues, and to encourage innovation and experiment would seem almost irresistible. With a few additional conditions it probably would be. One such condition is recognizing that students seriously interested in earning advanced degrees need to know ahead of time the schedule they can reasonably expect to follow and the financial support they can count on receiving.

For many years our teaching appointments have been a successful attraction to the best students in the nation. The pay at Berkeley has been in line with that in other large universities, which vary in matters of tuition waivers and other fringe benefits. At several, however, the expected work load is now less than half-time, an attractive consideration. Still more important, Teaching Assistants' salaries are low compared with the stipends of many of the fellowships and research grants now available both here and elsewhere. It is true that some Teaching Assistants would not trade their first year of teaching for research appointments worth a good deal more money. But one year of teaching is all that most Teaching Assistants would choose, and one cannot blame them for preferring non-teaching fellowships, or those research assistantships in which, especially in business administration, the sciences, agriculture, and engineering, the financial return is coupled with direct progress toward the degree. We have recommended the extension of teaching to all classes of graduates, and the inclusion of some teaching in the degree curricula, and these may act as equalizing devices. But an increase in the stipends of Teaching Assistants is also necessary. We endorse and repeat here the policy recommendation of the Committee on Educational Policy, approved by the Berkeley Division on November 9, 1965:

Recommendation 42: An increase is needed in the stipends for graduate students assigned to teaching, so as to recruit the ablest candidates to the University, to provide them an attractive alternative to the now more rewarding research assistantships, and to remunerate them in a manner fully commensurate with the difficulty and quality of the duties they perform.

XII.

UNFINISHED BUSINESS

IN MAKING the preceding recommendations, we do not pretend to have completed the blueprint for an ideal university at Berkeley. We have been conscious of writing at a time of unusual ferment on the campus, and have judged it important to limit our scope rather than postpone our response unduly. We have felt particularly free to omit comment on problems which seem already in course of solution. For example, in the light of the rapidly ameliorating atmosphere of University-wide relations, and above all the recent increases in local campus autonomy, we have said nothing about the relation of the campus to the state-wide University. The question of re-organizing and possibly de-centralizing the College of Letters and Science is currently being reviewed by the faculty itself; our remarks on this important topic have been submitted directly to the Executive Committee of the College. The College has established its own Special Committee on Academic Program, which will have *inter alia* to make detailed recommendations with respect to breadth and language requirements. Apart from the general ideas recorded in Chapter IX, our comments about breadth requirements have already been directly communicated to this committee through memoranda and informal meetings.

The problem of foreign language requirements has appeared to us worthy of a more extended review than we could undertake. The Foreign Language Council has recommended that this Committee consider the feasibility of stating the foreign language breadth requirement in terms of achievement expected at the end of a two-year (six-quarter) sequence of College language work. In replying to the Council, we have suggested that any proposal for change in the foreign language requirement would be best brought before the faculty accompanied by broad investigation of the whole subject of foreign language teaching, including fresh consideration of such subjects as the variety of departmental offerings; methods of instruction; selection, training, and treatment of Teaching Assistants; graduate programs in relation to preparation of college teachers; and the like. The Committee was not equipped to handle these topics with requisite authority, but the research we have done on such related subjects as Teaching Assistants and graduate study suggests that there is some room for re-examination and possible renovation. We hope that some agency such as the Foreign Language Council will conduct an investigation on its own initiative.

There are several other major and enduring problems to which similar close attention should also be directed. The Library has latterly had great difficulties in meeting the increased demand for services resulting from our development as a center of graduate study and research. The new Undergraduate Library is urgently needed; but neither it nor the various existing special libraries will answer the expected future pressures on our library resources. Indeed, insofar as the campus moves toward the more personalized and more independent study programs we recommend for all students, these pressures can be expected to increase still further. The same can be said for the problem of space and architecture on the campus. Contact between students and faculty is in many instances seriously inhibited by the lack of available facilities for informal meetings. We have discussed the ways in which space shortages depress the morale and efficiency of our Teaching Assistants, and in Appendix J we describe the discrepancies in the study space allocated to graduate students in different departments. We must now add that a progressively more humane community of teachers and students will inevitably demand a more humane architecture, with lounges and offices large enough for group meetings and tutorials, with more round tables and fewer lecterns.

It would not be difficult to cite a list of other topics, both larger and smaller, which the Committee might have discussed. This Committee's study of grading was only able to touch peripherally on the equally important subject of examinations. The campus needs a close study of the way in which University policy affects the attitudes of non-academic personnel, and the way in which non-academic personnel are in turn influenced in their dealings with students. We should investigate the possibility of attracting and educating much larger numbers of disadvantaged students. Financial support of graduate students, particularly in the humanities, is dangerously deficient; we need a long-range plan for its improvement. One very large question which preoccupied the Committee was whether lower-division education can ever succeed at a large public university with both our commitment to graduate studies and research on the one hand and our existing faculty-student ratios on the other. Such an issue cannot be settled until the faculty has made a more serious effort to promote close faculty-student contact on every level of the University; and we have therefore limited ourselves to this more proximate objective.

If we take the long perspective of educational history, it can be said that the search for mass higher education of good quality, which only began about a century ago, is still in its experimental stages. What can be accomplished at Berkeley will surely not be irrelevant in making that experiment succeed, and we commend the task to our colleagues and successors.

ADDENDUM—A MINORITY REPORT

BY

PROFESSOR GEORGE C. PIMENTEL

A minority report suggests an onerous message of unresolvable disagreement. In that sense, this section is not fully a minority report. True, there are some specific disagreements but, more generally, it represents a different view of the problem faced by the Select Committee on Education. It differs more on premises and emphases than in specifics. Despite the most considerate and patient attention from his colleagues, the writer remained as a minority element, not quite contented with the misfit of deliberations based on one set of premises when evaluated on the foundation of another set.

This controversy over the starting point for our examination of the possible need for educational reform at Berkeley is encapsulated in the word "reform." After prolonged consideration of the criticisms that have been made of education at Berkeley, I remain convinced that the word "reform" had no place in the deliberations. The starting point, relative to other noted institutions, is one of general excellence. The majority report does not adequately convey this message. "Innovation" and "creative development" are both needed on this campus, as they always will be. However, proposals for sweeping changes that might imperil for dubious gain a precious position of preeminence must be approached deliberately. Only with clear recognition that our students are presently offered magnificent and widely varied educational opportunities should we begin our investigation into ways to polish and widen them. The majority report directs only passing attention to existing variety, flexibility, and opportunity. Only with full acknowledgment to the outstanding quality of the faculty and to their devotion to the

University should we proceed to inquire into the optimum use of their creative talents. The majority report treats graduate education and the needs of the major in a manner too casual to be appropriate to their primacy on the Berkeley scene. It little considers the special ways in which a research-oriented faculty ought to be engaged in undergraduate education so that the undergraduates will benefit most from this research orientation. It sidesteps the knotty question of how much attention the faculty can devote to undergraduate education (e.g., in freshman seminars) before graduate education begins to suffer.

There are, then, four aspects of the majority report which evoked this minority report:

. . . its reluctance to paint a clear picture of our excellent starting point

. . . its unbalanced emphasis upon non-major education and relative neglect of our primary responsibilities in graduate and major education

. . . its excessive advocacy of permissiveness unaccompanied by validation of academic performance

. . . its structuring of the Board of Educational Development: a University within a University

This Addendum begins, then, with a different cast that the majority report. It leads to some agreements, some disagreements, and a few distinct conclusions. It would not be fair to the Committee for the reader to assume that my colleagues disagree with all of this section. They have had no opportunity to respond favorably or unfavorably. It is in the nature of things that the majority report speaks with the louder voice but the minority report has the last, albeit hastily written, word.

GEORGE C. PIMENTEL
Professor of Chemistry
Member, Select Committee on Education

Higher Education in Our Time

Here in the Western United States we see in sharp focus an educational change that prevails across the country. Higher education is no longer the prerogative of a privileged few. The small, private colleges, with their highly select student bodies, no longer constitute the mainstream of higher education. *Everyman* is seeking more knowledge, more insight, more opportunity to develop his mind and intellectually enjoy his existence. Huge numbers of young folk demand more education. They can be dealt with only at large State Universities, like the University of California; they will not be satisfied with less than the best possible institutions. We suddenly realize that the large State Universities have moved to the fulcrum in our society's continuing effort to improve itself.

The State System of Higher Education

In that setting, the State of California can take justifiable pride in its magnificent and much copied State System of Higher Education. We find here a well-conceived pyramidal educational structure that provides its citizens with appropriate variety and ample capacity at all levels for their educational needs. The structure is laudable in all its parts, but we shall concentrate on the University of California, which is placed at the apex of the State System. Here the qualified California citizen can obtain education of the very highest calibre, both at the undergraduate and the graduate level—he can obtain his precious opportunity irrespective of calling, wealth, race, or any other artificial barrier.

Berkeley: One of the Jewels in the Crown

The excellence of the University of California is epitomized here at Berkeley. Over the past three decades, the Berkeley campus has emerged as one of the leading intellectual centers of the world. This hard-won and enviable position can be attributed to the progressive and cumulative effects of a variety of factors: enlightened and generous public support, the magnificent supporting structure of State and Junior Colleges, a favorable climate, an education-oriented urban environment and, most of all, a preeminent faculty and a select, highly motivated student body.

It is our task to guarantee that Berkeley retains its well-deserved reputation for excellence. This guarantee will not be realized if we merely bask in the glow of past victories—we must look to the pressing needs of the present and the changing needs of the future. Inevitably these changing needs will dictate and direct an evolution in our educational methods, perhaps even our aims. Improvements and innovations in curricula must constantly be sought and explored. We must not be reluctant to consider significant deviations from time-honored patterns. This must be a continuing search in which all of the University community partcipates. Our position of national leadership in education makes heavier our responsibility in this search.

Outlook for the Future

As we examine and reshape our activities, we must peer into the future and prepare for it. Demographic projections tell us that California's population will more than double in the next 35 years. At the same time we are intimidated by the products of our own genius, automation, cybernation, and our technological power. It is timely to ask if a complete reassessment of the educational goals of the campus is required in the light of the probable social impact of these changes. We can even ask who should be educated here at Berkeley and at what should their education aim.

The most obvious of the changes that we can foresee is that many citizens will have much more leisure time. One hears such expressions as, "We must educate for leisure." Is that "we" here at Berkeley? But we find an opposite change in certain quarters. The onset of technological change has given some citizens less leisure time! This group contains the political leaders, the business leaders, the technical specialists and the creative artists who serve society by keeping its frontiers alive. During the course of the twentieth century, we have seen the 60–70 hour working week transferred from the "working class" to the "leader-specialist" class. The 35 hour, leisure-rich week has already appeared for the "blue collar" worker because of automation. It will soon appear for the "white collar" worker because of cybernation. There is no sign, however, of it coming for the leaders of society. There will be an intensification of the demands made on this group—for increased initiative, energy, creativity, and dedication.

Berkeley's Future Role in Education

Our answer to the changing face of our society must, then, be influenced by the role we see for ourselves in serving society. To this writer, there seems no question that the University and, most particularly, Berkeley, must take as its primary mission to provide society with an ample supply of those who will lead society, those who will provide the new knowledge on which the society of the future will thrive, those who will take the lead in shaping our culture, and those who will enrich mankind through creative contribution in the arts.

The Optimum Berkeley Student

If we accept this as our role, we can picture the type of student that we would like to attract to the campus. As observed in the majority report, Berkeley's student population should be shaped by self-selection according to a "style," a style that is consistent with our aspirations. We must seek to attract those who are most intelligent, most creative, most highly motivated and most self-confident. These are the qualities that are needed for leadership in our society.

After listing so glibly these common desiderata, we must recognize that a wide spectrum of types and talents will be involved. A corresponding range of educational opportunities will be needed. A creative person in the arts may need an extremely free selection in the content of his study whereas a creative person in science may need the opportunity to concentrate much of his study in technical areas. We must avoid the temptation to design a curricular mold that is expected to be useful across the campus. We must avoid the temptation to judge one discipline by criteria more useful to another. But we must also avoid characterizations that segregate "achievement-orientation" and "morality." Our humanists must be achievement-oriented if they are to influence and guide our culture. We must observe, and without chagrin, that achievement-oriented individuals command leadership in all facets of society, be it government, science, the arts, or business. Our mission is to attract individuals who are creative, moral, *and* achievement-oriented, to prepare them for their roles of leadership, and to guarantee that their character development makes them worthy of their roles.

The Optimum Berkeley Education

With a vast spectrum of types of students and an array of future roles for them, what common requisites can be specified? Perhaps this wide-ranging question actually has an answer. Each of our students has two needs. He should leave Berkeley equipped to assume a valuable and personally fulfilling role in society and he should leave with an intellectual foundation that will guide him in his execution of this role. Speaking very crudely, we can say that *every* student's experience here should contain a strong element of vocational education and a strong element of liberal education. In our eagerness to assure the latter, we must not deprecate or undervalue the former.

These two elements, vocational and liberal education, are not and must not be mutually exclusive. The heavy demands of many professional curricula must not expel the fresh air provided by courses in the humanities. Neither should an education centered in the humanities leave the student at its end with neither a sense of purpose nor of direction. The latter point is of timely importance because we find many of our alienated students in the humanities searching for purpose and direction. Though they might deride the thought, they are in need of vocationalism. Both elements of the University education are needed, as much by them as by the engineer or the science student. Across the campus and across the disciplines, vocational and liberal education must be melded and made compatible.

Beyond this there is another specification we can make for Berkeley education. It should be directed at the best students—the ones most motivated to learn—the ones most creative—the ones most able to benefit from their educational opportunities. The State System is designed to avoid the possibility that in our zeal to educate all of our new citizens, we do not meet the special needs of the most capable individuals. The responsibility falls squarely upon the University to guarantee that somewhere in our educational system the exceptional student can receive an exceptionally fine education. We must be energetic in seeking out these select ones and bold in trying to satisfy their special needs. Here is, perhaps, where our most unique contribution can be made.

Where Are We Now?

The year 1966 finds the Berkeley campus at a turning point. Ever since its birth there has been growth—sometimes fast, sometimes slow, but always uncontrolled. The size of the student body, its distribution among the disciplines and its distribution as to level, lower division, upper division, and graduate—was fixed by the undirected influence of society, working in a *laissez faire* educational marketplace.

Now we shall enter a period in which the size of the student body will be static and its composition will be at our command. We will have to make decisions—this applicant can enter, that one must go elsewhere. We will have to decide whether this discipline will be stimulated (by favoring its student enrollment) and that one will be limited. These decisions will determine the face of the campus, the "style" of our students; we cannot, in good conscience, leave them entirely to the irrational whim of extra-University social forces.

We enter this new period with about one fifth of our students in the lower division, two fifths in the upper division, and two fifths in graduate study. These students are admitted from every walk of life. They include many brilliant and creative persons, but also many who have great difficulty here. One of our major concerns must be to redefine our admissions goals and to refine our admissions policies to reach them.

We also enter this period with a magnificent faculty. Its quality is impartially specified by the fact that the Berkeley campus in 1965 received 50% more Guggenheim fellowships than any other single University. There is hardly a discipline in which one cannot find preeminence. In fact, *if any single factor should dominate our educational evolution, it must be the desire to retain this faculty while directing its activities to maximum advantage to the students.*

Finally, we enter this period with rich curricular offerings spanning most of man's knowledge. The majority report stresses the need for variety and flexibility in a fashion that leaves the reader only faintly aware of the existing rich variety and flexibility. Probably few of our students and fewer still of the citizens of the State fully realize the range of opportunities available to them here—a range virtually unmatched at any other educational locale in the country. Complaints from some of our students that their education is excessively rigid and that they do not find what they wish within the catalogue can be evaluated only after examining the abundant choice offered to the Berkeley student. He can choose from among five Colleges and nine Professional Schools. Graduate activities are enriched by the presence of thirteen research institutes, most of them with strong interdisciplinary aspects. Within the College of Letters and Science, the student may opt any one of 43 organized Departmental Major Programs that span knowledge both literally and figuratively from A (Anthropology) to Z (Zoology). There are also Group Major Programs and Field Major Programs to provide interdisciplinary opportunities for the undergraduate who desires "interdepartmental programs" (Group Major Programs; see catalogue) or "whose intellectual interests are of broader scope than are provided for in the major programs" (Field Major Programs; see catalogue). Finally there is the privately tailored "Individual Major" Program, described in the catalogue as follows: "The College recognizes that there are a few superior students whose intellectual needs can be met better by an especially designed individual major program."

Within each one of these possible study avenues, the student has still further freedom he can exploit according to his interest. It is instructive to examine a few, typical student programs in terms of four categories of courses:

a. Required courses within the major
b. Required courses in major-related subjects
c. Electives restricted to non-major (breadth) courses
d. Absolutely free electives

These quantities are shown in Table I for an L and S English major, History major and Physics major, for a College of Chemistry major and, finally, for a College of Engineering Electrical Engineering major. We see that in the humanities, a student finds that one third of his program is unfettered by restrictive requirements. Taking into account that he selected his major to suit his own interest, these free electives indicate that roughly two thirds of his education is quite personalized. At the other extreme is the Engineering area in which there is virtually no freedom except limited choice among major-related technical courses. The physical and biological sciences fall between these extremes.

A superficial consideration of Table I would suggest that student discontent would center in the technical areas, with its maximum intensity in the rigid engineering major and with its minimum in the

TABLE I

The Structure of Some Typical Major Programs

	a. Units in Required Courses within the Major	b. Units in Required Courses in Major-Related Subjects	c. Units in Electives Restricted to Non-Major Breadth Courses	d. Units in Absolutely Free Electives
L and S English	20 + 18 elective (32%)	0 (0%)	42 (35%)	40 (33%)
L and S History	12 + 22 elective (28%)	0 (0%)	48 (40%)	38 (32%)
L and S Physics	35 (29%)	26 (22%)	39 (32%)	20 (17%)
College of Chemistry	46 (37%)	33 (27%)	29 (23%)	16 (13%)
College of Engineering Electrical Eng.	51 + 21 elective (58%)	38 (10%)	12 (30%)	2 (2%)

permissive humanities curricula. It is interesting and significant that the opposite is the case.

But What of Student Discontent?

To many of us who were here during the student demonstrations of 1964 and 1965, there was no surprise in the students' idealism nor in their readiness to conclude that they have at last invented morality while their elders are disciples of hypocrisy. Memories of our own undergraduate idealism are kept alive through constant contact with brilliant young students as they awaken to a questioning attitude, their expectations untarnished and their aspirations undamaged by the contradictory realities of existence. Surely one of our most rewarding tasks is to promote this questioning attitude and to strengthen these noble aspirations.

What did come as a surprise was the intensity and extent of student alienation to the University that could be developed. As the leaders of a battle over political activism sought to gain numerical strength, they were able to exploit a variety of essentially irrelevant reservoirs of student discontent. In the context of this report, it is political activism that is irrelevant and these reservoirs of student discontent that must be understood and to which we must respond. It does no good to remind the student that he selected Berkeley, presumably because he preferred it to other alternatives. If, in fact, a growing number of high-calibre students lose their motivation and dissipate their educational opportunities while here at Berkeley, we must seek constructive changes.

To the writer, the majority section entitled "The Drop-out and the Rebel" came as a penetrating analysis of this type of student. The statistics cited there amply document the fact that a sizeable fraction of these students are of such high quality that it would be an irreparable loss to society if their needs were ignored. The statistics also serve to help us locate those parts of the campus in which changes are most likely to be helpful and those other parts of the campus which provide effective and successful models. We can look with pride on the fact that in many disciplines large numbers of students are enjoying and benefitting to the full from their experiences here at Berkeley. While seeking improvements in some areas, we can perhaps borrow from these disciplines and, in any event, take care not to damage these successful areas with sweeping and revolutionary changes.

To conclude this section, it would be satisfying to enumerate and clarify the causes of current student discontent. Many contributions have been cited that might sum to a critical accumulation of difficulties: the size of the University is a favorite oversimplification, impersonality, too little student-faculty contact, too much paternalism, limitations of the lecture system, lack of relevance of studies to everyday life, absence of interdisciplinary relationships. Each of these may contribute; none was invented yesterday. What is new may well be brought to the scene by the student himself. That these are not of his making nor within our control does not reduce the importance of recognizing them and listing them with candor. These factors, in the writer's eyes, are two in number—many potentially excellent students arrive at Berkeley without personal motivation and they arrive without the traditional foundation upon which to build that motivation. The first difficulty is an appendage of our education-oriented society. Its desirable insistence on more education for its youth has altered the social climate in which a student enters the University. No longer does he regard it as a rare privilege to receive higher education. Since childhood the recurrent theme has not been "whether" he would go to college, but "where." Over twelve years of his early education, he has struggled for grades "so he can get into college." He arrives at the University and gradually realizes that he doesn't know why he is there.

Even more fundamental is the second difficulty, the absence of foundation for motivation. In the affluence of the last two generations, many of our students have never suffered want. The question isn't, "How will I be able to assure security for myself and my family?" but rather, "Why isn't the world a better place when security is so easily acquired?"

We must find ways to provide a fruitful educational experience for these students, as well as the many who continue to arrive with strong drive, clear direction, and ample motivation. Here is another significant challenge we face—the University must aid the student to find himself, to verify his reason for being here, and to choose the direction for his life.

Evolution at Berkeley

From generalities, we must proceed to particulars. In the majority report, these particulars appear in the form of over forty recommendations. Some of these are taken up below, and some new are added.

Graduate Education

The University has one unique function in the State System of Education: to provide excellent education at the doctoral level. Not only is this our special responsibility, it is the most difficult educational endeavor we attempt. How to stimulate individual creativity is an elusive prescription. There is only one specification that is readily made: creativity is best nurtured in a climate of creativity. This then puts the lie to the uninformed criticism of the University embodied in the glib words "publish or perish." This phrase, which connotes a feverish pressure for publications with the empty motivation of advancement, can only be uttered by an individual who has not lived among creative people. Truly creative individuals are creative because they cannot help themselves. They do not create new knowledge for tenure or for a salary raise. They may value recognition from other creative persons, but mostly they create for the sheer joy of discovery. They may enjoy winning the respect of their admired peers, but mostly they make their penetrating analyses and exhaustive studies for the self-satisfaction that comes with enlightenment. It is these qualities that foster creativity in the qualified graduate student. If the faculty possesses these qualities in rich abundance, the graduate enterprise is bound to be successful in some measure. Without them, the effort is foredoomed.

Criteria for Faculty Selection

Immediately we see why such great emphasis is placed upon creativity as a criterion for selection of our faculty. Even if potential creativity were used as the sole criterion for tenure, many members of a faculty would fail to some extent to live up to expectations. Originality is such a rare commodity and so essential to graduate education that we can little afford to give heavy weight to alternate criteria for selection. This last remark seems heretical when it comes from an educator and it warrants further explanation. Concerning public service, there is no reason to be alarmed that Berkeley's service to the public might wither if it is lightly treated among advancement criteria. Our faculty is so heavily engaged in public service that they are unjustly criticized for absenteeism from the campus. Concerning teaching, our greatest challenge is to transfer to a new generation the qualities of creativity and originality. This proves to be a highly personal matter not at all readily measured, particularly by forensic skill or personality. In fact, I believe that the only generalization that can be made is that *a potentially creative graduate student should have frequent and intimate contact with a creative faculty member*—they will find their own way to communicate. Ultimately the most important lessons may be learned through example, and without articulation.

It follows that traditional measures of "teaching ability such as course outlines, forensic style, student popularity, etc. may be quite irrelevant at the graduate level where we find our unique educational role. Thus the Select Committee's Recommendation No. 1 is badly aimed. Our criteria should honestly put first things first. Recommendation No. 1 should be replaced by A-1.

Recommendation A-1

That the Instructions to Appointment and Promotion Committees be amended to clarify the fact that no candidate should be considered for promotion to tenure rank unless his research creativity guarantees that his presence on the faculty will contribute significantly to graduate education. When this guarantee is reasonably assured, other criteria, teaching and public service must be weighed as well.

Duration of Graduate Study

We turn now to the present quality of our graduate education. Here the majority report identifies great variation, both in the nature of the graduate experience and its duration. This is corroborated in Table II for several departments. The next to last column lists the number of Ph.D. students enrolled in 1963–64 divided by the number of Ph.D. degrees granted during that academic year. The great variation indicates that the average time of study for the Ph.D. must differ by a factor of two among the eight departments examined. Accepting the last column at face value, this average ranges from four to eight years. Many students in the humanities must receive the Ph.D. as they near the age of 30. It is no consolation if some of this period was spent in part-time or in interrupted study in order to replenish depleted financial resources. The Ph.D. period is thus only fragmented and excessively prolonged.

It is essential that each discipline introspectively reconsider its Ph.D. requirements, particularly those whose graduate students require more than six years to receive the Ph.D., *as urged in the Committee's Recommendation 34.* Here, perhaps, is an opportunity for gain through inspection of contrasts among the disciplines. It is readily discovered that prolonged graduate study tends to be a characteristic of disciplines in the humanities and that, generally, the sciences are able to meet their educational objectives in a shorter span of time. That graduate education is highly successful in the sciences can hardly be questioned. Berkeley graduates in the sciences command the same high respect throughout the country as our graduates in the humanities. What differences are there between graduate studies in the sciences and the humanities?

Disciplinary Contrasts

One undoubted factor that works to the advantage of the scientific areas is the availability of generous financial support for qualified students. It would be unwise, however, to place all the explanation there in order to set aside this worrisome problem. Indeed there are other factors that must be called to the fore and dealt with squarely. *The majority Recommendations 32 and 37 work in this direction and deserve the faculty's close attention.*

There is, however, one aspect of graduate study not considered in the majority report, the nature of the Ph.D. dissertation. In this central requirement, there is a striking contrast between the sciences and the humanities. Graduate study in the sciences is most often essentially a collaborative investigation at the frontiers of knowledge in which the graduate student and a professor pool their ingenuity, insight and enthusiasm. This is tangibly displayed at the end by coauthored publication of parts of the thesis. Such coauthorship is notably absent in the humanities. In the humanities, the thesis is often written by the graduate student in a one or two year period *after he has departed from the campus.* While thesis guidance is available to the student whenever he solicits it, faculty-student contact is sporadic and the professor's role is distinctly that of an external advisor. This absence of close collaboration defines a philosophically different attitude toward the thesis.

It is one thing to notice this difference and another to decide which, if either, route is preferable. From one point of view, the classical view of the Ph.D. thesis is that it must be completely independent, creative work. The extent to which the research supervisor deserves coauthorship of thesis-related publication is taken by some to be a measure of the invasion of the thesis integrity. From another point of view, the collaborative aspects of thesis study can be regarded as the richest part of graduate study. This collaboration brings the student into continuous contact with the research supervisor. The student has the opportunity to obtain an intimate view of the research director's creative talent at work. He becomes a partner in a research study whose significance is likely to be proportional to the professional standing of the research director, since this research forms the base of the faculty member's reputation. Thus the student feels that the profession awaits his work. He is likely to be given the opportunity to present his work at meetings of learned societies, with the double burden of representing himself and the prestigious heritage of his research director. The student immediately feels the full advantage of the preeminence of his research director and the department; he is pushed forward into the thick of current intellectual melees in the speciality the student has chosen.

Whatever the debate about these two representations concerning collaborative research, it is clear that many of the problems associated with graduate study in the humanities, prolonged duration, isolation, impersonalization, and alienation are ameliorated or totally eliminated through collaborative thesis study. It is an inevitable result of the thesis

TABLE II
Ph.D. Students and Ph.D. Degrees Conferred in 1963-1964

Major Field	Number of Ph.D. Students	Number of Ph.D. Degrees Granted	No. Students / No. Degrees	Estimated Average No. Years to Ph.D.
Electrical Engineering	135	22	6.1	(4)*
Chemistry	273	44	6.2	3.8
Anthropology	89	12	7.4	(5)
Physics	357	48	7.5	5.2
History	212	26	8.2	(5.5)
Mathematics	238	26	9.2	(6)
Political Science	142	12	11.8	(8)
English	182	15	12.1	(8)

*Parenthetical entries are estimated, assuming the same relationship between the fourth and fifth columns as for Chemistry and Physics, for which actual data were available.

pattern found in the sciences that the graduate-conducted research influences the flow of the director's own research. This identifies research director and student interest and directly affects the student's graduate education in the following crucial ways.

Student Status: The student enjoys the full status of a research collaborator. The student's fresh point of view and his intimate "fingertip" knowledge of his problem meld with the professor's accumulated experience, insight, and wisdom. The student-faculty relationship is that of two-way learning.

Identity: The student has the direct attention of a regular faculty member. At the same time, he becomes an integral part of a comfortably small peer group, the research professor's group of graduate students. These students generally meet regularly in "group seminars" to discuss research progress and to hear expository presentations of the latest research work closely touching their thesis problems. Within this small assembly, each individual moves in time from novitiate to a position of intellectual seniority; each individual learns from the others and, in turn, contributes to their learning. There is no problem of loss of identity under these circumstances.

Time of Graduate Study: In collaborative research study, the research professor is conscious at every moment of the student's progress (or lack thereof) toward the degree. It is a matter of active concern to him if a student's progress is blocked for an extended period, whether by technical detail or a psychological barrier, such as self-doubt, flagging motivation, or depleted enthusiasm. Every influence of the collaborative aspect is to sustain the graduate student's enthusiasm in his work and to encourage the completion of the study in a reasonable period. Thus the time spent on the thesis tends to be shortened without any arbitrary time limit impositions.

Advising: In addition to his regular faculty adviser, the student benefits from the highly personalized advice of his research professor. In week-to-week discussions of research problems, the faculty member becomes sharply conscious of the student's strengths and weaknesses—his most urgent educational needs. This intimate knowledge influences not only the formal course and seminar activity urged toward the student, but also it usually affects the thesis content. The thesis study can be guided to optimum balance between development of the student's talents of excellence and encouragement to add to his strength in areas of relative weakness. Of greatest importance is the fact that the close communication protects the student from an extended dissipation of his graduate study on a trivial aspect of a problem or one with negligible promise for success.

Having noted these rather obvious and undeniable advantages, we turn to the question of whether these could be realized in the humanities. Is creative work in these areas so personalized that collaborative activity is not only undesirable, but even self-defeating? Sometimes this may be so: to take an extreme example (and one not suited to thesis content), it is difficult to contemplate coauthorship of a poem. It is not difficult, however, to conceive a mutually profitable and highly educational collaborative study of, say, the influence of the industrial revolution on the literature of the latter part of the 19th Century. It is idle to assume that such a collaboration would necessarily stifle the student's creativity, or, conversely, that the professor's contribution could not be sufficient to warrant credit without defeating the intent of the thesis requirements. In practice, the professor, as an educator, insists that the study must offer ample avenue to creative development. Problems of credit and recognition are surprisingly rare; when the professor's contribution proves to be small, he unhesitatingly withdraws his name from the title page. Generally, collaborative research is a richly rewarding and mutually satisfying blending of complementary talents.

Undoubtedly the value of this type of thesis study in the humanities can be learned only through deliberate and voluntary experimentation. Its success will surely vary from individual to individual. Those who are able to decide in advance that a process they have not tried cannot succeed might as well participate vicariously by watching the results of their more venturesome colleagues' experience.

Recommendation A-2

Interested faculty in the humanities and the social sciences should be encouraged to direct a measured number of graduate students to-

ward collaborative thesis problems with the preconceived and clearly understood expectation that faculty-student coauthored publication (which would be an integral part of the Ph.D. thesis) would result.

Undergraduate Education

The Optimum Use of Our Faculty

Our research orientation attracts to this campus one of the most outstanding faculties in the entire world. How can their reservoir of knowledge be made available to the undergraduate? How can their participation in undergraduate instruction best be balanced relative to their research activities in graduate instruction? These are difficult questions and their answers are not entirely a matter of free choice. If a department aspires to recruit to its faculty the world's foremost authority on field theory, it may or may not be able to insist that he teach an introductory course in Physics for Non-scientists. It certainly will not be able to insist that he have a resonant lecturing voice and a captivating way with students. What it can expect is that when he is speaking about field theory, the lecture room will be well-filled and the attention will be intense no matter what the timbre of his voice. There is our clue to the optimum use of our faculty. We should try to assure that each faculty member's instructional activities center on his area of special competence. When he teaches in this area, his enthusiasm, his insight, even the anatomy of his thinking are made available to the student.

Lectures: Much Maligned and Too Little Valued

We would have no difficulty accomplishing this if there were only a few students for each professor. It seems, however, that when an Oppenheimer or a Tolman lectures, dozens, or even hundreds of listeners appear. Should ninety be excluded and only ten admitted to "personalize" the education of the lucky ten? This involves difficult choices and loss to many in order to benefit the few. No, we cannot abandon the others, even if a special opportunity is arranged for a carefully chosen ten. Then we must ask if the value of exposure to this great man's knowledge is destroyed for an individual student if ninety-nine others enjoy it simultaneously? Again the answer is no. If that student brings to the lecture an attentive, receptive mind and a strong interest, he will be alone anyway with the Oppenheimer or the Tolman. He will still leave with new insight that would not have been evoked in a hundred dialogues with lesser men. At his leisure and in company with his peers, the student can contemplate these new ideas, he can plumb the depths of his own, and then reshape them with the profundity we would have be our hallmark.

Indeed, we are caught in this situation. We have an outstanding faculty—inevitably they will attract large numbers of qualified students. *It is implied that the lecture course must consciously remain the basic building block as we remold our curricula.* It is, with our faculty, a building block that needs no apology. It is the medium by which we can exploit the special insight so uniquely abundant here. Hence the majority recommendation 3 is both unrealistic and unsound: "It should be the policy . . . [to decrease] the proportion of lecture courses in favor of discussion sections, small classes, seminars, tutorials, preceptorials. . . . ." Instead, we should measure our faculty resources carefully and devote what effort we can to small sections with the deliberate and overt intention of improving the student's receptiveness to lectures. We must not deprecate, in his eyes, the large lecture, but rather, assure that he appreciates the opportunity they offer. Even independent study should not be pictured as a mechanism to evade hearing faculty members discussing their specialties. Students should be encouraged to engage in individual study to the extent their self-discipline warrants *in addition* to partaking of the opportunities they will leave behind when they graduate. *Lectures represent the means we have for extending the special knowledge of the Berkeley faculty to all of our students.*

With this premise, the problem is clear, but the solution is not. We must get the research-oriented faculty authority in front of the undergraduate, he must be talking about his specialty, and the experience must be intellectually rewarding to a large number of students drawn from a variety of disciplines. No small order.

One possible answer is to engage two or three faculty members in a single lecture course, these individuals being selected so that the lecture material is readily divided according to their special competences. Each participant would be obligated to mesh his material with that presented earlier by his compatriots but otherwise he would have complete control of his own lecture content. Thus his participation would be concentrated where he would give the most stimulating presentation, in the area of his greatest interest and knowledge. The value to the student is obvious. If, at the same time, teaching credit were held at the same level as if he gave all of the lectures, this lower-division course would become a choice assignment. Thus, at a stroke we would improve the lectures, increase interest to the student, and attract the most able researchers to the lower-division courses.

Recommendation A-3

That large lower-division lecture courses engage two or three faculty members each with partial lecture responsibility but with full

teaching credit so as to attract the tenure staff and to inject authoritative insight into the lower-division courses.

Involvement of the Faculty

The majority report describes well the primary ingredient of good teaching. It is an ethos that exists now in many departments and which we want to be campus-wide. Such an ethos cannot be legislated. Worse yet, it cannot be coerced. Hence I have qualms about the Committee's recommendation 7 which imposes compulsory student evaluations even upon the unwilling instructor. Some faculty members are actually made uncomfortable in their own classroom by unkind and uncritical complaints. In a normal psychological reaction, fifty glowing responses are needed to neutralize one vituperative insult from a disgruntled student hiding in his anonymity. To the extent that the instructor feels that student critiques raise a wall between him and his students, his teaching is impaired.

Recommendation 7 should be made optional by adding the italicized expression: "of all undergraduate courses *whose instructors consent* in the winter quarter, 1967, . . ."

There is one compelling leverage which we have at our disposal to improve teaching and it should be used. If we wish to engage more tenure staff in lower-division instruction, we need only make it a mechanism for gaining research time. An example has been given and is embodied in Recommendation A-3. In general, lower-division courses and innovative undergraduate courses should be counted more heavily in assessing teaching load. Perhaps teaching a two-quarter large lecture course (or an innovative experiment) should automatically command a quarter without any formal teaching load. Outstanding contribution to lower-division instruction could even be rewarded through acceleration of sabbatical leave privileges. I believe that improvement in teaching is needed, but that it can be obtained through positive encouragement much more effectively than by surreptitious "visitations," dossiers, collections of course outlines, or threats of delayed advancement. Such proposals misjudge the creative person's mind. There is nothing quite so alien to creativity as coercion. It suggests and would lead to only one result—departure to a locale more characterized by trust and respect.

Recommendation A-4

That each department reweight its computation of teaching loads to ensure that undergraduate (particularly lower division) instruction is weighted so as to constitute a reduced teaching load.

Special Opportunity for Exceptional Students

If our "style" is to attract, as suggested earlier in this Addendum, the most intelligent, creative, motivated, and self-confident students, then we must give these select individuals special opportunities appropriate to their intellectual potentialities and to their educational maturity. Generally speaking, there are three primary goals we should set for ourselves:

1. To direct the outstanding student toward more advanced literature, including research literature. As early as possible, we should break the artificial bounds of the homework assignment and the assigned textbook. Reading in the advanced literature will whet his appetite to learn.

2. To direct the outstanding student into individual study, *with time to contemplate* what he is learning. Thus, we shall attempt to break into the "routine" of the modern university in which keeping up with homework and passing the exams seem to be the goals. We want these students to read widely and to think deeply about the problems that interest and challenge them.

3. To bring these students into tutorial contact with outstanding faculty.

Generally speaking, these special opportunities are more demanding on resources and, in particular, on faculty time than more conventional instruction. Hence we will have to make choices and exert preferences. The guiding principle of the Honors Program is, to this writer, the optimum. Privilege and opportunity should be directed to those students who indicate by their performance and initiative that they will most benefit. The selection of these students need not be based upon grades alone—indeed, subjective faculty evaluations ought to be weighted heavily when available. But the final distribution of special opportunity should be frankly competititive, a doctrine not clearly evident in the majority report. If the special opportunity is to be directed toward the most able student, criteria must be applied to decide who are the most able students, criteria which may differ from discipline to discipline. After selection, the student's performance should be periodically examined to validate his right to occupy, hence deny to another student, the position of special opportunity.

Recommendation A-5

There should be increased attention paid to the special needs of exceptionally able undergraduate students; new dimensions should be

added to our honors program, both in the criteria by which students are admitted and in the opportunities made available to them. Even with new criteria, possibly differing from discipline to discipline, admission should be frankly competitive and should be periodically validated through appropriate measures of performance.

Some specific possible additions to our present honors programs are as follows:

a. within courses, release for the exceptional student from regular homework assignments, tests and papers with the privilege and obligation of substituting course-relevant material according to his own interest;

b. assignment to the exceptional student of responsibility for instruction such as leading section discussions and presenting lecture-style reports;

c. extension of special library or laboratory privileges;

d. earlier involvement of such able students in individual, but faculty-guided study, with a measured and sensibly limited fraction of his activity so directed;

e. increased use of fourth quarter individual study programs for small numbers of exceptional students, these programs to carry no unit credit or grades, to be accompanied by scholarship stipends, to include close faculty contact, and to be counted in faculty teaching load.

Student Involvement in Teaching

Learning is at once an exciting and challenging process. Few students realize that one of the greatest appeals of academic life to the faculty is the opportunity to continue their own learning. Most of this continued education comes implicitly in the attempt to convey knowledge to another person, particularly if that other person is a bright, critical student to whom old ideas are new and, hence, readily questioned.

Thus one of the most rewarding educational experiences we can offer on campus is the opportunity to teach. It benefits the student-teacher but also the whole educational climate for it encourages every student to question more openly. He is much more likely to expose a lack of understanding or to challenge a dictum when addressing a fellow student. Gradually he loses reluctance to do either and opens the way to his own education. When the undergraduate begins to see learning and teaching as reciprocal and mutually supportive activities, he begins to benefit most fully from his opportunity here at Berkeley.

There are a variety of avenues by which talented undergraduates can become involved in teaching. Some have been mentioned in the previous section. Funds to supplement teaching assistant funds should be sought to permit reimbursement of undergraduate readers and laboratory assistants.

Recommendation A-6

Means should be sought to engage talented undergraduates in teaching within the regular educational structure of the University, both in classes they are taking and in courses they have completed.

University Permissiveness:
Not a Substitute for Student Motivation

This section, more than any other in this Addendum, constitutes a real dissenting opinion to a significant theme of the majority report. There are a number of recommendations made and with supporting discussion that constitute, in the eyes of the writer, an attempt to meet the problems of some of our non-conformist students with permissiveness. For example, the recommendations include:

a. "Advisers should be authorized to permit students at *any stage of their experience* to undertake supervised independent study involving *any proportion of their time.* (Rec. 2) (italics added)

b. ". . . advising . . . should be largely voluntary . . ." (Rec. 13)

c. ". . . with the consent of the student's major department [Pass-Fail] courses . . . [can even] . . . satisfy requirements of the major . . ." (Rec. 14) (Notice that this wording constitutes an implicit suggestion in a negatively worded recommendation.)

d. ". . . the administration should arrange for *Ad Hoc* courses . . ." (Rec. 22)

e. ". . . schools, colleges, and departments should be given wider latitude in accrediting field study . . ." (Rec. 25)

f. "Departments should have wide latitude in determining requirements for foreign language and other skills, and should . . . [relate] . . . the requirements flexibly to the actual studies being conducted by the individual student." (Rec. 33)

Individually, each of these proposals has merit. In fact, the writer would subscribe to most of them if their proposal were securely connected to the principle that these are privileges earned by the student through demonstrated motivation and regularly validated through performance criteria. There is, however, the disquieting thought that in some cases, the permissive removal of conventional evaluation and regulating procedures is offered as an answer to the alienated and unmotivated student's lack of direction and his unwillingness to perform (which *he* might vocalize "conform"). These measures may well encourage unmotivated students to remain unmotivated. There is little doubt that much of the student criticism of grading and curricular rigidity comes from a minority group that enters the discussion in a mood of alienation to the University (indeed, to our whole society). It is significant that these students tend to center in the humanities (see majority report, pp. 18, 24), *the disciplines that are already the most permissive* and least restrictive in their curricular requirements (see Addendum, Table I). It seems unlikely that the needs of an alienated and intellectually unmotivated student are well met in the diffuse world of independent study, field work, and emotion-charged *Ad Hoc* courses, all loosened by removal of grades as validating devices. Independent study requires both a self-discipline and an introspective self-evaluation that are notably absent in many of these students. I believe that the faculty cannot abdicate its responsibilities to decide course and curricular content (*Ad Hoc* courses, unlimited independent study), to monitor closely the scholarly level of its offerings (wide latitude ... in field study) and to validate regularly, on the basis of intellectually significant performance criteria, the student's right to occupy a position at the University.

Grading

The Committee has distributed two discussions on grading. One analysis consists of a detailed and merciless indictment of grades and the conclusion that they should be eliminated or reduced to Pass-Fail. The other analysis concludes that grades should be retained but refined by the addition of narrower grade increments. Each of these documents is sufficiently polarized in its premises that neither alone nor even the two together readily serve to place the issue in perspective. Only the complexity of the question is revealed in the thoughtful, but poles-apart changes proposed in these two reports.

There are three valid educational functions of a grading system.

a. To aid the student assess his own abilities and performance relative to those of his peers, thus to evaluate himself as he sets his life goals and career aspirations;

b. to provide a substantial evaluative record that can be used to aid the student gain admittance to graduate school, to aid him to transfer, if he wishes, to another educational institution, and to provide him with credentials as he seeks employment;

c. to validate the student's readiness to proceed to more advanced work, his right to the special opportunities afforded to honors students, and his right to retain a position in the University.

Each of these is an essential function. It would not be fair to our students to propose changes in our grading patterns that do not include a satisfactory substitute for each.

What are the disadvantages of grades? There is only one objection of substance—grades can become to the student the end and all of his education, substituting for the desire to know and the desire to strengthen his areas of weakness. That grading is fallible is a vacuous complaint; no exercise of judgment is infallible, but judgments must still be made. That letter grades should be supplanted by prose letters is another rather imperceptive suggestion. Any faculty member who has served on a scholarship committee and, hence, has attempted to psycho-analyze hundreds of letters of recommendation knows their weakness. He would know that their principal value lies in whatever quantitative and comparative data they contain ("he was 10th in a class of 37"; "he is about as bright as the best of the three students we sent you last year"). Proposals that grading should be less frequent do not remove grades as a false goal but they increase the decisiveness of any erroneous judgments that might be made.

The majority report contains three recommendations (No. 14, 15, and 16) that propose expansion of Pass-Fail usage. It is not clear that these recommendations, if implemented, will substantially affect the attitude of the students toward grades. Our students arrive at the University already indoctrinated in their attitudes. Whatever evaluation scheme we use to achieve the three inescapable functions that grades serve, we will have to reorient the student through subtle and persistent persuasion. Our own devotion to knowledge for its own sake must be prominently displayed. Our uses of grade point averages as validation criteria must be sufficiently flexible to accommodate good sense and fairness. Our interpretations of grades should be sensitive to trends and significant patterns and not merely to the over-all average. Ultimately the student will feel he has been dealt with fairly if he *is* dealt with fairly. He will become devoted to learning for the pure joy of learning if we who know that joy frequently share it with him.

Facilitating Innovation

The majority report amply justifies the desirability of establishing on this campus formal machinery to facilitate and encourage innovation. I subscribe wholeheartedly to this concept and join with the majority in the qualitative aspects of its proposal.

Structural Aspects of the Board of Educational Development

There are, however, severe doubts that the Committee has proposed the optimum structure. As pictured in Recommendations 19, 20, and 21, the Board of Educational Development has an awesome aspect that defies comparison with any existing unit within the entire University. First, it has the prestige and implied power of a Vice-Chancellor as its administrative head. This, presumably, defines a unit with somewhat closer administrative relation to the principal campus officer, the Chancellor, than is now possessed by any College. The administrative head is placed at a level equal to an existing office, the Vice-Chancellor for Academic Affairs, whose jurisdiction would seem to encompass educational innovation. The Board has the preconceived mission of soliciting from external sources most of the funds which will ultimately define its scope and impact upon the campus. Unlike the Organized Research Units that also depend for their existence upon the availablity of external funding, there is no specific provision for periodic review. Nor is there opportunity for faculty influence in the interests of educational impact, to limit or control the extent of its activities. It has powers to set up courses subject to no control whatsoever by our conventional means of validating the educational merit of a proposed new course. The Board can establish courses that no College is willing to house and which the Committee on Courses has not even viewed. Faculty salaries can be provided outside of any department for educational experiments that might have five year duration, posing difficult questions of faculty advancement in rank and to the tenure level. To complete this rather strange organism, the Board even has access to degree-granting authority through its membership on the Council.

We have here a University within a University—its own Vice-Chancellor—its own (and probably lucrative) fund sources—its own courses subject to no prior review—its own faculty insofar as it chooses to establish curricula that are incompatible with existing Colleges—even its own degrees, through the Council. We may well find it difficult to live with our own creation.

Relatively minor restructuring will suffice to meliorate these disadvantageous facets and to set the new unit in more constructive relationship to existing administrative and divisional apparatus. Adequate administrative prestige and leadership would be provided by an Assistant-Chancellor, placed in the office of and under the Vice-Chancellor for Academic Affairs. The Board should automatically include representation from both the Committee on Educational Policy and the Committee on Courses. Ultimately all successful experimental innovation ought to be woven into our regular curricula and this will be facilitated by making these two important committees party to the considerations which led to experimentation and, then, to evaluation. Finally, a complementary relationship between the Board of Educational Development and the Committee on Educational Policy should be clearly defined in which the Board seeks to improve education through innovation in reasonable harmony with the long range campus educational policy established by the Committee on Educational Policy.

To achieve these gains, the following recommendations are offered as substitute proposals [bold face type indicates additions] for the majority recommendations 19, 20, and 21 [italic type indicates deletions].

An Alternate Structure of the Board of Educational Development
Recommendation A-7

We formally propose the following addition to the By-Laws of the Academic Senate:

Board of Educational Development. This board consists of **eight members,** [*six members*] **six appointed by the Committee on Committees** to serve three-year staggered terms, **one member elected by the Committee on Educational Policy from its own membership, one member elected by the Committee on Courses from its own membership,** and the campus-wide administrative officer most responsible for educational development, all voting. Its duties are:

1. To stimulate and promote educational experimentation and innovation in all sectors of the Berkeley campus **while being sensitive to long range educational policy framework recommended by the Committee on Educational Policy;** to sponsor, conduct, and direct, with use of an Office of Educational Development and in liaison with the Committee on Educational Policy, continuing studies of the needs and opportunities for educational development; and to maintain liaison with the Committee on Courses of Instruction, Committee on Educational Policy, Graduate Council, and executive committees of the Colleges and Schools on matters of educational effectiveness, innovation, and for the initiation of experimental courses, programs, and curricula.

2. To receive, encourage and authorize experimental instructional proposals for which neither departmental nor college support is appropriate or feasible; to initiate and administer such experimental instructional programs pending their adoption by a department or other recognized faculty group, for a period not to exceed five years, subject to policies prescribed by **the Committee on Educational Policy;** [*the Division*] and to provide all possible accessory services for experimental programs initiated within departments, Schools, and Colleges.

3. To initiate and sponsor the securing of extra-mural funds for the support of experimental courses and curricula, and to administer such funds for this purpose as may be allocated to the board or to the Office of Educational Development.

Recommendation A-8

Assistant Chancellor [*Vice-Chancellor*] for Educational Development. It is recommended that an **Assistant Chancellor** for Educational Development be appointed **in the office of and under the Vice-Chancellor for Academic Affairs.** He shall become an *ex officio* voting member of the Board of Educational Development. [*Under the policy guidance of the Board of Educational Development.*] He shall:

1. Administer the policies and programs of the Board of Educational Development.

2. Consult with all appropriate members of the academic community concerning deficiencies in or possible development of existing offerings, and encourage new offerings where they are considered necessary.

[*3. Consult with Deans and Departmental Chairmen concerning desirable recruitments and promotions conducive to campus educational development.*]

3. Provide general administrative and incidental assistance to studies and experimental programs.

4. Secure funds for these purposes from private, foundation, University, and government sources.

Recommendation A-9

We propose the following addition to the By-Laws of the Academic Senate:

Council for Special Curricula. This council comprises the eight faculty members of the Board of Educational Development and the **members of the** Committee on Educational Policy, with the Registrar as its secretary. It is authorized to serve as a sponsor for the Bachelor of Arts and Bachelor of Science degrees, substituting in this capacity for a College or School, in the manner specified below. Where the council finds an experimental program of courses acceptable in intellectual content and quality as part or all of a four-year curriculum, but no College or School is ready to accept it, the council may take the following action to support the program.

a. The council shall insure the acceptability of credit toward a degree to students in the experimental program, subject to successful completion of the program and of other requirements established by the council in general conformity with the practice of the most relevant College or School. For administrative purposes the student shall enroll in that relevant unit. In any one calendar year the number of students whose programs the council may insure shall not exceed five per cent of the graduating class of the preceding year. The decision to insure a program shall require a favorable vote of at least three-quarters of the members.

b. When a student in an insured program has completed all such degree requirements within an eight year period after starting the program, his degree shall be recommended by the council, provided that he does not qualify instead for a degree in the relevant College or School.

c. The council shall inform the Berkeley Division of all experimental programs for which it has insured the granting of degrees, as soon as it has given this insurance.

[2. *Where the Berkeley Division has approved a specific program and has delegated the guidance of it to this council, students completing the program shall be recommended for their degrees by the council.*]

Recommendation A-10

That in the sixth year of the Board of Educational Development's operation, the Committee on Committees shall appoint an ad hoc committee to examine the extent and effectiveness of the Board's activities to recommend changes in its structure if needed, and to report to the Division during that year.

XIII.

APPENDICES

A. Tentatively Projected Enrollment, 1965–1975[1]

	BERKELEY		TOTAL UNIVERSITY	
	Average Enrollment	% of Total	Average Enrollment	% of Total
1965-66 Total (incl. est. Spring)	27,075		79,665	
Lower Division	6,025	22.3	26,025	32.7
Upper Division	10,650	39.3	27,225	34.2
Masters, Professional,				
1st Doctoral[2]	6,250	23.1	14,345	18.0
2nd Doctoral[3]	4,150	15.3	7,685	9.6
Medical & Health Sciences	....	......	(4,385)	(5.5)
1970-71 Total (incl. est. Spring)	27,500		109,145	
Lower Division	6,000	21.8	31,095	28.5
Upper Division	9,000	32.7	38,420	35.2
Masters, Professional,				
1st Doctoral	7,500	27.3	27,525	25.2
2nd Doctoral	5,000	18.2	12,105	11.1
Medical & Health Sciences	....	......	(6,608)	......
1975-76 Total (incl. est. Spring)	27,500		130,541	
Lower Division	5,500	20.0	31,190	24.0
Upper Division	8,400	30.6	46,247	35.4
Masters, Professional,				
1st Doctoral	8,200	29.8	36,339	27.8
2nd Doctoral	5,400	19.6	16,765	12.8
Medical & Health Sciences	....	......	(8,913)	......

[1] Data from Office of Analytical Studies. These figures represent tentative estimates. Only total enrollment figures for each year have been adopted officially by the University. Their official adoption, however, by no means precludes future adjustments.
[2] First-stage doctoral students have neither 24 units, nor Master's, nor advancement to candidacy.
[3] Second-stage doctoral students have either 24 units, or Master's degree, or candidacy.

B. BERKELEY ENROLLMENT FIGURES, FALL 1965[1]

	Total	Men	Women
Freshmen	3,307		
Sophomores	3,349		
Special Status	2		
Total Lower Division	6,658		
Juniors	5,311		
Seniors	4,581		
Special Status	60		
Total Upper Division	9,952		
Total Undergraduate	16,610	9,837	6,773
Professional	1,904		
Masters	3,506		
1st Doctoral	827		
2nd Doctoral	3,987		
Total Graduate	10,224	7,569	2,655
Total Students	26,834	17,406	9,428

C. UNDERGRADUATE STUDENTS BY SCHOOL OR COLLEGE AND MAJOR, FALL 1965

Agriculture
Agricultural Business
   Management 11
Agricultural Economics . 111
Agricultural Science ... 6
Agronomy 1
Dietetics 38
Dietetics and Nutrition 1
Entomology 3
Entomology and
   Parasitology 10
Food Science 9
Genetics 6
Nutrition 17
Plant Pathology 4
Poultry Husbandry 1
Preforestry 24
Preveterinary Medicine . 5
Soil and Plant Nutrition 2
Soil Science 4
Unclassified 15
   Total 268

Business Administration . 612
Chemistry 438
Criminology 121
Engineering
   Biological 1
   Ceramic 7
   Civil 222
   Electrical 434
   Engineering Geoscience 1
   Engineering Mathe-
     matical Statistics 2
   Engineering
     Mathematics 17
   Engineering Physics ... 66
   Geological 4
   Industrial 49
   Mechanical 270
   Metallurgical 13
   Mining 1
   Petroleum 8
   Unclassified 533
   Total 1628

[1] Data from office of the University Dean of Educational Relations, *Statistical Summary: Fall Term 1965*.

Environmental Design
Architecture 601
Landscape Architecture 48
Unclassified 317
    Total   966
Forestry   81
Letters and Science
American Culture 1
American Studies:
Colonial to the Civil
War 1
Anatomy 1
Anthropology 289
Art 194
Astronomy 24
Bacteriology 68
Biochemistry 98
Biological Sciences
Field Major 191
Biophysics 4
Botany 19
Chemistry 80
Classics 10
Communications and
Public Policy 53
Comparative Literature 55
Computer Science 3
Design 63
Dramatic Art 51
Economics 281
English 734
French 185
Genetics 13
Geography 52
Geology 22
Geophysics 6
German 80
Greek 9
History 754
Humanities Field Major 79
Italian 22
Journalism 24
Journalistic Studies . . . 16
Latin 7
Latin American Studies. 4
Linguistics 44
Mathematics 252
Mathematics for
Teachers 19

Molecular Biology 1
Music 63
Music Education 1
Near Eastern Languages 11
Oriental Languages . . . 20
Paleontology 10
Philosophy 119
Physical Education 26
Physical Sciences
Field Major 9
Physics–Chemical
Biology 1
Physics 233
Physics and Biology. . . . 10
Physiology 45
Political Science 747
Political Theory and
Ethics 1
Problems of Developing
Nations 1
Psycho-Biological
Science 1
Psychology 475
Religion 1
Scandinavian Languages
and Literature 3
Slavic Languages
and Literature 42
Social Problems 1
Social Sciences Field
Major 298
Social Welfare 112
Sociology 255
Spanish 111
Speech 75
Statistics 16
Structural Perspectives. 1
Totalitarianism in
International Affairs . 1
Urban Studies 1
Zoology 292
Unclassified 5536
    Sub-total 12,327
    Double Majors 57

    Total 12,384
Optometry 86
Public Health 26
    TOTAL 16,610

D. GRADUATE STUDENTS BY MAJOR, FALL 1965

Agricultural Chemistry 9
Agricultural Economics 57
Anatomy 16
Animal Physiology 3
Anthropology 147
Applied Mathematics 21
Architecture 30
Art 70
Asian Studies 37
Astronomy 42
Atmospheric and Space Science 4
Bacteriology 34
Biochemistry 76
Biophysics 76
Bioradiology 7
Biostatistics 20
Botany 66
Business Administration 438
Chemistry 287
Child Development 7
City and Regional Planning.. 64
Classical Archeology 6
Classics 29
Comparative Biochemistry ... 15
Comparative Literature 115
Comparative Pathology 1
Criminology 95
Demography 11
Design 10
Dramatic Art 52
Economics 307
Education 1,224
Endocrinology 3
Engineering
  Chemical 109
  Civil 301
  Electrical 378
  Hydraulic 1
  Industrial 114
  Mechanical 237
  Metallurgical 11
  Mineral Technology 117
  Naval Architecture 25
  Nuclear 86
  Petroleum 1
  Sanitary 2
English 496
Entomology 77

Environmental Health Sciences 6
Epidemiology 6
Folklore 7
Food Science 2
Forestry 31
French 67
Genetics 33
Geography 56
Geology 51
Geophysics 17
German 79
Greek 2
History 388
History of Art 53
International Relations 2
Italian 15
Journalism 16
Landscape Architecture 21
Latin 5
Latin-American Studies...... 1
Law 827
Librarianship 192
Linguistics 55
Logic and Methodology of
  Science 13
Mathematics 297
Medical Physics 7
Microbiology 12
Molecular Biology 31
Music 76
Near Eastern Languages..... 18
Nutrition 47
Optometry 31
Oriental Languages 28
Paleontology 32
Parasitology 10
Philosophy 96
Physical Education 12
Physics 391
Physiological Optics 6
Physiology 56
Plant Pathology........... 31
Plant Physiology 12
Political Science 266
Psychology 193
Public Administration 17
Public Health 194
Range Management 2

APPENDICES / 229

Romance Languages and
Literatures 68
Romance Philology 4
Scandinavian Languages
and Literatures 15
Slavic Languages and
Literatures 46
Social Welfare 338
Sociology 217

Soil Science 24
Spanish 32
Speech 3
Statistics 87
Virology 4
Wood Science and Technology 2
Wood Technology 6
Zoology 119
Double Majors .\...........115

E. University of Michigan Rating Form

THE UNIVERSITY OF MICHIGAN
College of Literature, Science and the Arts
STUDENT OPINION OF COURSES AND TEACHING

To the Student:

The act of evaluating the educational process is not a simple one for either the teacher or the student. However, the faculty has found that both teacher and student benefit from the careful and honest opinions given by our students. It is, therefore, the policy of the College to conduct this inventory of course objectives and teaching procedures every other year. Your thoughtful responses to this questionnaire will assist the College in improving the methods and objectives of our common educational endeavors.

FILL IN:

Department and Course Number..

Section Number ....

Name of Teacher..

School or College in which Enrolled..

Class (Circle one): Fresh., Soph., Junior, Senior, Grad., Special

Field of Major Interest or Concentration..

Overall Grade Point Average at University of Michigan...........................

Please do not sign your name.
This form will not be returned to the instructor until after grades have been reported.

TO SAVE YOU TIME, READ THE INSTRUCTIONS FOR ALL SECTIONS of this form BEFORE you begin to answer any one. This will help you avoid unnecessary or inappropriate answers.

1. What do you think are the objectives of this course as emphasized by the instructor? Here is a list of statements which can be used to identify this emphasis as given in most of our College courses. First read through the entire list and then underline as many phrases as you believe represent the main emphasis of this course. Use a double underline for the one, two, or three statements that are especially applicable.
   a) Learning new terminology or vocabulary
   b) Acquiring specific and factual information
   c) Learning rules, procedures, techniques, or methodology
   d) Learning concepts, principles, or theories

   e) Applying facts, procedures, principles, or other knowledge and skills
   f) Analytic or critical thinking; that is, learning to analyze or make evaluative judgments about data, ideas, arguments, or theories
   g) Creative thinking; that is, learning to combine facts, ideas, and procedures, or produce original material
   h) Changing or developing your interests in this field
   i) Changing or developing your attitudes or values
2. Are you satisfied with these course objectives; if not, how would you wish them to be changed?
3. Summarize briefly one of the more specific ways that this course has influenced or changed your interests, attitudes, or values
4. Ten attributes of instruction have been listed below. For each attribute, circle the word or phrase which is nearest to your impression of this course, i.e., which best describes that aspect of the course for you. Where appropriate, give reasons or examples to support your opinion. Not all of the attributes apply equally to each course in the College, so you may wish to make some qualifying comments in the space near each item.
   a) The use of class time was:
      very effective   satisfactory   unsatisfactory at times
   b) The pace of classroom presentation of material, for the most part, was: too slow   too fast   about right
   c) Individual help or further discussion outside of class:
      was encouraged by instructor   was normally available
                        should have been more available
   d) The integration of lectures with other course material was:
      somewhat lacking   good   excellent
   e) The assigned material was on the whole:
      too difficult   fine for me   too easy
   f) In my opinion the class procedure was:
      well organized   moderately well organized   poorly planned
   g) The instructor stimulated my interest in the subject matter:
      a great deal   somewhat   very little
   h) The instructor's enthusiasm for the subject matter was:
      strong and sincere   adequate   somewhat lacking
   i) The feeling between the instructor and the student was:
      somewhat antagonistic   cordial   especially close and friendly
   j) The instructor's description, explanation or analysis of the subject matter was: seldom clear   sometimes clear   consistently clear
5. Keeping in mind that the returns from this questionnaire will be used by the instructor in the process of improving his teaching, please mention ANY OTHER ASPECTS OF THE COURSE OR INSTRUCTOR not covered in previous questions which you consider to be especially good or poor. For example, consider any of the following list which are relevant: text and outside readings; lectures; recitation or discussion; laboratory; papers, projects and examinations; course procedure; instructor. Offer any suggestions that you have for improving this course.

F. Replies to Grading Questionnaire
"How Well Do You Think the Grading System at Berkeley Reflects the
Students' Actual Knowledge and Understanding of the
Subjects Studied?"
(Replies by 2,112 returning students at registration, Fall 1965)

Grade-Point Average	No Answer or "Don't Know"	"Very Well"	"Fairly Well"	"Only Slightly"	"Not at All"	Total
3.5 +	4	16	163	69	13	265
	(1.5%)	(6.0%)	(61.5%)	(26.0%)	(4.9%)	
3.0-3.4	3	15	304	225	24	571
	(0.5%)	(2.6%)	(53.2%)	(39.4%)	(4.2%)	
2.5-2.9	6	23	323	312	25	689
	(0.9%)	(3.3%)	(46.9%)	(45.3%)	(3.6%)	
2.0-2.4	2	13	196	209	34	454
	(0.4%)	(2.9%)	(43.2%)	(46.0%)	(7.5%)	
1.9 & under	2	4	52	68	5	131
	(1.5%)	(3.1%)	(39.7%)	(51.9%)	(3.8%)	
Unknown			1		1	2
Total	17	71	1,039	883	102	2,112
	(0.8%)	(3.4%)	(49.2%)	(41.8%)	(4.8%)	

G. Curricular Programs for Some Professional Colleges and Schools on the Berkeley Campus[1]

College/School	Quarter Units Required for Bachelors Degree	Major Plus Preprofessional Requirements	Humanities Social Science Requirement	Other Courses and Electives
AGRICULTURE				
Agricultural Economics	180	87	32	61
Agricultural Science	180	112	32	36
Entomology	180	116	29	35
Genetics	180	111	36	33
Plant Nutrition	180	123	18	39
CHEMISTRY	180	111	27	42
ENGINEERING[2]				
Civil	183	150[2]	27	6
Electrical	180	151	27	2
Mechanical	180	147	27	6
ENVIRONMENTAL DESIGN[3]				
FORESTRY	201	149	24[4]	27
LETTERS & SCIENCE[5]				
Physics	180	87	36	57

[1] Data for this table were taken from departmental sources and from *The Provisional General Catalogue* of the University of California at Berkeley, 1966-1967. It became apparent that numerous errors and omissions exist in the provisional catalogue. The Committee has rectified these as far as possible.
[2] Less than 50% of the major requirements within Engineering are taken in the College of Engineering. The remainder are taken in technical areas of other colleges and schools.
[3] The curriculum of the Architecture Department in the College of Environmental Design is undergoing radical revision from a five-year to a six-year program at this time, and detailed curricula are not available.
[4] But this may include some military, naval, or air science.
[5] The curriculum of the Physics Department is included in this table to provide a highly structured program within Letters and Science for comparison with the professional curricula.

H. GRADUATE DEGREES AWARDED IN 16 SCHOOLS
(In each column, the bracketed figure on the right represents

Year[1]	Degree	Physical Sciences			Biological Sciences		Social Sciences	
		Chemistry (incl. Chem. E.)	Physics	Mathematics (incl. Applied Math.)	Biochemistry (incl. Comp. Biochem.)	Zoology	Economics	Poli. Sci.
1955–6	Masters	9 [164]	22 [221]	7 [98]	7 [64]	10 [105]	17 [125]	17 [170]
	Doctoral	19	35	8	7	13	24	9
1956–7	Masters	15 [187]	26 [249]	12 [117]	5 [57]	13 [94]	20 [132]	22 [161]
	Doctoral	34	35	9	3	5	15	9
1957–8	Masters	11 [216]	20 [292]	20 [142]	2 [65]	15 [118]	13 [145]	29 [199]
	Doctoral	37	22	5	15	12	10	7
1958–9	Masters	13 [255]	29 [341]	23 [172]	3 [59]	10 [110]	17 [162]	37 [216]
	Doctoral	34	31	8	16	9	11	5
1959–60	Masters	22 [270]	21 [355]	19 [213]	5 [58]	13 [121]	23 [189]	45 [244]
	Doctoral	42	45	7	14	13	7	9
1960–1	Masters	21 [307]	19 [371]	22 [277]	1 [63]	15 [146]	44 [211]	59 [279]
	Doctoral	40	42	19	10	20	13	11
1961–2	Masters	26 [361]	25 [421]	47 [316]	3 [71]	15 [145]	35 [258]	44 [341]
	Doctoral	53	48	26	8	10	10	7
1962–3	Masters	41 [402]	28 [404]	42 [323]	– [69]	15 [140]	29 [295]	122 [360]
	Doctoral	48	51	24	5	10	11	12
1963–4	Masters	33 [461]	18 [399]	37 [328]	4 [82]	13 [148]	55 [335]	80 [270]
	Doctoral	59	52	29	15	14	15	13
1964– June '65	Masters	33 [440]	15 [396]	44 [337]	7 [85]	17 [138]	71 [328]	64 [253]
	Doctoral	53	32	16	5	12	13	8

[1] The year is defined as going from the fall term through the following summer session, e.g., degrees awarded in Summer 1956, are reported under 1955–56, not 1956–57.

AND DEPARTMENTS, FALL 1955–SPRING 1965
the total of graduate registrants in the Department.)

Humanities		Languages			Professions[2]			
English	History	German	French	Spanish	Engineering	Education	Law	Business Adm.
19 8 [184]	45 13 [226]	3 7 [29]	7 _ [28]	2 6 [19]	96 17 [315]	69 26 [903]	1 1 [319]	10 _ [198]
33 7 [164]	44 13 [193]	5 5 [24]	5 4 [28]	– 3 [22]	121 15 [394]	78 23 [751]	5 _ [361]	70 _ [225]
32 6 [210]	50 6 [243]	2 1 [27]	11 3 [29]	4 1 [21]	153 14 [512]	64 32 [887]	5 _ [403]	63 _ [252]
35 5 [272]	76 18 [283]	4 2 [33]	6 3 [30]	4 _ [31]	165 16 [583]	67 31 [1004]	2 _ [465]	95 _ [284]
53 8 [278]	78 14 [279]	1 1 [40]	13 3 [36]	9 2 [26]	170 34 [643]	66 31 [973]	8 _ [500]	90 1 [281]
66 13 [397]	70 15 [340]	5 2 [42]	16 1 [41]	6 4 [28]	223 43 [843]	64 35 [1050]	7 _ [569]	110 2 [333]
68 10 [444]	82 25 [356]	6 3 [58]	7 5 [41]	6 3 [33]	274 42 [970]	46 44 [1160]	4 _ [628]	104 8 [350]
97 12 [440]	47 18 [339]	5 2 [70]	18 3 [49]	12 3 [36]	304 58 [1095]	59 41 [1226]	12 _ [712]	119 10 [366]
87 12 [460]	65 30 [392]	18 3 [91]	15 3 [47]	14 5 [34]	334 65 [1188]	53 45 [1311]	4 _ [802]	180 7 [435]
70 10 [497]	73 22 [396]	20 2 [92]	17 3 [54]	9 4 [32]	270 68 [1252]	37 35 [1395]	12 1 [803]	199 8 [494]

[2] Figures for the professional schools include professional as well as academic degrees.

I. Graduate Students Fully Supported from Official Sources, Spring 1965

	Total Grad. Enroll.	Fellowships[1]		Employment Equivalent to Support[2]								Total Graduate Student Support	
		Total	%	Act. Instr.	Assoc.	TF	TA	RA	Junior Specialist	Total	%	Total Supported	% Supported
Chemistry (incl. CE)	396	107	27.04	1	0	0	98	64	0	163	41.16	270	68.20
Physics	374	75	20.05	0	0	0	100	61	0	161	43.04	236	63.09
Math	302	86	28.50	4	0	6	61	62	0	133	44.03	219	72.53
Biochemistry	82	33	40.24	0	0	0	7	23	0	30	36.58	63	76.82
Zoology	131	28	21.37	1	5	0	52	7	0	65	49.61	93	70.99
Economics	293	54	18.43	4	0	0	41	0	0	45	15.35	99	33.78
Political Science	230	40	17.39	0	0	0	49	37	2	88	38.26	128	55.65
English	429	44	10.25	2	5	0	70	0	0	77	15.61	121	25.86
History	346	44	12.71	4	0	0	57	0	0	61	17.62	105	30.33
German	83	2	2.40	3	0	5	68	0	0	76	91.56	78	93.96
French	90	2	2.22	8	3	8	51	0	0	70	77.77	72	79.99
Spanish	45	0	0.00	0	0	0	35	0	0	35	77.77	35	77.77
Engineering	1162	155	13.33	3	1	20	107	197	24	352	30.29	507	43.62
Education	1126	14	1.24	0	0	5	8	21	3	37	3.28	51	4.52
Law	779	114	14.63	0	5	0	0	18	0	23	2.95	137	17.58
Bus. Ad.	411	21	5.10	2	3	2	24	27	0	58	14.11	79	19.21

[1] Under this category are fellowships from the University of California, Woodrow Wilson Foundation, National Science Foundation, NDEA, NASA, Public Health, and grants-in-aid. Also included are various agencies which provide substantial support along with the tuition and fees of certain graduate students (i.e., Dept. of Health, Education, and Welfare; Agency for International Development; Air Force, etc.). Since all sources of major fellowship support cannot be identified, the figures given are probably lower than the actual totals.

[2] Readerships are not included, since they do not normally provide full support for graduate students.

J. Graduate Study Space

A quantitative survey of graduate study facilities was made for the Select Committee in December of 1965; it covered sixteen of the departments and colleges principally engaged in graduate education: Chemistry, Physics, Mathematics, Biochemistry, Zoology, Economics, Political Science, English, History, German, French, Spanish, Engineering, Education, Law, Business Administration.

Perhaps the most significant finding of this survey is the need for decentralization of graduate study facilities. Graduate students, who usually do most of their work and studying in one department, must have study space conveniently located. If a graduate student has an hour or two in between classes, it is preferable that he do his studying in a place adjacent to his department.

Of the sixteen departments and colleges surveyed, only six were found to have departmental libraries, five of which were either science departments or professional schools: Engineering, Law, Chemistry, Physics, Biochemistry, and French. The other professional schools, the social sciences, and Zoology all belong to interdepartmental library complexes: The Education-Psychology Library, the Hans Kelsen Library, the Biology Library, and the Astronomy-Mathematics-Statistics Library. Most of the humanities departments are relegated to the Main Library, which must also serve the needs of the entire campus. The Humanities Graduate Service reading rooms provide only 124 seats for 17 departments having 1,600 potential graduate student users. The Main Library carrels provide only 415 spaces on a first-come first-served basis to all continuing Berkeley graduate students.

There is a "descending scale" of facilities among the departments studied, with the physical sciences and professional schools at the top, the social sciences in the middle, and the humanities at the bottom. For example, all the laboratory sciences provide each of their students with personal space in the laboratories; the College of Engineering, with almost thirteen hundred students, provides individually assigned spaces to approximately two-thirds of its students, with additional unassigned spaces available; the social sciences have access to the Hans Kelsen Memorial Library, which has perhaps the most attractive facilities on campus; the humanities, on the other hand, have generally inadequate departmental study facilities. The English Department, for example, has almost five hundred graduate students, but provides a total of only seventy-five desks, thirty-five for Teaching Assistants and readers, and forty reserved for advanced Ph.D. candidates.

Even those departments, such as Engineering and Zoology, which have a high ratio of study space to graduate students, do not necessarily meet the need for adequate space, since this ratio gives only a quantitative and not a qualitative evaluation: for example, the Spanish Department has one desk for every Teaching Assistant, but these desks are inconveniently located in places such as the Department's mimeograph room, and are unsuitable for consultation with students, let alone for study; the Biology Library, which has a large number of volumes and study desks, is nonetheless found to be defective because of bad ventilation, lack of washroom facilities, and very poor lighting.

In addition to the need for better library study facilities for graduates, there is also a need for departmental graduate lounges where students can study, relax, eat, or meet and talk with members of their departments. Only one of the departments studied, Business Administration, has a lounge reserved for graduates (the English and Zoology Departments have plans for graduate lounges); however, this lounge does not meet the needs, since it only holds about twenty in a Department with four hundred and fifty-three graduate students.

This quantitative survey can only scratch the surface—a more extensive study would be needed to assess accurately the adequacy of graduate student facilities on the campus. But even from a preliminary survey, it is evident that our graduate study space is generally inadequate and that there are great quantitative and qualitative inequalities among the facilities of different departments.

K. SOURCES OF NEW GRADUATE STUDENTS IN 16 SCHOOLS AND DEPARTMENTS: 1960 (FALL), 1964–65 (FALL AND SPRING), 1965 (FALL)

Students coming from:	Year:	Physical Sciences						Bio-Sciences				Social Sciences				Humanities				Languages						Professions							
		Chemistry #	Chemistry %	Physics #	Physics %	Mathematics #	Mathematics %	Bio-Chemistry #	Bio-Chemistry %	Zoology #	Zoology %	Economics #	Economics %	Political Science #	Political Science %	English #	English %	History #	History %	German #	German %	French #	French %	Spanish #	Spanish %	Engineering #	Engineering %	Education #	Education %	Law #	Law %	Business Adm. #	Business Adm. %
1. U. C. Campuses	1960 (F)	2	2.4%	16	17.6%	18	16.4%	1	6.6%	5	17.9%	7	11.5%	19	24.4%	24	14.7%	16	13.8%	4	33.3%	4	19.0%	5	20.8%	79	21.1%	172	52.6%	111	42.4%	40	26.0%
	1964-5	6	4.4%	11	11.2%	31	25.6%	—	—	13	37.1%	13	12.3%	16	21.3%	26	12.1%	33	25.0%	5	20.8%	15	40.5%	5	27.8%	169	28.0%	304	45.4%	97	33.2%	81	29.2%
	1965 (F)	4	5.5%	22	27.8%	16	17.6%	2	11.1%	6	27.3%	20	20.8%	22	24.7%	22	13.7%	31	25.4%	7	36.8%	10	27.0%	1	10.0%	94	19.3%	302	53.8%	103	34.2%	51	25.6%
2. Calif. State Colleges	1960 (F)	3	3.5%	4	4.4%	7	6.4%	1	6.6%	1	3.6%	3	4.9%	1	1.3%	3	1.8%	5	4.3%	1	8.3%	2	9.5%	1	4.2%	3	.9%	28	8.6%	22	8.4%	5	3.2%
	1964-5	1	.8%	—	—	6	4.9%	1	4.2%	4	11.4%	8	7.5%	5	6.6%	7	3.2%	4	3.0%	1	4.2%	—	—	—	—	16	2.7%	73	10.9%	21	7.2%	18	6.9%
	1965 (F)	1	1.4%	3	3.8%	7	7.7%	—	—	—	—	3	3.1%	4	4.5%	4	2.5%	7	5.7%	1	5.3%	—	—	—	—	14	2.9%	57	10.2%	23	7.6%	4	2.0%
3. Thirteen "Leading" American Universities*[1]	1960 (F)	10	11.8%	12	13.2%	18	16.4%	2	13.3%	—	—	7	11.5%	13	16.6%	30	18.4%	30	25.9%	—	—	2	9.5%	4	16.7%	33	9.8%	27	8.3%	46	17.6%	23	14.9%
	1964-5	22	16.2%	27	27.5%	22	18.2%	9	37.5%	2	5.7%	23	21.7%	19	25.3%	44	20.5%	24	18.2%	3	12.5%	3	8.1%	—	—	45	7.5%	59	8.8%	52	17.8%	27	9.7%
	1965 (F)	5	6.8%	14	17.7%	12	13.2%	3	16.7%	1	4.5%	10	10.4%	14	15.7%	32	20.0%	13	10.7%	1	5.3%	—	—	1	10.0%	17	3.5%	32	5.7%	44	14.6%	25	12.6%
4. Twenty-six "Leading" American Small Colleges[2]	1960 (F)	3	3.5%	4	4.4%	5	4.5%	1	6.6%	2	7.1%	1	1.6%	8	10.3%	23	14.1%	10	8.6%	—	—	1	4.8%	—	—	6	1.8%	9	2.7%	4	1.5%	4	2.6%
	1964-5	5	3.7%	11	11.2%	6	5.0%	1	4.2%	3	8.6%	8	7.5%	4	5.3%	27	12.6%	10	7.6%	4	16.7%	3	8.1%	—	—	—	—	25	3.7%	20	6.8%	2	.7%
	1965 (F)	5	6.8%	3	3.8%	6	6.6%	1	5.6%	1	4.5%	5	5.2%	7	7.9%	17	10.6%	5	4.1%	1	5.3%	1	2.7%	—	—	4	.8%	23	4.1%	20	6.6%	4	2.0%
5. M.I.T. / C.I.T. / Cal. Tech.	1960 (F)	6	7.1%	11	12.1%	4	3.6%	—	—	—	—	2	3.3%	—	—	—	—	—	—	—	—	—	—	—	—	18	5.4%	—	—	4	1.5%	3	1.9%
	1964-5	7	5.1%	12	12.2%	2	1.7%	1	4.2%	—	—	1	.9%	—	—	—	—	—	—	—	—	—	—	—	—	20	3.3%	1	.1%	1	—	1	.4%
	1965 (F)	1	1.4%	8	10.1%	3	3.3%	—	—	—	—	—	—	—	—	2	1.2%	—	—	—	—	—	—	—	—	16	3.3%	1	.2%	1	.3%	—	—
6. Oxford / Cambridge / Toronto	1960 (F)	—	—	1	1.1%	—	—	—	—	1	3.6%	—	—	1	1.3%	2	1.2%	1	.9%	—	—	1	4.8%	—	—	1	.3%	—	—	1	.4%	2	1.3%
	1964-5	2	1.4%	2	2.0%	—	—	—	—	—	—	4	3.8%	1	1.3%	2	.9%	4	3.0%	—	—	1	2.7%	—	—	3	.5%	1	.1%	—	—	2	.7%
	1965 (F)	—	—	—	—	1	1.1%	—	—	—	—	1	1.0%	1	1.1%	2	1.2%	1	.8%	—	—	—	—	—	—	4	.8%	1	.2%	1	.3%	1	.5%
7. All other Foreign Schools	1960 (F)	15	17.7%	7	7.7%	21	19.1%	5	33.3%	4	14.3%	12	19.7%	11	14.1%	4	2.5%	4	3.4%	1	8.3%	—	—	6	25.0%	93	27.7%	7	2.1%	4	1.5%	22	14.3%
	1964-5	23	16.9%	12	12.2%	15	12.4%	5	20.8%	5	14.3%	20	18.9%	8	10.7%	11	5.1%	4	3.0%	3	12.5%	3	8.1%	3	16.7%	214	35.5%	20	3.0%	17	5.8%	50	18.0%
	1965 (F)	7	9.6%	13	16.5%	22	24.2%	2	11.1%	2	9.1%	33	34.4%	9	10.1%	7	4.4%	9	7.4%	—	—	2	5.4%	2	20.0%	207	42.4%	9	1.6%	20	6.6%	41	20.6%
8. All other American Schools[3]	1960 (F)	46	54.1%	36	39.6%	37	33.6%	5	33.3%	15	53.6%	29	47.5%	25	32.1%	77	47.2%	50	43.1%	6	50.0%	11	52.4%	8	33.3%	103	30.6%	84	25.7%	70	26.7%	55	35.7%
	1964-5	70	51.5%	23	23.5%	38	31.4%	7	30.0%	8	22.9%	29	27.4%	22	29.3%	98	45.6%	53	40.2%	8	33.3%	12	32.4%	10	55.6%	136	22.6%	187	27.9%	85	29.0%	96	34.7%
	1965 (F)	50	68.5%	16	20.3%	24	26.4%	10	55.6%	12	54.5%	24	25.0%	32	36.0%	74	46.2%	56	45.9%	9	47.4%	24	64.9%	6	60.0%	132	27.0%	136	24.2%	89	29.6%	73	36.7%
Totals for all 8 categories	1960 (F)	85		91		110		15		28		61		78		163		116		12		21		24		336		327		262		154	
	1964-5	136		98		121		24		35		106		75		215		132		24		37		18		603		670		292		277	
	1965 (F)	73		79		91		18		22		96		89		160		122		19		37		10		488		561		301		199	

*Of 13, Harvard, Yale, Columbia, Michigan, and Wisconsin apply to all Depts. Illinois to all but Economics. The 7 others differ by department:

Chemistry	Physics	Mathematics	Bio-Chemistry	Zoology	Economics	Political Science	English	History	German	French	Engineering	Law
Princeton	Princeton	Chicago	Indiana	Indiana	Chicago	Chicago	Princeton	Princeton	Penna.	Penna.	Chicago	Chicago
Chicago	Chicago	Princeton	Cornell	Johns Hopkins	Stanford	Princeton	Chicago	Chicago	Texas	North Carolina	Princeton	Minnesota
Cornell	Stanford	NYU	Penna.	Princeton	Princeton	Minnesota	Cornell	Cornell	Indiana	Princeton	Stanford	Stanford
Minnesota	Cornell	Stanford	Johns Hopkins	Chicago	Johns Hopkins	Cornell	Johns Hopkins	Johns Hopkins	Chicago	Ohio State	Cornell	Cornell
Northwestern	Minnesota	Cornell		Penna.	Minnesota	Stanford	Penna.	Penna.	Cornell	NYU	Minnesota	Princeton
Washington	Penna.	Ohio State		Cornell	Northwestern	Johns Hopkins	Indiana	Minnesota	Northwestern	Johns Hopkins	Penna.	Penna.
Stanford	Ohio State	Minnesota		Stanford	Duke	Duke	Stanford	Northwestern	Ohio State	Indiana	Indiana	Northwestern
					Penna.							

[1] The lists of 13 are different and appear separately for each of the 16 departments. Five schools, Harvard, Yale, Columbia, Michigan, and Wisconsin, are in *all* the departmental lists. Berkeley, which ranks from one to five in these departments, is excluded from this category (see #1, above). Selections for this category rely on Hayward Keniston's survey of graduate chairmen (University of Pennsylvania, 1957). Although individual rankings in this survey have been criticized, it is not likely that the composite group is much in error. The lists should be compared with the survey by the American Council on Education which will soon be published.

[2] These small colleges are well known for the numbers of students they send on to graduate schools. The list is taken from a selection made for the Select Committee by the Center for the Study of Higher Education:
Amherst, Antioch, Bard (N. Y.), Bennington, Bryn Mawr, Carleton (Minn.), Dartmouth, Grinnell (Iowa), Haverford, Kenyon, Lawrence U., Middlebury, Mt. Holyoke, Oberlin, Occidental, Pomona, Radcliffe, Reed, Raymond (Univ. of the Pacific), Sarah Lawrence, Smith, Swarthmore, Vassar, Wellesley, Wesleyan (Conn.), Williams

[3] It should not be inferred that the eighth category includes no excellent schools; some arbitrary drawing of lines was necessary for organizing this report.

XIV.

EPILOGUE:
FINAL ACTION

Final Action Taken on Recommendations
of the Select Committee on Education's Report, EDUCATION AT BERKELEY, by
the Academic Senate, Berkeley Division
Spring 1966–Winter 1967

Recommendation 1 (pp. 39–44). The following resolution based on the
recommendation was adopted November 8, 1966:

The Berkeley Division of the Academic Senate directs its Committee
on Budget and Interdepartmental Relations and Committee on
Teaching to:

1. Prepare, in consultation with the Vice-Chancellor of Academic
Affairs, a statement of concrete suggestions which will help chairmen
to submit tangible evidence of deficient, satisfactory, or outstanding
performance in various areas of teaching.

2. Make it clear, in appropriate ways, that recommendations for
promotions which contain only perfunctory evidence on teaching
will be unacceptable to Senate review committees; and

3. Report back to the Division, before the end of the current academic year, what steps have been taken to comply with articles 1
and 2 of this motion.

The following resolution was passed on May 16, 1967:

The review committees and the Budget Committee make their recommendations, and the Chancellor his decisions, on appointments and
promotions to tenure rank in accordance with established University
policy:

*Superior intellectual attainment, as evidenced both in teaching and
in research or creative achievement, is an indispensable qualification
for appointment or promotion to tenure positions.*

Thus a candidate's teaching performance, whatever its other qualities
may be, must evidence superior intellectual attainment. Departments

will bear in mind, of course, that there are many types and styles of teaching. Each discipline or subject is likely to present special pedagogical problems and to offer opportunities for different approaches, and each teacher will be inclined to adopt goals and methods in accord with his particular interests. Consequently it is essential that reviewers take into account the objectives the teacher sets for himself, as well as the more obvious features of his performance.

Some of the teaching qualities mentioned by reviewers include:

1. Command of subject
2. Continued growth in the subject
3. Ability to organize material for presentation
4. Capacity to present material with logic and force
5. Ability to arouse interest in subject, and to relate the subject to other fields of knowledge
6. Grasp of fundamental objectives and values
7. Enthusiasm for learning and teaching
8. Effectiveness in guiding and stimulating discussion
9. Ability to stimulate advanced students to creative work
10. Readiness to experiment with new teaching techniques

Some of the kinds of evidence that reviewers have found useful in evaluating teaching include:

1. Reports of colleagues, or other scholars, who have been associated with candidate in oral examinations, joint teaching programs, or curriculum revision
2. Reports of colleagues, or other scholars, who have visited a course taught by the candidate or who have observed him in some type of actual teaching
3. Reports of colleagues or others who have attended conferences, panel discussions, research reports, public lectures, or colloquia in which the candidate was a participant
4. Reports on the number and quality of theses and dissertations written under the supervision of the candidate
5. Written or oral comments volunteered by students and former students
6. Student questionnaires
7. Textbooks, source books, syllabi, etc., written or edited by the candidate
8. Course plans
9. Reading assignments
10. Problem assignments

Each department is urged to be on the alert for new ways of improving and evaluating teaching, and for better methods of obtaining recognition for good teaching.

Recommendation 2 (pp. 48–49). Adopted in amended form February 6, 1967 as follows:

The Berkeley Division endorses the principle that academic deans should be authorized to permit students at any stage of their experience to undertake supervised independent study involving any proportion of their time justifiable by sound educational reasons, and directs the Committee on Courses to frame appropriate legislation and submit it to the Division by the winter quarter, 1968.

Recommendation 3 (pp. 48–50). Received and placed on file February 6, 1967:

It should be the policy of the administration and faculty to increase the opportunity of all students for learning based on dialogue and on cooperative student self-instruction by decreasing the proportion of lecture courses in favor of discussion sections, small classes, seminars, tutorials, preceptorials, and similar teaching arrangements.

Recommendation 4 (50–54). Approved as a sense motion February 6, 1967 in the following revised form:

Departments with markedly low levels of faculty participation in their lower division courses should restructure their patterns of teaching in order to give greater faculty attention to the lower division. Faculty time indirectly directed at lower division instruction through such activities as graduate teaching colloquia, teaching seminars, and supervision of teaching assistants should be credited in any evaluation of faculty participation in lower division instruction.

Recommendation 5 (pp. 54–56). Received and placed on file February 6, 1967:

Systematic study of the educational role of Organized Research Units on the Berkeley campus should be undertaken as part of the Campus Academic Plan. Such study should attempt to document the past and current educational activities of such Units, the policy considerations that have facilitated or interfered with the development of these activities, and should consider what changes might be effected to enhance the educational functions of the Units.

Recommendation 6 (pp. 54–57). Received and placed on file February 6, 1967:

Consideration should be given to giving credit to students and faculty members for the educational activities carried on within Units. To the extent that Units are engaged in educational activities—which is apparently considerable—they should be recognized as educational as well as research units. Research personnel who contribute importantly to the supervision, training, and instruction of students should be given official recognition, perhaps through increased use of appropriate titles, such as Lecturer and Senior Lecturer.

Recommendation 7 (pp. 57–60). Adopted in the following form May 17, 1966:

The Committee on Teaching is directed to design and administer an experimental student evaluation of all undergraduate courses offered in the winter quarter, 1967, to be sent by students directly to individual faculty members, as the basis for later faculty consideration of a permanent system of student evaluation of courses.

Recommendation 8 (pp. 60–63). Adopted as policy in the following form May 17, 1966:

The faculty and administration should regularly consult students' views on educational policy both in campus-wide and in departmental affairs. Campus-wide, the students have the major responsibility to develop effective channels of communication; within each department, however, the chairman and faculty should take the initiative.

Recommendation 9 (pp. 60–63). The Committee withdrew this recommendation as redundant after having supported the passage of the following resolutions of the Committee on Student Affairs, May 17, 1966:

A. That the present Committee on Student Affairs of the Academic Senate be expanded to include three student members, one graduate, one undergraduate, and the President of the Associated Students of the University of California, *ex officio.*

That the Senate of the Associated Students of the University of California appoint one graduate student and one undergraduate student to the Committee on Student Affairs of the Division.

That in the case of vacancy the procedure for selecting student members will be the same as outlined above.

That the membership of the faculty be reduced from 5 to 4 (3 members and Chairman) to create a committee of effective size.

That the student representatives be given a standing invitation to attend the Academic Senate meetings as guests.

B. That the Berkeley Division extend the regular privilege of speech at its meetings to the President of the Associated Students of the University of California (Berkeley) for the purpose of informing the Division of student affairs and activities relevant to its concerns.

That the new agenda item be included under "IV. Other Announcements."

That the President of the Associated Students may delegate this function either to the First Vice-President of the Associated Students or to the Second Vice-President of the Associated Students.

Recommendation 10 (pp. 69–71). Adopted April 25, 1966 in the original form:

The high school student's record for admissions should include a more sensitive analysis of his course record for academic strengths and weaknesses; the results of aptitude and achievement tests; recognition of significant extracurricular achievement; and evaluations from high school officials.

Recommendation 11 (pp. 71–72). Adopted April 25, 1966 in the original form with the stipulation that this resolution must be approved in turn by the University-wide Academic Senate and by the Board of Regents.

Admission standards should be made more flexible by allowing each campus full discretion in admitting or rejecting candidates whose high school grade-point averages now fall in the range 2.8 to 3.2.

Recommendation 12 (pp. 72–73). Adopted in its original form April 25, 1966:

The campus should improve its recruitment of able candidates through the use of alumni, faculty, and students, and an improved program of scholarship assistance.

Recommendation 13 (pp. 77–89). Referred to the College of Letters and Science February 6, 1967 in its original form:

The advising system in the College of Letters and Science should be made largely voluntary through the adoption of such improvements as mechanizing the record-keeping, reforming the orientation procedure, simplifying the rules and liberalizing their application, providing ample printed materials, establishing a Campus Information Service, appointing advising specialists, promoting combinations of advising and teaching, and encouraging participation of student advisers.

Recommendation 14 (pp. 98–99). The following Regulation of the Berkeley Division based on this recommendation was adopted May 5, 1966:

1270. Any undergraduate student in good standing may enroll in one course each quarter on a *Passed* or *Not Passed* basis, subject to the following limitations and to such additional regulations as may be adopted by the faculties of the various schools and colleges:

(a) Courses which are required in the student's major or prerequisite to the major may be taken on a *Passed* or *Not Passed* basis only upon approval of the faculty of his college or school.

(b) After a student has twice failed to pass courses attempted on a *Passed* or *Not Passed* basis, he may not enroll in further courses on that basis.

(c) A part-time student may enroll in courses on a *Passed* or *Not Passed* basis in the same proportion of his total program as permitted to a full-time student.

(d) Units earned by passing such a course count toward the degree requirement, but the course is disregarded in computing the student's grade-point average.

Recommendation 15 (pp. 99–100). The following Regulation of the Berkeley Division based on this recommendation was adopted May 5, 1966:

1271. For a period of five years beginning with the fall quarter, 1966, departments may offer graduate or undergraduate courses on a *Passed* or *Not Passed* basis, subject to the following limitations:

(a) An instructor may be in charge of no more than one such course in any quarter on a *Passed* or *Not Passed* basis.

(b) A student may not enroll in more than one course in any quarter on a *Passed* or *Not Passed* basis.

(c) Units earned by passing such a course count toward the degree requirement, but the course is disregarded in computing the student's grade-point average.

Faculty members taking part in this experiment are expected to report their findings to the Committee on Educational Policy and the Board of Educational Development.

Recommendation 16 (pp. 100–101). The following Regulation of the Berkeley Division based on this recommendation was enacted on October 28, 1966:

A1262. In the Berkeley Division for a course extending over more than one quarter, where evaluation of the student's performance is deferred until the end of the final quarter, provisional grades of *In Progress* shall be assigned in the intervening quarters. The provisional grades shall be replaced by the final grade, if the student completes the full sequence. The Berkeley Division is authorized to regulate the award of credit in cases where the full sequence is not completed.

Recommendation 17 (pp. 101–102). A resolution based on this recommendation—to count units of credit but to disregard grade points in courses taken in an undergraduate's first quarter of residence—failed to pass on May 5, 1966.

Recommendation 18 (pp. 102–103). The following Resolution was adopted May 25, 1966:

Departments, colleges and schools are encouraged to conduct further experiments in grading, including refinements of the present system.

Recommendation 19 (pp. 112–115). This recommendation was approved with amendments and enacted as By-Law 15 of the Berkeley Division on March 31, 1966 as follows:

By-Law 15. Board of Educational Development. This board consists of six appointed members who serve three-year staggered terms, and the campus-wide administrative officer most responsible for educational development, all voting. Its duties are:

1. To stimulate and promote experimentation in all sectors of the Berkeley campus, and to support innovation wherever it is needed; to sponsor, conduct, and direct, with use of an Office of Educational Development, continuing studies of the needs and opportunities for educational development; and to maintain liaison with the Committee on Courses of Instruction, Committee on Educational Policy, Graduate Council, and the executive committees of the colleges and schools, on matters of educational effectiveness, innovation, and for the initiation of experimental courses, programs and curricula.

2. To receive, encourage, and authorize experimental instructional proposals for which neither departmental nor college support is appropriate or feasible; to initiate and administer such experimental instructional programs pending their adoption by a department or other recognized faculty group, for a period not to exceed five years, subject to policies prescribed by the Berkeley Division; and to provide all possible accessory services for experimental programs initiated within departments, schools, and colleges.

3. To initiate and sponsor the securing of extramural funds for the support of experimental courses and curricula, and to administer such funds for this purpose as may be allocated to the Board or to the Office of Educational Development.

4. That in the sixth year of the Board of Educational Development's operation, the Committee on Committees shall appoint an *ad hoc* committee, to examine the extent and effectiveness of the Board's activities, to recommend changes in its structure if needed, and to report to the Division during that year.

Recommendation 20 (pp. 112–116). Adopted in the following amended form on March 31, 1966:

Assistant Chancellor for Educational Development. It is recommended that an Assistant Chancellor for Educational Development be appointed in the office of and under the Vice-Chancellor for Academic Affairs. He shall become an *ex officio* voting member of the Board of Educational Development. Under the policy guidance of the Board of Educational Development, he shall:

1. Administer the policies and programs of the Board of Educational Development.

2. Consult with all appropriate members of the academic community concerning deficiencies in or possible development of existing offerings, and encourage new offerings where they are considered necessary.

3. Consult with Deans and Departmental Chairmen concerning desirable recruitments and promotions conducive to campus educational development.

4. Provide general administrative and incidental assistance to studies and experimental programs.

5. Secure funds for these purposes from private, foundation, University, and government sources.

Recommendation 21 (pp. 112–118). Adopted as By-Law 18 of the Berkeley Division and Regulations 1300–1303 of the Berkeley Division on April 19, 1966; amended on May 25, 1966 to read as follows:

By-Law 18. Council for Special Curricula.—This council comprises the members of the Board of Educational Development and seven members of the Committee on Educational Policy, with the Registrar as its secretary. It is empowered to fix the requirements for experimental programs leading to the Bachelor of Arts or Bachelor of Science as specified in Regulations 1300–1303, and to recommend for degrees the students who have satisfied those requirements, substituting in such capacity for a college or school.

Regulations 1300–1303

1300. Students in special curricula shall have been duly admitted to a relevant college or school, and shall register in that academic unit. Procedures for study-list approval shall conform to the practices of the college or school, and to any additional provisions of the Council for Special Curricula.

1301. A special curriculum leading to the Bachelor of Arts or Bachelor of Science degree may be established by the Council upon favorable vote of at least three-quarters of its members, incorporating an experimental program of courses which the council finds to possess intellectual content and quality appropriate to part or all of a four-year curriculum, but to have no college or school ready to accept it. At the time each such special curriculum is established, the Council shall prescribe the requirements for graduation that are to be met by students who follow the experimental program either in full or in part, corresponding as closely as practicable to requirements for a relevant school or college and conforming to the general requirements of the University and the Berkeley Division. Students in a special curriculum shall complete the degree requirements within eight years after starting in it.

Immediately after establishing a special curriculum, the Council shall report its action to the Berkeley Division, and shall arrange for publication of the curriculum requirements in the General Catalogue or in other suitable announcements.

1302. The Council shall prescribe the conditions for admission to each special curriculum. The total number of students admitted to special curricula in any one calendar year shall not exceed five percent of the graduating class of the preceding year, except by express consent of the Berkeley Division.

1303. The Council's recommendations for degrees, to be awarded in the Council's name, shall have identical standing with recommendations from schools and colleges. Each student completing a special curriculum to the Council's satisfaction shall be recommended by the Council for the bachelor's degree, either in accordance with the Council's established requirements or under suspension of certain requirements. However, if the requirements for a special curriculum are accepted by the relevant college or school, or if a student completing a special curriculum also satisfies the regular degree requirements of that college or school, the degree shall be recommended by that academic unit rather than by the Council.

Recommendation 22 (pp. 126–128). Withdrawn October 31, 1966 by the Committee as redundant to Recommendation 19, section 2. Recommendation 22 read as follows:

The administration should arrange for *Ad Hoc* Courses, the topics of which may be determined from term to term by the Board of Educational Development, to supply the relevant scholarly and intellectual background to subjects of active student concern.

Recommendation 23 (pp. 128–131). Referred to the Board of Educational Development on October 17, 1966 as follows:

The Division should establish a new category of interdisciplinary University Courses, each subject to the regular review of the Committee on Courses. The Division should also develop appropriate means of special administrative support for such courses, where such means do not already exist.

Recommendation 24 (pp. 135–136). A modified version of this recommendation was adopted October 31, 1966 as follows:

An experimental program of freshman seminars should be offered by the fall quarter, 1967.

Recommendation 25 (pp. 136–140). Adopted in the following revised form October 20, 1966:

The Division endorses in principle the desirability of expanding opportunities for faculty-supervised off-campus field study for qualified students. To this end: a) schools, colleges and departments are urged to exercise wider latitude in accrediting such field study under already-existing authorizations; b) the Committee on Courses and the Board of Educational Development are jointly charged with framing of new legislation and procedures which would facilitate the expansion of such opportunities, and to report to the Division before the end of the current academic year.

Recommendation 26 (pp. 140–141). Approved October 17, 1966 as a sense motion in the following form:

The University should create a small number of new Professorships of the University, devoted to study and teaching of the general human significance of the results of scholarship.

Recommendation 27 (pp. 141–146). Approved February 6, 1967:

Each professional college and school should explore with the College of Letters and Science the value and feasibility of optional undergraduate programs leading to combined degrees and report to the Division by the end of Spring Quarter, 1968.

Recommendation 28 (pp. 141–146). Referred to the College of Letters and Science on February 6, 1967 for study and report to the Division by the Spring Quarter, 1968 in the following revised form:

The College of Letters and Science should explore with the professional schools and colleges means of providing more effective general courses and programs in humanities and social science suitable for undergraduate students in the professional schools and colleges.

Recommendations 29, 30, and 31 (pp. 149–155). Referred to the College of Letters and Science on February 6, 1967 in their original form. The following motion based on Recommendations 28, 29, 30, and 31 was approved by the Division February 6, 1967:

> The Berkeley Division, recognizing that breadth requirements and breadth offerings throughout the campus are interdependent and should be subjected to periodic review, directs each college and school to review and to prepare a detailed report on its breadth requirements and to circulate the report to all members of the Division by the spring quarter, 1968.

Recommendation 32 (pp. 161–162). Received and placed on file in the original form on February 6, 1967:

> Departments should provide graduate programs in which comprehensive coverage of the department's territory gives way early in the graduate student's career to individually designed, integrated programs of study suited to the student's special interests.

Recommendation 33 (pp. 161–163). Referred to the Graduate Council on February 6, 1967 for study and report:

> Departments should have wide latitude in determining requirements for foreign languages and other skills and should consider relating the requirements flexibly to the actual studies being conducted by individual graduate students.

Recommendations 34 and 35 (pp. 163–165). Referred to the Graduate Council on February 6, 1967 for study and report.

> *Recommendation 34:* Departments should make certain that capable full-time students having a sound preparation can earn the Master's degree in three to five quarters, and the Ph.D. in three to four years. The Graduate Council should periodically review all current graduate programs and report whether these norms are in effect.

> *Recommendation 35:* The faculty should encourage interdisciplinary graduate study by promoting courses organized around specific problems, and by permitting students to pursue interdisciplinary programs of study under departmental or interdepartmental supervision.

Recommendation 36 (pp. 165–167). Received and placed on file February 6, 1967 as follows:

> Departments should allow all graduate students to participate in undergraduate teaching appropriate to their skills, and should grant course credit to graduate students for work designed to relate the graduate curriculum to the problems of teaching.

Recommendation 37 (pp. 167–168). Referred to the Graduate Council for study and report on February 6, 1967 as follows:

We should decrease the number of hurdles in the graduate curriculum by elevating admissions standards, then simplifying examination requirements correspondingly.

Recommendation 38 (pp. 169–171). The following motion based on this recommendation was approved on April 25, 1966:

The Berkeley Division directs the Graduate Council to investigate and report to the Division by the regular meeting of November, 1966, the merits of creating a new degree to require preparation equivalent to that normally required for advancement to candidacy for the Ph.D., but without requiring a dissertation of the kind required for the Ph.D. degree.

The subsequent Report of the Graduate Council submitted to the Division November 8, 1966 by C. Hand, Chairman, reads as follows:

II. In the Spring of 1966 the Berkeley Division directed the Graduate Council to investigate and report to the Division the merits of creating a new degree to require preparation equivalent to that normally required for advancement to candidacy for the Ph.D., but without requiring a dissertation of the kind required for the Ph.D. degree.

In considering the range of proposals for a Doctor of Arts or similar degrees, the Graduate Council was struck by the fact that the main force of the arguments on their behalf come from the present exigencies of the academic marketplace rather than from a considered theory of graduate education. The Council finds that insofar as Berkeley has fallen short of its potential for providing a large number of new university and college teachers annually, it has not done so because of curricular wastefulness or "research-oriented" rather than "teacher-oriented" doctoral programs. Doubtless, certain doctoral programs at Berkeley are in need of modernization; nevertheless, when modernized they will continue to be Ph.D. programs. It is overwhelmingly apparent, however, that the single most needful step for an increase in the percentage of graduate students granted the doctorate annually is an improved level of financial support for graduate students, especially those in the Humanities and Social Sciences. Such improved support, our studies indicate, will be immediately reflected in the number of college and university teachers graduated from Berkeley; without such increased support, no mere change in doctoral programs will suffice. Therefore, while continuing to encourage experimentation and modernization in Ph.D. programs, and while continuing to explore all available means of increasing the level of financial support of graduate students, the Council passed the following motion:

The sense of the Graduate Council is that there is no reason to create the Doctor of Arts degree at this time.

Because of straitened finances, and less frequently, because of a diminished desire to pursue intensive research over a period of years, many graduate students annually enter upon full-time college teaching before their doctorates have been granted. A considerable number of them do so upon advancement to candidacy for the doctorate. Since advancement to candidacy does represent a significant level of achievement beyond the Master's degree, and since, in most departments, it marks the stage at which the student has acquired a comprehensive control of his field and now lacks only his dissertation for fulfillment of the requirements for the doctorate, the Council believes that upon advancement to candidacy for the Ph.D. the student should be awarded a Candidate's degree. Those colleges that emphasize their desire to engage "teachers" rather than "scholars," the Council is satisfied, will respect this degree. Moreover, the Candidate's degree will suggest to the student that he may satisfy his personal and professional ambitions without continuing his graduate career into the dissertation stage unless he so wishes, but, at the same time, will not block his advancement to that stage, and it will allow departments to recognize a unified body of achievement beyond the Master's without compelling them to establish a separate terminal program or in any other way to conduct courses of study that are susceptible to the label "second class."

Therefore:

The Graduate Council recommends to the Berkeley Division of the Academic Senate that steps be taken to create a new degree, Candidate in ...., as marking a definite stage of progress in our present Ph.D. program, and that this degree be awarded upon advancement to candidacy.

The recommendation was approved by voice vote unanimously on November 8, 1966 and referred to the Universitywide Coordinating Committee on Graduate Affairs. The Coordinating Committee, on February 14, 1967, approved enabling legislation to establish the degree of Candidate in Philosophy which will be forwarded to the Assembly of the Academic Senate for approval and referral to the President for final action by the Regents.

Recommendations 39, 40, and 41 (pp. 178–184). Received and placed on file on February 6, 1967 in their following original forms:

Recommendation 39: Teaching promise should be a major criterion for student appointments that involve teaching or tutoring, and teaching responsibilities should always be commensurate with the student's state of preparation. It follows that sustained classroom teaching should generally be reserved to the second year of graduate study and later.

Recommendation 40: Frequent regular meetings between professors and Teaching Assistants, including graduate teaching colloquia or teaching seminars where appropriate to the discipline, should be part of the regular program in each department, and should be counted as teaching credit of faculty and course or service credit of students.

Recommendation 41: All departments using Teaching Assistants should foster a climate of professional respect through (a) providing assistants with adequate physical facilities for both their teaching duties and their own studies; (b) assigning work with careful attention to avoiding duties that are too heavy or unnecessarily menial, and with periodic review of appropriateness of assignments; and (c) establishing student-faculty discussions of standards of appointment, workable ways of handling students' requests, and other matters of common professional concern.

Recommendation 42 (pp. 185–187). Received and placed on file on February 6, 1967:

An increase is needed in the stipends for graduate students assigned to teaching, so as to recruit the ablest candidates to the University, to provide them an attractive alternative to the now more rewarding research assistantships, and to remunerate them in a manner fully commensurate with the difficulty and quality of the duties they perform.